Modern Critical Views

Modern Critical Views

Katherine Mansfield
Christopher Marlowe
Andrew Marvell
Herman Melville
George Meredith
James Merrill
John Stuart Mill
Arthur Miller
Henry Miller
John Milton
Yukio Mishima
Molière
Michel de Montaigne
Eugenio Montale
Marianne Moore
Alberto Moravia
Toni Morrison
Alice Munro
Iris Murdoch
Robert Musil
Vladimir Nabokov
V. S. Naipaul
R. K. Narayan
Pablo Neruda
John Henry Newman
Friedrich Nietzsche
Frank Norris
Joyce Carol Oates
Sean O'Casey
Flannery O'Connor
Christopher Okigbo
Charles Olson
Eugene O'Neill
José Ortega y Gasset
Joe Orton
George Orwell
Ovid
Wilfred Owen
Amos Oz
Cynthia Ozick
Grace Paley
Blaise Pascal
Walter Pater
Octavio Paz
Walker Percy
Petrarch
Pindar
Harold Pinter
Luigi Pirandello
Sylvia Plath
Plato

Plautus
Edgar Allan Poe
Poets of Sensibility & the
    Sublime
Poets of the Nineties
Alexander Pope
Katherine Anne Porter
Ezra Pound
Anthony Powell
Pre-Raphaelite Poets
Marcel Proust
Manuel Puig
Alexander Pushkin
Thomas Pynchon
Francisco de Quevedo
François Rabelais
Jean Racine
Ishmael Reed
Adrienne Rich
Samuel Richardson
Mordecai Richler
Rainer Maria Rilke
Arthur Rimbaud
Edwin Arlington Robinson
Theodore Roethke
Philip Roth
Jean-Jacques Rousseau
John Ruskin
J. D. Salinger
Jean-Paul Sartre
Gershom Scholem
Sir Walter Scott
William Shakespeare
    Histories & Poems
    Comedies & Romances
    Tragedies
George Bernard Shaw
Mary Wollstonecraft
    Shelley
Percy Bysshe Shelley
Sam Shepard
Richard Brinsley Sheridan
Sir Philip Sidney
Isaac Bashevis Singer
Tobias Smollett
Alexander Solzhenitsyn
Sophocles
Wole Soyinka
Edmund Spenser
Gertrude Stein
John Steinbeck

Stendhal
Laurence Sterne
Wallace Stevens
Robert Louis Stevenson
Tom Stoppard
August Strindberg
Jonathan Swift
John Millington Synge
Alfred, Lord Tennyson
William Makepeace Thackeray
Dylan Thomas
Henry David Thoreau
James Thurber and S. J.
    Perelman
J. R. R. Tolkien
Leo Tolstoy
Jean Toomer
Lionel Trilling
Anthony Trollope
Ivan Turgenev
Mark Twain
Miguel de Unamuno
John Updike
Paul Valéry
Cesar Vallejo
Lope de Vega
Gore Vidal
Virgil
Voltaire
Kurt Vonnegut
Derek Walcott
Alice Walker
Robert Penn Warren
Evelyn Waugh
H. G. Wells
Eudora Welty
Nathanael West
Edith Wharton
Patrick White
Walt Whitman
Oscar Wilde
Tennessee Williams
William Carlos Williams
Thomas Wolfe
Virginia Woolf
William Wordsworth
Jay Wright
Richard Wright
William Butler Yeats
A. B. Yehoshua
Emile Zola

Modern Critical Views

EMILY DICKINSON

Edited with an introduction by

Harold Bloom

Sterling Professor of the Humanities
Yale University

CHELSEA HOUSE PUBLISHERS
New York

PROJECT EDITORS: Emily Bestler, James Uebbing
EDITORIAL COORDINATOR: Karyn Gullen Browne
EDITORIAL STAFF: Sally Stepanek, Linda Grossman, Gilda Abramowitz, Claudette Gayle, Peter Childers, Enid Stubin
DESIGN: Susan Lusk

Cover illustration by Peterson Design.

Printed and bound in the United States of America

10   9   8   7   6   5   4   3   2

Library of Congress Cataloging-in-Publication Data

Emily Dickinson, modern critical views.
 Bibliography: p.
 Includes index.
  1. Dickinson, Emily, 1830–1886—Criticism and interpretation—Addresses, essays, lectures.
I. Bloom, Harold.
PS1541.Z5E38   1985   811'.4   84-23085
ISBN 0-87754-605-3

Contents

Editor's Note

This volume offers a representative selection of the most helpful literary criticism accorded to Emily Dickinson during the last quarter-century. As the "Introduction" sets forth, Dickinson is a supremely difficult poet, because of her originality and her cognitive power. Her critics struggle both with her conceptualizations and with her verbal figures, and perhaps only now begin to see the dimensions of her subtle and complex visions. Charles R. Anderson, still the best of her close readers, accurately describes her unique capabilities as a poet of despair. The essays by Albert Gelpi and David Porter contextualize her early phases in the most relevant tradition, that of New England. Robert Weisbuch's study relates her characteristic inwardness to the Romantics' internalization of quest-romance, a relation also explored in Sharon Cameron's brilliant essay. Margaret Homans and Joanne Diehl bring forward the insights of contemporary feminist criticism, in two parallel attempts to differentiate Dickinson from her male precursor poets. Finally, Shira Wolosky examines the poet's innovations in syntax and in poetic form as instances of deviation from inherited religious modes under the impact of the Civil War, our American national crisis.

Introduction

It is not a rare quality for great poets to possess such cognitive strength that we are confronted by authentic intellectual difficulties when we read them. "Poems are made by fools like me," yes, and by Dante, Milton, Blake and Shelley, but only God can make a tree, to reappropriate a rejoinder I remember making to W.H. Auden many years ago, when he deprecated the possibilities of poetry as compared with the awful truths of Christian theology. But there are certainly very grand poets who are scarcely thinkers in the discursive modes. Tennyson and Whitman are instances of overwhelming elegiac artists who make us fitful when they argue, and the subtle rhetorical evasions of Wallace Stevens do not redeem his unfortunate essay, "A Collect of Philosophy."

Of all poets writing in English in the nineteenth and twentieth centuries, I judge Emily Dickinson to present us with the most authentic cognitive difficulties. Vast and subtle intellect cannot in itself make a poet; the essential qualities are inventiveness, mastery of trope and craft, and that weird flair for intuiting significance through rhythm to which we can give no proper name. Dickinson has all these, as well as a mind so original and powerful that we scarcely have begun, even now, to catch up with her.

Originality at its strongest—in the Yahwists, Plato, Shakespeare and Freud—usurps immense spaces of consciousness and language, and imposes contingencies upon all who come after. These contingencies work so as to conceal authentic difficulty through a misleading familiarity. Dickinson's strangeness, partly masked, still causes us to wonder at her, as we ought to wonder at Shakespeare or Freud. Like them, she has no single, overwhelming precursor whose existence can lessen her wildness for us. Her agon was waged with the whole of tradition, but particularly with the Bible and with romanticism. As an agonist, she takes care to differ from any male model, and places us upon warning:

> I cannot dance upon my Toes—
> No Man instructed me—
> But oftentimes, among my mind,
> A Glee possesseth me,
>
> . . . .
>
> Nor any know I know the Art
> I mention—easy—Here—
> Nor any Placard boast me—
> It's full as Opera—
>
> [326]

The mode is hardly Whitmanian in this lyric of 1862, but the vaunting is, and both gleeful arts respond to the Emersonian prophecy of American Self-Reliance. Each responds with a difference, but it is a perpetual trial to be a heretic whose only orthodoxy is Emersonianism, or the exaltation of whim:

> If nature will not tell the tale
> Jehovah told to her
> Can human nature not survive
> Without a listener?
>
> [1748]

Emerson should have called his little first book, *Nature*, by its true title of *Man*, but Dickinson in any case would have altered that title also. Alas, that Emerson was not given the chance to read the other Titan that he fostered. We would cherish his charmed reaction to:

> A Bomb upon the Ceiling
> Is an improving thing—
> It keeps the nerves progressive
> Conjecture flourishing—
>
> [1128]

Dickinson, after all, could have sent her poems to Emerson rather than to the nobly obtuse Higginson. We cannot envision Whitman addressing a copy of the first *Leaves of Grass* to a Higginson. There is little reason to suppose that mere diffidence prevented Miss Dickinson of Amherst from presenting her work to Mr. Emerson of Concord. In 1862, Emerson was still Emerson; his long decline dates from after the conclusion of the War. A private unfolding remained necessary for Dickinson, according to laws of the spirit and of poetic reason that we perpetually quest to surmise. Whereas Whitman masked his delicate, subtle and hermetic art by developing the outward self of the rough Walt, Dickinson set herself free to invest her imaginative exuberance elsewhere. The heraldic drama of her reclusiveness became the cost of her confirmation as a poet more original even than Whitman, indeed more original than any poet of her century after (and except) Wordsworth. Like Wordsworth, she began anew upon a *tabula rasa* of poetry, to appropriate Hazlitt's remark about Wordsworth. Whitman rethought the relation of the poet's self to his own vision, whereas Dickinson rethought the entire content of poetic vision. Wordsworth had done both, and done both more implicitly than these Americans could manage, but then Wordsworth had Coleridge as stimulus, while Whitman and Dickinson had the yet more startling and far wilder Emerson, who was and is the American difference personified. I cannot believe that even Dickinson would have written with so absolutely astonishing an audacity had Emerson not insisted that poets were as liberating gods:

Because that you are going
And never coming back
And I, however absolute,
May overlook your Track—

Because that Death is final,
However first it be,
This instant be suspended
Above Mortality—

Significance that each has lived
The other to detect
Discovery not God himself
Could now annihilate

Eternity, Presumption
The instant I perceive
That you, who were Existence
Yourself forgot to live—

These are the opening quatrains of poem 1260, dated by Thomas Johnson as about 1873, but it must be later, if indeed the reference is to the dying either of Samuel Bowles (1878) or of Judge Otis Lord (1884), the two men Richard Sewall, Dickinson's principal biographer, considers to have been her authentic loves, if not in any conventional way her lovers. The poem closes with a conditional vision of God refunding to us finally our "confiscated Gods." Reversing the traditional pattern, Dickinson required and achieved male Muses, and her "confiscated Gods" plays darkly against Emerson's "liberating gods." Of Emerson, whose crucial work (*Essays, The Conduct of Life, Society and Solitude,* the *Poems*) she had mastered, Dickinson spoke with the ambiguity we might expect. When Emerson lectured in Amherst in December 1857, and stayed next door with Dickinson's brother and sister-in-law, he was characterized by the poet: "as if he had come from where dreams are born." Presumably the Transcendental Emerson might have merited this, but it is curious when applied to the exalter of "Fate" and "Power" in *The Conduct of Life,* or to the dialectical pragmatist of "Experience" and "Circles," two essays that I think Dickinson had internalized. Later, writing to Higginson, she observed: "With the Kingdom of Heaven on his knee, could Mr. Emerson hesitate?" The question, whether open or rhetorical, is dangerous and wonderful, and provokes considerable rumination.

Yet her subtle ways with other male precursors are scarcely less provocative. Since Shelley had addressed *Epipsychidion* to Emilia Viviani, under the name of "Emily," Dickinson felt authorized to answer a poet who, like herself, favored the image of volcanoes. Only ten days or so before Judge Lord died, she composed a remarkable quatrain in his honor (and her own):

> Circumference thou Bride of Awe
> Possessing thou shalt be
> Possessed by every hallowed Knight
> That dares to covet thee
>
> [1620]

Sewall notes the interplay with some lines in *Epipsychidion*:

> Possessing and possessed by all that is
> Within that calm circumference of bliss,
> And by each other, till to love and live
> Be one:—
>
> [549–52]

Shelley's passage goes on to a kind of lovers' apocalypse:

> One hope within two wills, one will beneath
> Two overshadowing minds, one life, one death,
> One heaven, one Hell, one immortality,
> And one annihilation . . .
>
> [584–87]

In his essay, "Circles," Emerson had insisted: "There is no outside, no inclosing wall, no circumference to us." The same essay declares: "The only sin is limitation." If that is so, then there remains the cost of confirmation, worked out by Dickinson in an extraordinary short poem that may be her critique of Emerson's denial of an outside:

> I saw no Way—The Heavens were stitched—
> I felt the Columns close—
> The Earth reversed her Hemispheres—
> I touched the Universe—
>
> And back it slid—and I alone
> A Speck upon a Ball—
> Went out upon Circumference—
> Beyond the Dip of Bell—
>
> [378]

"My Business is Circumference—" she famously wrote to Higginson, to whom, not less famously, she described herself as "the only Kangaroo among the Beauty." When she wrote, to another correspondent, that "The Bible dealt with the Centre, not with the Circumference—," she would have been aware that the terms were Emerson's, and that Emerson also dealt only with the Central, in the hope of the Central Man who would come. Clearly, "Circumference" is her trope for the Sublime, as consciousness and as achievement or performance. For Shelley, Circumference was a Spenserian cynosure, a Gardens of Adonis vision, while for Emerson it was no part of us, or only another challenge to be overcome by the Central, by the Self-Reliant Man.

If the Bible's concern is Centre, not Circumference, it cannot be because the Bible does not quest for the Sublime. If Circumference or Dickinson is the bride of Awe or of the authority of Judge Lord, then Awe too somehow had to be detached from the Centre:

> No man saw awe, nor to his house
> Admitted he a man
> Though by his awful residence
> Has human nature been.
>
> Not deeming of his dread abode
> Till laboring to flee
> A grasp on comprehension laid
> Detained vitality.
>
> Returning is a different route
> The Spirit could not show
> For breathing is the only work
> To be enacted now.
>
> "Am not consumed," old Moses wrote,
> "Yet saw him face to face"—
> That very physiognomy
> I am convinced was this.
>
> [1733]

This might be called an assimilation of Awe to Circumference, where "laboring to flee" and returning via "a different route" cease to be antithetical to one another. "Vitality" here is another trope for Circumference or the Dickinsonian Sublime. If, as I surmise, this undated poem is a kind of proleptic elegy for Judge Lord, then Dickinson identifies herself with "old Moses," and not for the first time in her work. Moses, denied entrance into Canaan, "wasn't fairly used—," she wrote, as though the exclusion were her fate also. In some sense, she chose this fate, and not just by extending her circumference to Bowles and to Lord, unlikely pragmatic choices. The spiritual choice was not to be post-Christian, as with Whitman or Emerson, but to become a sect of one, like Milton or Blake. Perhaps her crucial choice was to refuse the auction of her mind through publication. Character being fate, the Canaan she would not cross to was poetic recognition while she lived.

Of Dickinson's 1,775 poems and fragments, several hundred are authentic, strong works, with scores achieving an absolute aesthetic dignity. To choose one above all the others must reveal more about the critic than he or she could hope to know. But I do not hesitate in my choice, poem 627, written probably in her very productive year, 1862. What precedents are there for such a poem, a work of un-naming, a profound and shockingly original cognitive act of negation?

The Tint I cannot take—is best—
The Color too remote
That I could show it in Bazaar—
A Guinea at a sight—

The fine—impalpable Array—
That swaggers on the eye
Like Cleopatra's Company—
Repeated—in the sky—

The Moments of Dominion
That happen on the Soul
And leave it with a Discontent
Too exquisite—to tell—

The eager look—on Landscapes—
As if they just repressed
Some Secret—that was pushing
Like Chariots—in the West—

The Pleading of the Summer—
That other Prank—of Snow—
That Cushions Mystery with Tulle,
For fear the Squirrels—know.

Their Graspless manners—mock us—
Until the Cheated Eye
Shuts arrogantly—in the Grave—
Another way—to see—

It is, rugged and complete, a poetics, and a manifesto of Self-Reliance. "The poet did not stop at the color or the form, but read their meaning; neither may he rest in this meaning, but he makes the same objects exponents of his new thought." This Orphic metamorphosis is Emerson's, but is not accomplished in his own poetry, nor is his radical program of un-naming. Dickinson begins by throwing away the lights and the definitions, and by asserting that her jocular procreations are too subtle for the Bazaar of publication. The repetition of colors (an old word, after all, for tropes) remains impalpable and provokes her into her own Sublime, that state of Circumference at once a divine discontent and a series of absolute moments that take dominion everywhere. Better perhaps than any other poet, she knows and indicates that what is worth representing is beyond depiction, what is worth saying cannot be said. What she reads, on landscapes and in seasons, is propulsive force, the recurrence of perspectives that themselves are powers and instrumentalities of the only knowledge ever available.

The final stanza does not attempt to break out of this siege of perspectives, but it hints again that her eye and will are receptive, not plundering, so that her power to un-name is not Emersonian finally, but something different, another way to see. To see feelingly, yes, but beyond the arrogance of the self in its war against process and its stand against other selves. Her interplay of perspectives touches apotheosis not in a Nietzschean or Emersonian exaltation of the will to power, however receptive and reactive, but in suggestions of an alternative mode, less an interpretation than a questioning, or an othering of natural process. The poem, like so much of Dickinson at her strongest, compels us to begin again in rethinking our relation to poems, and to the equally troubling and dynamic relation of poems to our world of appearances.

CHARLES R. ANDERSON

Despair

Emily Dickinson was no visionary intent on escaping the prison of this flesh. What gives weight to her poems that tug to be free and soar is her solid sense of reality, not just of scene and thing but of thought and feeling. More than most of her contemporaries she knew how to discriminate between vision and fact, and was aware how small a part ecstasy makes in the sum total that comprises life. Her normal impulse is to load the scales against it, as in this early poem:

> The Heart asks Pleasure—first—
> And then—Excuse from Pain—
> And then—those little Anodynes
> That deaden suffering—. . .

Then permission to sleep and finally, if the 'Inquisitor' wills it, 'The privilege to die.' With a different emphasis, reversing the compensatory doctrine of heavenly reward for a life of suffering, she says in a late letter: 'To have lived is a Bliss so powerful—we must die—to adjust it.'

Her effect of reality is achieved not by an accent on pleasure or pain but by her dramatic use of their interaction. As an artist she took full advantage of contrast as a mode of definition, making the pleasure-pain antithesis a running strategy in her poetry. As 'Water is taught by thirst,' so 'Transport—by throe.' Again:

> Delight—becomes pictorial—
> When viewed through Pain—. . .
> Transporting must the moment be—
> Brewed from decades of Agony! . . .

And finally, from among her earliest efforts, there is a poem constructed entirely of such contrasts, in terms of intensity and duration, beginning:

> For each extatic instant
> We must an anguish pay
> In keen and quivering ratio
> To the extasy. . . .

'Time is a pain lived piecemeal,' as one critic astutely epitomizes this poem, 'and the sum of the pieces equals a moment of joy.' But this is just an exercise in hedonistic calculus.

There is a wide range of pain explored in her poetry. She distinguishes misery, as a hurt that can be relieved, from suffering which stresses the act of enduring. But these milder aches and griefs did not challenge her powers of analysis like the extreme forms from affliction to woe that are recurrent in her poems. She discriminates among them somewhat as her copy of Webster did. He defines 'agony' as the pain so excruciating as to cause bodily contortions 'similar to . . . the sufferings of our Savior in the garden of Gethsemane'; 'anguish' as any keen distress of the mind 'from sorrow, remorse, despair, and the kindred passions'; and 'despair' itself as the extremest form of all, resulting in hopelessness, though with only subordinate theological connotations. But the purpose of her poems is something far other than the niceties of the lexicographer. She simply separates the lesser pains that will heal from the greater pains that will not and chooses the latter as her special concern, noting with precision their qualities and above all their effects.

If she had emphasized their causes, as from a loss of love or fame or religious faith, there would be more justification for biographical inquiry. Even so, her very obsession with the theme of extreme pain has made inevitable the conjecture that some experience of unusual intensity was the source of it. There is scattered evidence for this in the letters, but only one explicit statement. Written to Higginson in 1862, at the beginning of her creative flood tide, it has often been taken as explaining why she turned to poetry as a career: 'I had a terror—since September—I could tell to none—and so I sing, as the Boy does by the Burying Ground—because I am afraid.' It is doubtful that the nature of this 'terror' will ever be clarified by further external data. But the poems of this period likewise seem to reflect an extreme emotional and psychological crisis that tempts speculation. Some fifty of them have been arranged recently by one of her biographers in an impressive display of the severity and many-sidedness of such a conjectured crisis.

A number of her poems, though not usually the best, seem to relate this extreme suffering to a loss in love. One of the quieter ones, written in 1864 on the theme of renunciation until 'He' and 'I' can be reunited, presumably in heaven, begins and ends with phraseology remarkably similar to her statement in the letter to Higginson just quoted: 'I sing to use the Waiting . . . To keep the Dark away.' Another, ten years later, makes a memorable song out of pain as one of the pressures that wrings poetry from the heart, though declining to name the instrumentality as love:

> Not with a Club, the Heart is broken
> Nor with a Stone—
> A Whip so small you could not see it
> I've known
>
> To lash the Magic Creature
> Till it fell,
> Yet that Whip's Name
> Too noble then to tell.
>
> Magnanimous as Bird
> By Boy descried—
> Singing unto the Stone
> Of which it died— . . .

Singing to conquer pain is again the theme. The images are sharp—'Club,' 'Stone,' 'Whip,' culminating in the evocative 'Magic Creature' that makes the heart a living person. Nor is the third stanza an extraneous prose trailer, but a flash that brings the whole into focus. The boy, Eros with a slingshot, kills the bird of his desire heedless of its song. But the very real stone here links back to the invisible one at the beginning, denied into a whip, which makes the smitten heart sing too, now that the oblivious lover-killer has faded out. The suffering has been mastered and the beauty remains.

Her most anguished record of a hopeless love, 'I cannot live with you,' never quite rises out of pain into poetry, though some of the lines sing. For the most part it is a discursive monologue (fifty lines, her longest single effort in verse), struggling vainly to resolve an impossible dilemma. I cannot live with you or without you; I cannot die, or go to heaven, or even desire heaven without you. Yet there is no hope of reunion in Paradise either, because of some obscure flaw in their love. The reader is shaken by an eruption of emotion that is threatening from somewhere behind the poem to break out into the text, but it is never sufficiently under control to be channeled into language except to a modest degree in the final stanza:

> So We must meet apart—
> You there—I—here
> With just the Door ajar
> That Oceans are—and Prayer—
> And that White Sustenance—
> Despair—

The prerequisite for mastery, as in all Dickinson's best poetry, was to abandon the cumulative and logical for the tight symbolic structure that was her forte. Closely connected with this was the narrowing of her concern to one emotion at a time. Two of her better poems on the pain of renunciation deal, respectively, with the acceptance of loss as an inescapable part of the human condition and with the sheer quality of the resulting agony. In both, the specific event of a love-parting is reduced to a generalized idea of deprivation. The first of these achieves conciseness of theme if not of form:

> I should have been too glad, I see—
> Too lifted—for the scant degree
> Of Life's penurious Round—
> My little Circuit would have shamed
> This new Circumference—have blamed—
> The homelier time behind.
>
> I should have been too saved—I see—
> Too rescued—Fear too dim to me
> That I could spell the Prayer
> I knew so perfect—yesterday—
> That Scalding One—Sabachthini—
> Recited fluent—here—
>
> Earth would have been too much—I see—
> And Heaven—not enough for me—
> I should have had the Joy
> Without the Fear—to justify—
> The Palm—without the Calvary—
> So Savior—Crucify—
>
> Defeat whets Victory—they say—
> The Reefs in Old Gethsemane
> Endear the Shore beyond—
> 'Tis Beggars—Banquets best define—
> 'Tis Thirsting—vitalizes Wine—
> Faith bleats to understand—

The search for peace begins creatively with two concentric symbols, one circle for the mortal lot and one for the heavenly expansion unattainable on earth. If they had been developed to control the whole poem, their interaction might have encompassed not only the fact and the vision but the adjustment between the two, in a more satisfying fusion of theme and form. Though this advantage is not followed through, the first stanza sets up the limits of the human condition as a realized center for measuring the pressure of pain to follow. Justifying to herself why she was deprived of ecstasy, the ecstasy of heavenly love presumably, she says that it would have made her unjustly disdainful of the 'penurious Round' of ordinary life. One cannot escape from the 'little Circuit' of petty realities by leaping directly into a 'new Circumference.' Had such heavenly bliss actually been bestowed on her she would have proved inadequate to it. Being still limited by the human capacity for expansion, she would have dishonored ('shamed') the potentialities of such love and could only have 'blamed' her failure on the deficient preparation of the 'homelier' life she had known before. The uplifting from a 'scant degree' to an exalted one is not so easily obtained. Mortal experience will never become a center from which the inner self can expand toward limitless joy. The geometry of earthly and heavenly circumference is drawn with inflexible and mutually exclusive precision.

Leaving these two encompassing images, the poem develops instead by linear argument to prove that the human way is not the easy but the hard one, the way that must go through pain to a fuller understanding of what heaven can be. Some sort of logical unity is preserved by the syntactical pattern. The conditional mood, 'I should . . . ,' is maintained throughout (except in the last stanza), giving the whole poem the quality of a hypothetical case history. Again, 'Too rescued . . . too saved' in the second stanza echoes 'Too lifted . . . too glad' in the first and is answered by 'too much' in the third. Once in a letter she used the syllogistic paradox with shock effect to argue: 'To be human is more than to be divine, for when Christ was divine, he was uncontented till he had been human.' Similarly here: as Jesus before reaching his divine expanse had to experience mortal suffering to the point of temporary despair and utter his *Sabachthani*, so must she in order to spell out the human prayer, 'My God, my God, why has thou forsaken me.' She can say it fluently now because she has been forsaken, though 'Recited' gives it the air of ritualistic formula, as if she were rehearsing the words of Another to make them her own.

A more important kind of unity derives from thematic linkages. The 'little Circuit—new Circumference' antithesis reappears at the beginning of the third stanza in the exalted earthly life that would blot out the heavenly. At its close the 'Scalding' prayer that gives the poem its center is balanced by a daring redaction of the historic renunciation in Gethsemane ('Not my will, but thine, be done') in her startling plea: 'So Savior—Crucify.' The personal intensity ends with this climactic juxtaposition of opposites that began with Joy and Fear, Palm and Calvary. The last stanza seems on the surface like a mere appendix of aphorisms in further illustration of the pleasure-pain contrast. But this is the truth as 'they say' it, and two submerged metaphors identify 'them' as the authors of the Gospel story. 'Gethsemane' recalls the night before the crucifixion, 'Defeat-Victory' the agony of Golgotha that must follow the triumphal entry into Jerusalem, 'Banquets' and 'Wine' the spiritual feast of the Last Supper. That this was also the celebration of the Passover evokes the image of the Paschal lamb, slain and eaten at that time, which reappears indirectly in the final line: 'Faith bleats to understand.' This brings to mind many Biblical references to the Savior as the Good Shepherd, but also in its plaintiveness links back to the cry from the cross that forms the poem's passionate center. If glory must first be denied into despair for Christ, how much more so for mortals? Pain and loss, sharpened by a momentary vision of ecstasy, constitute the human condition she has been trying to adjust herself to throughout. For all her attempt to verbalize this, in the end she can only cry as a sheep.

The nature of despair itself, rather than the story of how she rebelled against it or finally accepted it, called out her finest talents:

> The Auctioneer of Parting
> His 'Going, going, gone'
> Shouts even from the Crucifix,
> And brings His Hammer down—
> He only sells the Wilderness,
> The prices of Despair
> Range from a single human Heart
> To Two—not any more—

This poem comprises the most remarkable pun in nineteenth-century Anglo-American literature, reviving that clowning Elizabethan device for the purposes of serious poetry long before Joyce and Pound rediscovered its efficacy. What is being sold, what is 'Going,' is gone-ness itself. What is being knocked down from the cross—and the verbal play makes that horrific extension inescapable—is death, the symbolic last 'Parting' of all. The wooden rap of the ordinary auctioneer's gavel makes all sales final, and this one transformed into a 'Hammer,' such as drove the nails into God's body, has the finality of Fate. The purchaser cannot back out, he must take possession of what he has bought.

He has bought the 'Wilderness,' not in the American sense of a primeval forest but as in Biblical references to those waste places where life cannot be supported. Her Lexicon, differing from modern dictionaries, gives prominence to this definition, 'a barren plain . . . , uncultivated and uninhabited by human beings,' citing by way of example the deserts of Arabia in which the Israelites wandered for forty years. The presence of 'Crucifix' in her poem makes her meaning unmistakable: a desert where the lost wander. 'Wilderness' is her new designation for 'that White Sustenance—Despair,' the utter desolation of the human heart. That any one should buy the wilderness voluntarily may seem strange. Yet parting short of death is an act of free will, however desperate the circumstances that force the choice. The price of this 'death' is a living heart, two if both make the renunciation, a single one if the other is unaware of love's commitment. (It is only in these last two lines that there is any suggestion of a love-parting; otherwise the theme seems to be separation from God, made doubly poignant by its unuttered cry from the cross.) So the figure of the auction carries through to the end. The movement of the poem is unavoidably downward, dictated by the hammer's stroke. The powerful conceit reaches its climax in the second line, the devastation spends itself in the center, and the force of both is dissipated in the cool air of calculation at the end. The violent emotion comes to rest here in quiet analysis, it is true, but this is the mood that creates her best poems on the extremity of pain.

Her justification for such bold adaptations of the great Christian symbol to human agony is made explicit in another poem. 'One Crucifixion is recorded—only,' she says, but there are as many unrecorded ones as there are people: 'Gethsemane—/Is but a Province—in the Being's Centre.' The theme of her own 'Calvary' in many poems is generally taken to be her suffering through the frustration of an earthly love. Yet this assumption must be balanced against references to herself as a creature 'Of Heavenly Love—forgot' and the general tenor of poems like the two just discussed. Her use of 'Despair' sometimes comes close to the traditional Christian definition, the last one cited in her Lexicon: 'Loss of hope in the mercy of God.' Such a suggested meaning in these poems is usually supported by a pervasive religious language—Sabachthani, Calvary, Crucifix. In others she uses despair simply as the extremest form of mortal suffering, 'the anguish of despair' as Webster phrased the secular illustration, which is similar to but not identical with the soul's helplessness of heaven. It seems wisest to read the whole range of her poems on pain, as in the case of those on ecstasy, simply as poems, free of entanglement in autobiographical conjecture or the formalism of theology. Let the 'I' be fictive, the 'supposed person' who stands for Everyman, and let the pain be secular unless the evidence of the whole poem makes it otherwise.

Anguish confined entirely to this world can be devastating enough, by reason of its very intensity. It is aggravated by the realization that man can find no help for it outside himself, as he can with spiritual despair through the hope of God's grace. Contrary to many of the romantic poets who preceded her, she found no healing balm in nature for human hurt. The absolute cleavage between man and the external world was one of her basic convictions . . . and its indifference to his plight is the theme-song in many of her poems. Her best one on the theme of human suffering confronted by nature's gay parade seems on the surface to be in danger of a reverse use of the pathetic fallacy, for here the indifference is threatening at several points to break out into open hostility, but a close reading proves she has not lapsed into the error of making nature sentient. On the contrary, she has made deliberate use of emotional extravagance to create a sense of nightmare, such as might result when anguish had reduced its victim to irrational terror:

> I dreaded that first Robin, so,
> But He is mastered, now,

I'm some accustomed to Him grown,
He hurts a little, though—

I thought if I could only live
Till that first Shout got by—
Not all Pianos in the Woods
Had power to mangle me—

I dared not meet the Daffodils—
For fear their Yellow Gown
Would pierce me with a fashion
So foreign to my own—

I wished the Grass would hurry
So—when 'twas time to see—,
He'd be too tall, the tallest one
Could stretch—to look at me—

I could not bear the Bees should come,
I wished they'd stay away
In those dim countries where they go,
What word had they, for me?

They're here, though; not a creature failed—
No Blossom stayed away
In gentle deference to me—
The Queen of Calvary—

Each one salutes me, as he goes,
And I, my childish Plumes,
Life, in bereaved acknowledgement
Of their unthinking Drums—

She feared the sounds of spring would 'mangle' her, its colors 'pierce' her, and so on. Nature is not only personified but on the warpath, the poet's soul so hypersensitive it can be wounded by anything, her emotions exaggerated to the point of being ludicrous. These certainly seem like the signposts of sentimentalism, and the casual reader may easily misinterpret them. Aware she was using a precarious technique, she matched her skill to the risk. The overwrought center is deftly set apart by being related in the past tense and is provided with a frame of irony by the opening and closing stanzas, which enable her and the reader to view it objectively from the calmer present. The nightmare is confined to stanzas two through five. They record not what actually happened but what she 'dreaded' would happen. The past tense, and the subjunctive mood, shows that for this part of the story's enactment spring had not yet come; the section opens with the clue 'I *thought* if I could only live/Till. . . .' The events that follow never existed anywhere except in her deluded imagination, but in that interior world they constituted the whole of reality and they function with terrifying precision. For an adult to hide behind grass blades for protection against the spears of attacking daffodils would indeed be insane, but that is just the point. This and the other imagined events are paranoid images skillfully objectifying the hallucinatory world of her fears.

The initial image sets the tone by evoking the exact sense of unreality desired: 'Not all Pianos in the Woods/Had power to mangle me.' In one sense 'Pianos' is a metaphor for the treble of birds, the bass of frogs, and all the range of natural sounds in between, with their wild harmony and counterpoint. In a letter to Higginson she once said, 'the noise in the Pool, at Noon—excels my Piano.' In a lesser poem on the same theme she uses a similar figure, the black birds' 'Banjo,' accurate enough for their twanging monotone and with the added humor of an oblique reference to the Negro minstrels popular in that day. But the humor appropriate to anguish is macabre, not grotesque, and the 'Pianos' here give just that touch. For in another sense they are not metaphorical but real, or rather surrealistic, like the objects in a painting by Dali. Placed in the woods instead of in the parlor, by the distortion of terror, they could become instruments of torture. Caught behind the keyboard of a gigantic piano she would be 'mangled' by its hammers even as she was driven mad by the booming strings, helplessly dodging blows whose source, timing, and spacing she could not guess. This is indeed the world of nightmare, induced by dread when unbearable pain has unhinged the reason.

The framing stanzas are not for the purpose of ridiculing this terror or repudiating it as mere insanity. Their relation to the center of pain is much more intricate. The opening one is mainly in the present tense, after spring has come, but it begins with a throwback to the fear that had gripped her earlier, 'I dreaded that first Robin, so.' The following lines appear to modify the excess of terror by saying calmly, 'He is mastered, now,' all the more reassuring by being couched in homely idiom ('I'm some accustomed to Him grown'). But the reader is the one who is actually reassured, knowing that the creator of the poem has mastered herself rather than the robin, though the experience lingers vividly in her memory and still 'hurts a little.' He is now prepared to accept as true her account in the succeeding stanzas of the dread produced by coming spring, in all the intensity of its psychic reality. As her mind reviews that past time of nightmare her language breaks into the turgid and improbable. One surrealistic scene after another flashes before her in a fantastic parade, the shouting mob of birds, daffodils, grass, and bees she 'could not bear . . . should come.'

The conclusion returns to the quiet mood of adjustment, in the present tense, with which the poem began: 'They're here, though; not a creature failed.' Arrogating to herself the title 'Queen of Calvary' might seem to indicate that some of the distorted vision still remains, but this is undercut by irony. Her imagined subjects do not obey her wish by staying away 'In gentle deference' to her grief. Instead, they file past her with gay sounds and colors quite as 'foreign' to her present state as she had feared in the nightmare. This, of course, is not the parade conjured up by her terrified imagination. It is the orderly procession of spring, which follows winter just as a resurrection should follow her 'Calvary.'

Whether she desires it or not spring brings renewal of life to nature, taunting the stricken soul with its signs of health. It is only in this root sense that it 'salutes' her, the assumed deference of subject to sovereign being part of the calculated mockery. She can do nothing but accept this false promise of a return to well-being. Hence her 'bereaved acknowledgement' of spring's greeting by lifting her 'childish Plumes.' They are the insignia of her royalty and of her grief, as in the purple plumes of traditional monarchy and the black ones of hearse and horse in the funerals of her own day. Her recognition that both are childish is the mark of a certain stage of recovery, the awareness that at least her irrational terror is now dead. For all that she has outlived it, 'mastered' it, it was none the less real while it lasted. And the new wisdom she has gained from this adjustment is perhaps even more awesome. It is apparently the conviction that her anguish was not insane but the processes of nature are, in the sense that they have no relation to her interior world. Its loud and meaningless life continues to beat on her consciousness with 'unthinking Drums.' Any outward demonstrations of terror and grief in the face of nature's indifference are childish, just as man's claim of sovereignty over it would be. The anguish that remains, though not named, is her sense of the suffering mind's isolation in an alien Universe.

The pain that Dickinson explores in the major poems is of a sort the victim never fully recovers from. 'Split Lives—never "get well," ' she commented in a letter. 'It is simple, to ache in the Bone, or the Rind,' according to one of her poems, 'But Gimlets—among the nerve—/Mangle . . . terribler.' Such pain goes to the quick. It usually involves a 'death' to some part of the person's life and an awareness of change to a new dimension of being. There is nothing occult or morbid about all this. Certain basic human experiences are universally recognized as answering exactly to this description, though the resulting anguish is usually glossed by wit or otherwise played down in popular speech, probably because of its very intensity. The more obvious ones may be readily agreed upon: the struggle out of adolescence into maturity, with its loss of freedom; the breaking of the dream, whether of glory or love or joy; the benumbing discovery that the grave is not just for others, with the consequent first experience of 'dying.' The vocabulary of utility desperately applied to them (growing pains, disillusionment, common sense) stresses the gain in wisdom, but it cannot conceal the loss to the spirit. This kind of anguish, the distinguishing mark of the human consciousness as opposed to animal and vegetable being, is valid subject matter for the artist and she made it one of her special provinces. Though she rarely makes the experience specific, it may be indicated in a general way as that whole area of crisis, looming behind the record of the years 1859–1866, which transformed her from an obscure woman into a great poet.

Her best poetry is not concerned with the causes but with the qualities of pain, an emphasis that removes it effectively from the category of the sentimental. She even takes care to differentiate between the kind manufactured by poetasters and that which engages her attention: 'Safe Despair it is that raves—/Agony is frugal.' Her own approach at times seems almost clinical, but this is simply the mode she adopted to gain the proper distance between her personal emotions and her art. It separates her sharply from the subjective lyricism of an older tradition and reveals her kinship with the twentieth century. The qualities she sought to fix with greatest precision are its intensity, its duration, and the change it brings about. In several minor poems she used time as a measure of degree in defining the extremity of pain that was her real concern. To the readiest cliché of both the sentimentalist and the pragmatist, that 'Time assuages,' she replied, not when it is 'Malady'; and in a letter: 'to all except anguish, the mind soon adjusts.' Extreme suffering even changes the very nature of time, she demonstrated in a pair of dialectical quatrains: 'Pain—expands the Time— . . . Pain contracts—the Time.' It makes clock and calendar meaningless and annihilates the very idea of eternity; the true center of pain exists in a temporal vacuum, containing its own past and future. Spatially it is equally limitless and without definable locality: it 'ranges Boundlessness.' Unlike contentment, which resides lawfully in a 'quiet Suburb,' agony cannot stay 'In Acre—Or Location—/It rents Immensity.' It absorbs the whole of consciousness, condensed to a measureless, momentless point.

Pain is thus a quality of being that exists outside time and space, the only two terms in which it can possibly be externalized. Her dilemma in describing this formless psychic entity was how to contrive outward symbols that would make the internal condition manifest. In solving this difficulty she borrowed from the techniques of the theatre, man's supreme contrivance for presenting illusion by making scene and action a set of appearances through which the spectator must penetrate to the reality beneath. With the aid of this device, supplemented by the rituals of formal ceremonies like trials and funerals, the effects of extreme pain are rendered by her in a series of unusually interesting poems.

In the most extraordinary of them, the abstract concept of 'death' as inflicted on the consciousness by despair is projected in one of those courtroom scenes of nightmare made vivid to modern readers by Kafka. The victim is on trial for his life, though for some nameless crime, and the machinery of an inexorable justice grinds to its conclusion, without moving, in a kind of wordless horror:

> I read my sentence—steadily—
> Reviewed it with my eyes,
> To see that I made no mistake
> In its extremest clause—
> The Date, and manner, of the shame—
> And then the Pious Form
> That 'God have mercy' on the Soul
> The Jury voted Him—
> I made my soul familiar—with her extremity—
> That at the last, it should not be a novel Agony—
> But she, and Death, acquainted—
> Meet tranquilly, as friends—
> Salute, and pass, without a Hint—
> And there, the Matter ends—

The proliferation of pronouns here is not a sign of artistic confusion but a grammatical echo of the dream chaos, whose intricate meaning can be parsed readily enough if the analyst follows the mode of the subconscious drama. 'I,' 'Him,' and 'She' are all aspects of the persona of the poem, as in the dream all characters are projections of the dreamer.

The poem falls into two equal parts of eight lines each, though the climactic quatrain that introduces the second is written as an extended couplet, thus giving emphasis to the previously unnamed 'Agony.' This twofold division corresponds roughly to the duality of body and soul. The fictive 'I' stands for the whole of the mortal life that dominates the first half, as mind-heart-body react to the sentence of death. The extrapolated 'she,' the filmy protagonist of the second half, is the immortal part, this section being primarily concerned with the effect of the verdict on the soul. Yet both are spoken by 'I,' for Dickinson could not indulge in an outright *Debate between the Body and the Soul* as the medieval poet could, his belief in the absolute reality of both not being available to her. The law refuses to take any cognizance of such duality and addresses the reunited halves of the prisoner as 'Him,' though it does so at the very point where the jury in condemning his body to death makes use of a formula from traditional piety to recommend mercy on his soul. 'Him,' placed exactly at the juncture between the two halves of the poem, likewise unifies them and at the same time gives the persona wholeness of being for the duration of a single word, though even then only as the third person condemned in the nightmare, anonymous and detached from the agonized dreamer-narrator.

The legal language, concentrated in the first half, not only sets the scene but controls the meaning throughout. Brought up in a family of lawyers, she came by it naturally. But far more important than her precision in handling its terminology is the imaginative fitness with which she puts it to work. The dramatic appeal of a criminal trial comes from the contrast of the lawless emotions involved in the original actions and the ordered procedure by which the court re-enacts them, with the possibility that at any moment the violently human may erupt through the formalism of its jargon. From this situational irony she creates her strategy, giving it a unique twist by having one actor, the masking 'I', slip successively into all the leading roles—prisoner-in-the-dock, defense counsel, judge, jury, and courtroom spectators.

The poem opens with the flat statement that the unidentified speaker, completely subdued to the mechanism of the ritual, has read his sentence 'steadily,' or as her Lexicon defines it 'without tottering, shaking,' such as might be expected of one condemned to die. This air of professional disinterestedness holds throughout the first eight lines, as the speaker performs both judicial and counselling functions. 'Reviewed it' suggests that this is a court of appeal, perhaps of last resort, reviewing the decision of a lower trial court; also that the defense, counsel and client, are going over a familiar document, not wih the heart but 'with my eyes,' alert to any technicalities of 'date,' 'clause,' or 'manner' that might serve as a basis for requesting a reversal of the opinion; finally that the condemned is even looking for an extra-legal loophole in the one human phrase that has crept into this otherwise formally pronounced judgment, but the jury's vote of 'God have mercy' is just a 'Pious Form' without legal consequences. All the ingenuity of the profession and the meticulous care of the accused have revealed 'no mistake,' however, and the sentence stands in its 'extremest clause.' So ends the first scene.

The same elaborate device of a dream-trial is used in another poem in the form of a simile to stand explicitly for the 'death' that can come from 'Agony.' It crept nearer every day until the benumbed victim dropped 'lost [as] from a Dream.' Then, 'As if your Sentence stood—pronounced,' she says, and you were led from the luxurious doubts of the dungeon to the gibbet and sure death, suppose some creature should gasp 'Reprieve' at the last moment, would this lessen the anguish? Only temporary relief, not pardon and remission, is possible for the pain of the human condition, she is saying, and death itself might well be preferable. But in that poem the agony, being insufficiently controlled, shatters the form with fragmentary and conflicting images. The superior mastery of the one under consideration consists in the skill by which the metaphor of the legal nightmare becomes both cover and contents, so that the thematic meaning of pain can be gradually unfolded by what the poem enacts, clarified in the last part even as it is given a new direction.

Beneath the stylized language of this drama the speaker knows he is none of these other parties, judge or jury or attorney, not even the disinterested spectator, a role reserved for the reader. He is the one condemned to death. (The exigencies of discourse require the use of the third person throughout the rest of this discussion of what happens to the 'I' of the poem, but this must not be confused with her special use of 'Him' in line eight.) He is also aware that the whole ritual is simply a nightmarish image of another and worse kind of death, the dying of consciousness under the pressure of despair. But he has lost his sense of identity, and this is what accounts for his apparent apathy. His detachment is such that he can read his own death sentence as if it applied to someone else. As she put it elsewhere: 'A Doubt if it be Us' assists the mind, staggering under extreme anguish, until it finds a new footing.

To lose one's identity by such a living death is in a sense to be separated from one's soul, which justifies the colloquy in the second section. But the mortal part still does all the talking, 'I made my soul familiar' answering in uninterrupted sequence to the opening line, 'I read my sentence—steadily.' The continuity of speaker binds the two parts together, and this limited point of view provides a further irony by relating an immortal sequence in mortal terms. The soul, previously introduced only in the jury's callous formula, now becomes an entity, and the theme of death-dealing pain emerges with an effect of shock from the metaphor of a legal death-sentence. The scene has now dissolved from the courtroom to some shadowy anteroom, perhaps the death-cell or even the execution chamber itself, with that inconsequent shifting so familiar in dreams. Fearing that what killed his consciousness may also kill his soul, the speaker is solicitous that 'she' should be prepared for 'her extremity' so that in the end 'it should not be a novel Agony.' 'Novel' means not only unexpected, the final shock he wants to make her familiar with in advance, but also new, implying that she has gone through all his past agonies with him too.

In his ignorance of the nature of souls he apparently thinks they are subject to death as well as to suffering. So the last irony is that the 'novel Agony' is reserved for him, not her. 'She and Death' it turns out are old acquaintances, as symbols of mortality and immortality, but since they have no common ground save the moment of passing they simply 'Salute' courteously and go their respective ways, 'without a Hint' to him of what they are really like or where they have gone. His surprise discovery is that in this friendly meeting it is only he, 'the Matter,' which has been annihilated. His sentence has been executed not by legal but by verbal machinery. In the triple pun, 'And there, the *Matter* ends,' the fictive 'I' experiences a new death by losing his soul as well as his identity in the depths of despair, the curtain is rung down on the bad dream along with all the legal theatricalities that bodied it forth, and the poem destroys itself in a tour de force. The reader, if any one, suffers shock.

That Dickinson could make a macabre joke out of agony will offend only those who take poetry solemnly. Perhaps it was one mode of rescue, as literal death would have been another, from a pain that was unbearable. Still another kind of escape, into a state of trance, proved most fruitful of all to the maker of poems on pain. She put it succinctly once in prose: 'Anguish has but so many throes—then Unconsciousness seals it.' Again, as a compact metaphor:

> There is a pain—so utter—
> It swallows substance up—
> Then covers the Abyss with Trance—
> So Memory can step
> Around—across—upon it—
> As one within a Swoon—
> Goes safely—where an open eye—
> Would drop Him—Bone by Bone.

The alternations of substance and abstraction make an intricate structure here. The inner quality of suffering 'swallows up' the reality of self and world and turns them into a bottomless 'Abyss,' which her Lexicon illustrated by quoting the description of pre-Genesis chaos, 'Darkness was upon the face of the abyss.' To cover this nothingness, pain makes itself concrete in the insubstantiality of 'Trance,' so that consciousness can step upon it or around it and blot out the memory of it in a kind of living death. Otherwise, if the victim should materialize again, the intensity of the pain would drop him 'Bone by Bone.' This makes a striking definition of the mind's protection against its own suffering by falling into the blankness of 'Swoon,' but not a very memorable poem.

Her best poems on the extremity of pain, the kind producing a state of trance, make its quality of spiritual death concrete in terms of physical death and at the same time dramatize it in the ritual of burial. In the first of these, the levels of sinking down to unconsciousness follow step by step the ceremony so familiar in her village world:

> I felt a Funeral, in my Brain,
> And Mourners to and fro
> Kept treading—treading—till it seemed
> That Sense was breaking through—
>
> And when they all were seated,
> A Service, like a Drum—
> Kept beating—beating—till I thought
> My Mind was going numb—
>
> And then I heard them lift a Box
> And creak across my Soul

With those same Boots of Lead, again,
Then Space—began to toll,

As all the Heavens were a Bell,
And Being, but an Ear,
And I, and Silence, some strange Race
Wrecked, solitary, here—

And then a Plank in Reason, broke,
And I dropped down, and down—
And hit a World, at every Crash,
And Got through knowing—then—

The stage lies within the cortex of the brain, and the drama is rendered exclusively in terms of unarticulated sounds, transformed into motions which enact the pantomime through its inexorable progress to extinction.

The subdued step of mourners in the real world became in the first stanza a heavy relentless 'treading' to this tortured consciousness, until it feared that 'Sense was breaking through.' The twofold meanings here, of the mind giving way and of the sensations threatening to quicken again from their comfortable state of numbness, are picked up in the following stanza and the concluding one. When the funeral service began, its incessant droning made the mind at last actually begin 'going numb,' though with the disquieting echo of a pagan ritual in its beating 'Drum.' By the time the third stanza is reached, the mind is so dissociated it is now both the extinct life in the coffin and the agonized soul across which the pallbearers creak. 'With those same Boots of Lead, again' implies that the experience was re-enacted over and over yet simultaneously, with the lead of the coffin grotesquely transferred to the boot-soles of the attendants. This same duality of consciousness continues as the procession leaves the church and the funeral knell sounds, announcing the death of the body of agony and at the same time killing the listening spirit. This sound is so cosmic only the most extravagant simile will compass it: 'As all the Heavens were a Bell, / And Being, but an Ear.' Such a climax has an absolute rightness about it. For the poem has consisted exclusively of a succession of images all auditory and reiterated—treading, beating, creaking. And with this final tolling, the consciousness is 'Wrecked, solitary,' except for the companioning 'Silence,' more harrowing than any of the sounds had been.

For the mind to apprehend beyond the pale of death, even the hallucinatory death of obliterating pain, would be to go beyond the limits of judgment. To avoid this the poem ends with the mind simply giving way, but this too in terms of the last act of burial. Just as the coffin is about to be lowered into the grave, 'a Plank in Reason broke,' and the persona dropped down through level after level of unconsciousness, hitting a new 'World' of extinction 'at every Crash.' These were the last soundless sounds of agony, as the mind 'got through knowing.' Being has been swallowed up in trance. Perhaps the only flaw in this poem is that the metaphor of 'Funeral' comes near stealing the show. The powerfully dramatized ceremony, with all its ghastly detail, tends to draw the reader's attention away from the spiritual death it was intended to illuminate. That extreme form of mortal pain she likened to 'despair' did not need to be named as her theme, to be sure, but its qualities and effects should have been more vividly evoked as the final meaning of the whole sequence of images. Since this was not quite adequately done, there is some danger of the poem being misread as merely the fantasy of a morbid soul imagining its own death, which would certainly diminish its significance.

There are two kinds of death, however, not counting the death of the soul in the theological sense of 'despair.' One may literally die away from the world, but she never made the mistake of trying to embody her own decease in a serious poem. On the other hand, the world may die away from the perceiving consciousness under stress of pain, and the resulting death to the spirit can be experienced and rendered. Such pain overwhelmed Emily Dickinson during her last years, as death thinned the ranks of her intimate circle and all but extinguished her small world. The cumulative impact of all this brought on a nervous breakdown, which she recorded in almost clinical fashion:

> I saw a great darkness coming and knew no more until late at night. I woke to find Austin and Vinnie and a strange physician bending over me, and supposed I was dying, or had died, all was so kind and hallowed. I had fainted and lain unconscious for the first time in my life. . . . The doctor calls it 'revenge of the nerves'; but who but Death wronged them?

Such actual experiences do not produce poems but collapse, as she phrased it in another letter about the same time: 'Blow has followed blow, till the wondering terror of the Mind clutches what is left, helpless of an accent.' Twenty years earlier she projected her imagined spiritual death from excessive pain in 'I felt a Funeral, *in my Brain*.' No specific autobiographical source is needed to explain this poem, for its close similarity to the preceding and following ritual dramas makes its meaning unmistakable.

In her most remarkable poem rendering the extinction of consciousness by pain in terms of a funeral, the deftness of her strategy shows just what could be done with this technique. Its three stanzas faintly shadow forth three stages of a familiar ceremony: the formal service, the tread of pallbearers, and the final lowering into a grave. But metaphor is subdued to meaning by subtle controls:

After great pain, a formal feeling comes—
The Nerves sit ceremonious, like Tombs—
The stiff Heart questions was it He, that bore,
And Yesterday, or Centuries before?

The Feet, mechanical, go round—
A wooden way
Of Ground, or Air, or Ought—
Regardless grown,
A Quartz contentment, like a stone—

This is the Hour of Lead—
Remembered, if outlived,
As Freezing persons, recollect the Snow—
First—Chill—then Stupor—then the letting go—

This poem has recently received the explication it deserves, matching its excellence. But its pertinence to this whole group of poems is such as to justify a brief summary of the interpretation here.

'In a literal sense,' according to this critic, there is 'neither persona nor ritual, and since it describes a state of mind, neither would seem to be necessary.' Instead, as befits one who has lost all sense of identity, the various parts of the body are personified as autonomous entities (*the* nerves, *the* heart, *the* feet), belonging to no one and moving through the acts of a meaningless ceremony, lifeless forms enacted in a trance. As a result, attention is centered on the feeling itself and not on the pattern of figures that dramatize it. As the images of a funeral rite subside, two related ones emerge to body forth the victim who is at once a living organism and a frozen form. Both are symbols of crystallizaton: 'Freezing' in the snow, which is neither life nor death but both simultaneously; and 'A Quartz contentment, like a stone,' for the paradoxical serenity that follows intense suffering. This recalls her envy of the 'little Stone,' happy because unconscious of the exigencies that afflict mortals, and points forward to the paradox in another poem, 'Contented as despair.' Such is the 'formal feeling' that comes after great pain. It is, ironically, no feeling at all, only numb rigidness existing outside time and space.

In two final poems, her use of 'despair' seems to be unmistakably in the direction of the Christian meaning, though her treatment of this theological term is unorthodox to say the least. From the point of view of the poet, the chief problem is that despair is amorphous and needs to be bodied forth in some palpable form, such as the ritual drama she used so successfully, in order to be fully realized. But this may tend to restrict its meaning since, from another point of view, it is a protean condition. It feels somewhat like this and somewhat like that, like none and yet like all. To give shape to this quality she used the technique of throwing up a shower of varied images, the great feat of skill requisite being to make them at once discrete and sequential, capable of coalescing into an unexpected whole.

In one attempt the power of the separate images is undeniable, though the fusion is not quite made:

> It was not Death, for I stood up,
> And all the Dead, lie down—
> It was not Night, for all the Bells
> Put out their Tongues, for Noon.
>
> It was not Frost, for on my Knees
> I felt Siroccos—crawl—
> Not Fire—for just two Marble feet
> Could keep a Chancel, cool—
>
> And yet, it tasted, like them all,
> The Figures I have seen
> Set orderly, for Burial,
> Reminded me, of mine—
>
> As if my life were shaven,
> And fitted to a frame,
> And could not breathe without a key,
> And 'twas like Midnight, some—
>
> When everything that ticked—has stopped—
> And Space stares all around—
> Or Grisly frosts—first Autumn morns,
> Repeal the Beating Ground—
>
> But, most, like Chaos—Stopless—cool—
> Without a Chance, or Spar—
> Or even a Report of Land—
> To justify—Despair.

The opening and closing words, 'It was not Death' but it was 'Despair,' pose the problem and set up the surface dialectic. In between are a series of negations, or mere similes of possibility, each followed by an opposing statement or qualification. Occasionally they are interlocked in series by turning the affirmation of one pair into the thing denied in the next, notably in the second stanza. It becomes immediately apparent, however, that these are not statements at all but figures of speech, and the relations between them are far more poetic than their superficial resemblance to Hegelian logic indicates.

The first sequence begins with an image of the recumbent dead in contrast with her own erect figure, which rules out death as her status even while the quality of it is retained. This is picked up in the third stanza where her feeling of going through a living death recalls the figures of the dead she has seen 'Set orderly, for Burial.' Out of her local experience she undoubtedly knew about country funerals, where corpses were laid out in the parlor in unrelieved *rigor mortis*, but these are the dead that 'lie down.' This image is blended with one evoked out of her knowledge of old cathedrals, like

Westminster Abbey, with their stone effigies raised up above the horizontal sarcophagi. These are the erect 'Figures' of the dead whose cold semblance of life 'Reminded me, of mine.' This carries back to her own 'Marble feet' in the preceding stanza, which are lifeless enough to 'keep a Chancel cool, whether buried beneath its floor or standing in some niche nearby. The burial theme also follows over into the fourth stanza, without even a break in the syntax, 'As if my life were shaven,/And fitted to a frame.' In this image of death, seemingly nearer to the rural kind she was acquainted with, the body is not being placed in a box for burial, however. It is itself being carpentered into one, 'shaven and fitted,' and the new 'frame' into which the old one of bone and flesh is being transformed is a kind of humble wooden effigy answering to the marble ones of the great. The 'key' referred to in this passage may seem somewhat out of place since corpses are sealed in coffins rather than locked. But spirits are locked in bodies, and since coffin and corpse are one here, her vital life 'could not breathe without a key' to release it from the body of this despair.

Another set of relations works out from the second half of the opening stanza: 'It was not Night, for all the Bells/Put out their Tongues, for Noon.' The brilliance of midday, reinforced by the clangorous sound of bells and their swinging motion, seems the very image of life in contrast to the night of death, but there are overtones of irony in all this. 'Tongues,' borrowed directly from the folk metaphor for bell clappers, has the inevitable connotation of wagging, and the colloquial idiom 'put out' completes the suggestion of brazen mockery of her state. Bells also toll notably for death, which links this with the funeral imagery already pointed out. Though 'Noon' is the height of the day's life it is also the beginning of the sun's decline. For this reason it is a recurrent image for the escape out of time in her poetry, as in the conceit of the stopped clock which went out of decimals 'into degreeless Noon.'

In the present poem she also uses the other end of the clock's cycle for the moment of death and, after denying that her state was one of 'Night,' returns twelve lines later to admit that it was 'like Midnight, some.' This is the hour 'when everything that ticked—has stopped,' with no friendly reassurance from such commonplaces as the pendulum of measured time or the visible objects of a familiar room or landscape. Instead, 'Space stares all around' with the glazed eyes of death. Then the scene moves on from the midnight of black despair to the even more blank whiteness of an autumn morning when 'Grisly frosts . . . Repeal the Beating Ground.' The ticking life that had ceased in the silence of night is reinforced by more powerful phrasing, the pulsing life of earth abrogated by the coming death of winter. The sound effects from the verbal play of 'Beating' and 'Repeal' make this at last the actual funeral knell so long hinted at. There is also a final link back to the earlier 'Frost' that had been denied in line 5 as the true symbol of despair.

The obscurity of this second stanza is symptomatic of the risks inherent in the technique employed for this poem. The reader is left with more to explain than to experience in the unresolved disparity of its images: 'not Frost' but 'Siroccos,' not 'Fire' but—whatever it is that is going on in the 'Chancel.' She seems to have felt the need to clarify, for her only suggested revisions in the manuscript come exactly at this crucial point: 'on my Flesh > my Knees'... and 'just my > just two Marble feet'.... One can only clutch wildly at meaning. As the poet knelt at the chancel rail, beyond which sacrament and conviction are at white heat, did she feel first cold whiteness, then a hot oppressive wind off the desert, then fire that cooled her feet to marble? The functioning of the Eucharist in relation to 'Despair,' if such was her intention, never quite comes through. The very obscurity of the rite hinted at in this stanza suggests that she is trying to use despair here in the traditional Christian sense, for Holy Communion is exactly what would be beyond the reach of one who had lost hope in the mercy of God, and any attempt to partake of it would be baffled and confused. This theological doctrine was almost as unavailable to her as the sacrament would be to the lost, and they find only a dim embodiment in this poem.

The spate of images flows on, however, mostly similes. It was none of these—not death or night or noon, not stone effigies or flesh turned to wood, not blank silence whether black or white—'yet, it tasted like them all.' Is 'tasted' a final effort to bring off the communion metaphor: the sense organs must feed on and incorporate these sensations until substance and experience are one? The next to last image for despair is most harrowing of all, its effect increased by the insistent beat of four accented syllables in succession that fall like hammer blows: 'But, most, like Chaos—Stopless—cool— ... ' By extending measurable time into eternity and familiar locale into staring space, beyond the ordered universe, this image removes the last signs by which suffering man can identify himself as human. The cumulative effect of all this overwhelms the consciousness, but the images refuse to coalesce into a whole. The poem is as chaotic as despair itself, its only form being multiform formlessness. If the harried reader may be allowed one despairing quip, he may express his fear that the method itself as here employed is 'stopless.' For a final anticlimactic image of shipwreck is added ('Without a ... Spar—/Or even a Report of Land'), which fails even more to 'justify,' in the Miltonic sense, all this suffering.

The ultimate problem, then, was not to master despair, which she presumably succeeded in doing as a woman when she took the artist's path to peace, but to manage the images evoked by her sensibility so as to transform the experience into great poetry. The same technique used in the preceding attempt was brought under perfect control in her finest poem on despair:

> There's a certain Slant of light,
> Winter Afternoons—

That oppresses, like the Heft
Of Cathedral Tunes—

Heavenly Hurt, it gives us—
We can find no scar,
But internal difference,
Where the Meanings, are—

None may teach it—Any—
'Tis the Seal Despair—
An imperial affliction
Sent us of the Air—

When it comes, the Landscape listens—
Shadows—hold their breath—
When it goes, 'tis like the Distance
On the look of Death—

For more than half a century this poem was placed by her editors under the category of nature. But winter sunlight is simply the over-image of despair, inclosing the center of suffering that is her concern. Grammatically, the antecedent of the neutral 'it' whose transformations make up the action of the poem is this 'certain Slant' of light, but in figurative meaning 'it' is the 'Heavenly Hurt.' This is a true metaphor, sensation and abstraction fused into one, separable in logic but indistinguishable and even reversible in a poetic sense. The internal experience is not talked about but is realized in a web of images that constitutes the poem's statement, beginning with one drawn from nature, or rather from the firmament above it, and returning to it in the end with a significant change of meaning.

These multiple images exemplifying the protean condition of despair are vividly discrete, but they grow out of each other and into each other with a fitness that creates the intended meaning in shock after shock of recognition. Its amorphous quality is embodied at the outset in 'light,' a diffused substance that can be apprehended but not grasped. Further, this is a slanting light, as uncertain of source and indirect in impact as the feeling of despair often is. Finally, it is that pale light of 'Winter Afternoons,' when both the day and the year seem to be going down to death, the seasonal opposite of summer which symbolized for her the fullness and joy of living. It is when he feels winter in his soul, one remembers, that Melville's Ishmael begins his exploration of the meaning of despair. Next, by the shift of simile, this desolation becomes 'like the Heft/Of Cathedral Tunes.' The nebulous has now been made palpable, by converting light waves into sound waves whose weight can be felt by the whole body. The strong provincialism, 'Heft' (smoothed away to 'Weight' by former editors), carries both the meaning of ponderousness and the great effort of heaving in order to test it, according to her Lexicon. This homely word also clashes effectively with the grand ring of

'Cathedral Tunes,' those produced by carillon offering the richest possibilities of meaning. Since this music 'oppresses,' the connotation of funereal is added to the heavy resonance of all pealing bells. And since the double meaning of 'Heft' carries through, despair is likened to both the weight of these sounds on the spirit and the straining to lift the imponderable tonnage of cast bronze.

The religious note on which the prelude ends, 'Cathedral Tunes,' is echoed in the language of the central stanzas. In its ambiguousness 'Heavenly Hurt' could refer to the pain of paradisiac ecstasy, but more immediately this seems to be an adjective of agency, from heaven, rather than an attributive one. This hurt is inflicted from above, 'Sent us of the Air,' like the 'Slant of light' that is its antecedent. In this context the natural image takes on a new meaning, again with the aid of her Lexicon which gives only one meaning for 'slant' as a noun, 'an oblique reflection or gibe.' It is then a mocking light, like the heavenly hurt that comes from the sudden instinctive awareness of man's lot since the Fall, doomed to mortality and irremediable suffering. This is indeed despair, though not in the theological sense unless Redemption is denied also. As Gerard Manley Hopkins phrases it in 'Spring and Fall,' for the young life there coming to a similar realization, 'It is the blight man was born for.'

Because of this it is beyond human correction, 'None may teach it—Any.' Though it penetrates it leaves 'no scar,' as an outward sign of healing, nor any internal wound that can be located and alleviated. What it leaves is 'internal difference,' the mark of all significant 'Meanings.' When the psyche is once stricken with the pain of such knowledge it can never be the same again. The change is final and irrevocable, sealed. The Biblical sign by which God claims man for his own has been shown in the poems of heavenly bridal to be a 'Seal,' the ring by which the beloved is married into immortal life. But to be redeemed one must first be mortal, and be made conscious of one's mortality. The initial and overwhelming impact of this can lead to a state of hopelessness, unaware that the 'Seal Despair' might be the reverse side of the seal of ecstasy. So, when first stamped on the consciousness it is an 'affliction.' But it is also 'imperial . . . Sent us of the Air,' the heavenly kingdom where God sits enthroned, and from the same source can come Redemption, though not in this poem.

By an easy transition from one insubstantial image to another, 'Air' back to 'a certain Slant of light,' the concluding stanza returns to the surface level of the winter afternoon. As the sun drops toward the horizon just before setting, 'the Landscape listens' in apprehension that the very light which makes it exist as a landscape is about to be extinguished; 'Shadows,' which are about to run out to infinity in length and merge with each other in breadth until all is shadow, 'hold their breath.' This is the effect created by the slanting light 'When it comes.' Of course no such things happen in nature, and it would be pathetic fallacy to pretend they did. The light does not inflict this suffering nor is the landscape the victim. Instead, these are just images of despair.

Similar figures are used in two other poems. In one the declining motion of the sun seems just a symbol of the inexorability of death:

> Presentiment—is that long Shadow—on the Lawn—
> Indicative that Suns go down—
>
> The Notice to the startled Grass
> That Darkness—is about to pass—

But in relation to the whole body of her poetry such apprehensiveness of the coming of 'Darkness,' like a dreaded king whose approach has already been heralded, suggests that this 'Presentiment' is one of unbearable pain. In the other poem it is so named. When lives are assailed by little anguish they merely 'fret,' she says, but when threatened with 'Avalanches . . . they'll slant,'

> Straighten—look cautious for their Breath—
> But make no syllable—like Death—

So with the slant of light 'When it goes,' as the sun finally sets and darkness covers all, ''tis like the Distance/On the look of Death.' Such is the difference between the coming of despair and the aftermath of extinction. The latter calls up an image of the staring eyes of the dead, the awful 'Distance' between life and death, and, as the only relief in sight, the distance between the poet and her experience that has made this sure control of form and language possible. The final and complete desolation of the landscape is the precise equivalent of that 'internal difference' which the action of the poem has brought about.

Such is the mortal view of despair, the quality and effects of which are the exclusive theme of this poem. Yet certain ambivalent phrases in it, like 'Heavenly Hurt' and the great 'Seal' of God (which by implication, at least, has a reverse side), seem related to the curious conjoining of ecstasy and despair that pervades much of her writing. In one poem it is explicit. The moment of ecstasy, given then withdrawn, is rendered in a series of paradoxes culminating in the lines:

> A perfect—paralyzing Bliss—
> Contented as Despair—

This is strikingly similar to Andrew Marvell's conjunction of joy and pain in 'The Definition of Love.' Seeking to discriminate a love so rare that mortal hope could never reach it on 'tinsel wing,' he concludes:

> Magnanimous Despair alone
> Could show me so divine a thing.

Whether she was acquainted with this poem is not known but it is analogous to several of her own, in its shock imagery and the technique of juggled ambiguities more than in theme. For when she sought heavenly fulfillment for earthly denial it was directly through Biblical metaphor, without the mediating convention of the cult of Platonic love. Fortunately for her originality, she derives as an artist from the Calvinism of New England rather than from the tradition of metaphysical poetry.

For a final exploration of dual meaning, one may return to that ambiguous 'certain Slant of light' which pierced her from above with 'an imperial affliction.' It calls to mind the 'waylaying Light' that struck her once like lightning, and brought the heavenly 'gleam' with which the preceding chapter on 'Ecstasy' concluded. It is notable that she used exactly the same metaphor in another poem to describe a blistering pain, that came not once but continually and 'burned Me—in the Night':

> It struck me—every Day—
> The Lightning was as new
> As if the Cloud that instant slit
> And let the Fire through— . . .

By spiritual insight she had discovered the close relation between human despair and the yearning for heavenly ecstasy, just as a kind of primitive wisdom had led her back to the juncture of love and death in the instinctual world. But these were only motions of the heart, up and down.

Always thrusting itself between was the conscious mind, that flickering identity that tries to give meaning to the bafflingly familiar pilgrimage from cradle to grave by defining, discriminating, questioning. This is what saves her from the sentimentalism that would have resulted had she adopted either extreme of ecstasy or despair as her whole view. Instead, she created her poems out of the tensions that issue from the clash of such powerful opposites. Further, she declined the gambit of an easy escape into paradox, for she never made an exact equation between love and death, ecstasy and despair. In her poetry their relations are much more complex: they form interlocking and reversible sequences. What gives this especial novelty is the direction of her emphasis, which is the opposite of that taken by her New England predecessors in the orthodox handling of these ambiguities. For example, in place of the Puritan view that earthly suffering is the ordained path to a heavenly reward of bliss, she makes the momentary glimpse of ecstasy both measure and cause of the despair that is the essence of the human condition. As she wrote in a late stanza:

> The joy that has no stem nor core,
> Nor seed that we can sow,
> Is edible to longing,
> But ablative to show. . . .

To be human is to yearn for the heavenly ecstasy we are deprived of on earth, 'ablative' being the Latin term for the case of deprivation. And so with the subtle interrelations of love and death. When her friend Higginson lost his wife she said in her letter of consolation: 'Do not try to be saved—but let Redemption find you—as it certainly will—Love is its own rescue, for we—at our supremest, are but its trembling Emblems.' These themes, fused from polar opposites, permeate her writings in prose and verse.

Her absolute loyalty to mind was the instrument by which she achieved this balance and maneuvered her emotions into forms. But she rarely lost sight of the fact that it was merely a technique of control, not the source of her poems. It is true that in her later years she indulged her penchant for aphorism in a number of verses that tend to run off into sheer intellectualism, even as some of her earliest efforts had been pure expressions of personal sentiment. Her best poems, however, present their themes in the full context of intellect and feeling, concerned not with exploiting either as such but with rendering the experiences that fuse them both. An eminent critic has put this succinctly: 'Unlike her contemporaries, she never succumbed to her ideas, to easy solutions, to private desires . . . ; like Donne, she *perceives abstraction and thinks sensation.*' And he makes this the basis for a high claim to distinction, that she was probably the only Anglo-American poet of her century who achieved a fusion of sensibility and thought, attaining 'a mastery over experience by facing its utmost implications.'

Inevitably, her search for meaning within the self, as well as in the non-self outside, led to a search for rediscovery of the maker of these selves. A poem written in mid-career, of small intrinsic worth, has considerable interest as a statement of her progressive concern with nature, man, and God. At first she thought that 'nature' was a sufficient subject for her poetry, she says, until 'Human nature' came in and absorbed the other 'As Firmament a Flame'; then, when she had just begun her exploration of that, 'There added the Divine.' All of her major themes are listed here in order: the outer world and the inner, the other world and, by implication at least, the paradise of art as the nearest she could come to attaining the 'Divine.' As a schoolgirl she had explained her inability to make peace with God because 'the world holds a predominant place in my affections.' Her withdrawal from society after maturity merely changed the terms of her loyalty, first to external nature then to the interior world of the self. As a poet she concluded that this last was the only reality she could know. It was also, she discovered, her best instrument for perceiving the processes of time and for conceiving the stasis of eternity, so that the reader today sees the ultimate purpose of all her explorations as religious in the profoundest sense of that term. And she would have rejoiced in the confirmation of her world view by modern thinkers, as in the recent definition of religion by an eminent scientist as 'a search for the relation between human desire and purpose on the one hand and cosmic change and indifference on the other.'

In contrast with the orthodoxy of her own day this approach could only seem heretical, however, which explains her tendency to discountenance herself as a religious person, as in her terse self-portrait late in life, 'I am but a Pagan.' The letter containing this phrase encloses a poem which furnishes the title for this section and brings it to a fitting conclusion:

> Of God we ask one favor,
> That we may be forgiven—
> For what, he is presumed to know—
> The Crime, from us, is hidden—
> Immured the whole of Life
> Within a magic Prison
> We reprimand the Happiness
> That too competes with Heaven.

Her pained sense of estrangement from the religion of her fathers lingered to the end, but so did the integrity that gave her courage to go her own way, to continue her search for heaven through poetry rather than through a theology she could not accept. This debate frames her perfect image for the earthly paradise where she wrestled with her angel. The mind and heart, the consciousness, the self, the soul—whatever word one wishes—this was the 'Magic Prison' she always explored in her poetry. 'Immured the whole of Life' within its walls she accepted the mortal lot as inescapable, trapped in time and wavering perpetually between doubt and belief in another life beyond. There she dedicated herself to creating the one thing of absolute value that, in her view, the human being is capable of. It goes under the rather inadequate name of religion, or art, the vision that comes with man's utmost reach towards truth and beauty. Its essence is longing, with ecstasy at one end and pain at the other, the leap of the heart and the despair of the mind.

ALBERT GELPI

Seeing New Englandly: From Edwards to Emerson to Dickinson

Beneath Emily Dickinson's little jokes about being a "Pagan" there lay an honest recognition, but beneath her allusion, just a few years before her death, to her "Puritan Spirit," there lay a recognition equally honest. No commentary on Emily Dickinson can avoid the observation that despite her restlessness she was very much of New England. The crucial question asks precisely in what respects hers was a Puritan spirit in the larger evolution of the American character.

I

The Puritan's "vision" of himself and the cosmos was formulated into theological tenets the truth of which rested not on scriptural authority alone but on the individual's sense of things. To the Puritan, God was the self-existent Being who devised the magnificent harmony of Creation and sustained it in contingent existence while He reigned above in incomprehensible sovereignty. But God's plan had been ruined by man's original sin, through which he lost grace. The loss of grace, that projection of the divine whose indwelling presence united man and nature and God, left man in solitary need and ushered in death, pain, depravity—the consequences of man's descent to a merely natural existence. Blind and impotent, crippled in mind and will, he stood in cringing dependence before an unseen and now angry Jehovah, who could elect to strike him with thunderbolts or to confer

From *Emily Dickinson: The Mind of the Poet*. Copyright © 1965 by the President and Fellows of Harvard College. Harvard University Press, 1966.

through Christ's mediation the grace which, all undeserved, would span the gaping separation, raise man's faculties, and restore him to unity with his God and his world. The Scriptures were God's words to man, through which he could understand the truth of his plight and the nature of his regeneration. Man's duty was to ponder and elucidate God's message and to carry out His Commandments. Hence the single-minded concern of Puritan divines with applying man's reason to God's revelation; and the unrelenting labor to erect a vast theological system on which fallen man could rely and within which he could think and act.

Needless to say, at its best Puritanism amounted to more than an arid rationalism or an abject surrender to formulae. Within the theological structure, the obligation of the individual man strained his stamina to the uttermost. He had to confront the universe starkly and answer within the privacy of his heart all the basic questions: Who am I? What is my relation to the not-me? How must I live in the certitude of death? Have I grounds for hope or not? In this confrontation the noblest Puritans neither winced nor succumbed. On the contrary, within their theology they lived as individuals fully and passionately; universal religious truth and individual human experience were working not at cross-purposes but toward concentricity. One has only to turn to Bradford's *Of Plimmoth Plantation* or Winthrop's "Journal" or Nathaniel Ward or Samuel Sewall or the verse of poets as different as Anne Bradstreet and Edward Taylor to realize with what vigor and passion the Puritan could commit himself, mind and heart and soul, to life. Most splendidly, there is the fierce brightness of Jonathan Edwards, illuminating both worlds. He resolved "to live with all my might, while I do live," and so to strive for heaven "with all the power, might, vigour, and vehemence, yes violence I am capable of." He asserted the importance of the passions and the holiness of religious affections. He loved his wife and God's radiant world, while rejoicing all the more in the "Divine and Supernatural Light."

Only seventy-five years after Edwards' death it seemed to Emerson that the body of doctrine had become a corpse, devoid of feeling or response, stiffened by rigor mortis. What could a living person do but inter the dead? But then he was left to confront the cosmos without even the authority of the Scriptures or the protective framework of established truth. Moreover, Emerson started from a different philosophical viewpoint from Edwards: Emerson's epistemology was not based on Locke's inductive method but on the intuitive perception of the post-Kantian transcendentalists; his metaphysic found German idealism and Oriental mysticism more congenial than Christian dualism.

Nevertheless, Edwards' and Emerson's formulations bespeak continuity as well as change. Like a good New Englander, Emerson also began with a double awareness of things: there was, or seemed to be, Nature and Soul, matter and spirit, not-me and me, Understanding and Reason. There was an "inevitable dualism," and the purpose of life was to resolve the opposition—not in some hypothetical future but here and now. He could admit the appalling impingements and limitations which constituted "Fate"; he could concede that "there is a crack in every thing that God has made"; he could see the world as fragmented and out of joint. But for Emerson the remedy was right at hand. The Fall was an illusion; nor was man helpless and debased, except by choice. Man was the vessel of divinity and need only release his energies; he was "a god in ruins," and could be a god in fact, like Jesus Christ. Man's Fall was only his first realization of himself as an existence apparently distinct, but the process of living was the opening out of one's self to discover "an occult relation" with all other things. In moments of most expansive perception the divine energy flowing from "me" became one again with the divine energy surging from the "not-me." At such times "I am nothing; I see all; the currents of the Universal Being circulate through me; I am part or parcel of God." Each and all, matter and spirit are One.

What had happened over the years was that the masterful synthesis which Edwards represented—that glowing fusion of intellectual and emotional character, that precarious poising of delight in this world against commitment to the next, that careful balance between individual and church—had been split asunder, and the Puritan mind, unable to repair the damage, would not be whole again. Thus, however similar are the axiomatic assumptions of Edwards' "vision" and the "vision" of Emerson, they could hardly have projected more dissimilar views of man's situation. Both men would agree that the individual loses himself in the highest knowledge only through a supra-logical spiritual power which manifests itself in a movement of the affections. Edwards would call that power grace; and Emerson, Reason. Edwards would place its source in God, and Emerson would place it in man. Finally, Edwards would support even the perceptions of grace with a rational system and with a community, while Emerson would leave the self reliant only on intuitive "Reason" and the responsive heart. For Emerson, Reason made each man "full of grace," and instituted a new scheme of "redemption" (though Emerson would not have invoked the theological terms he had so conspicuously shed). Man was god; hence he saved himself; and then earth was heaven. For Edwards heaven was the transcendence of earth; for Emerson it was the fulfillment of earth.

From the beginning there had been in Protestantism the impulse to push the notion of private conscience to its final extreme—namely, unquestioned reliance on individual revelation. In America there had been the related heresies of Anne Hutchinson and Roger Williams and the Friends, and there had been Cotton Mather's concept of "a particular faith" and Solomon Stoddard's awed respect for the unfathomable workings of grace in the individual. For a long time the orthodox had been effective in restraining the tendency to fix on the "inner light" by controlling it within themselves and by driving the heretics out. Ironically, both Edwards and Emerson became, for their respectable contemporaries, irrational enthusiasts. However, while the conservative "Arminians" had successfully stamped out the fires that spread from Edwards' Northampton, their Unitarian grandchildren pitted themselves in a losing effort against the hotheads from Concord. Indeed, the momentum of the rebellious young Turks succeeded in routing a debilitated theological Protestantism and establishing the primacy of personal, innate, and now "secular" vision. Thereby the drama of "salvation," or rather fulfillment, was located in the individual consciousness—a word whose connotations are very different from those of the word "soul." The final step in the transition was the recognition of the poet as the priest and saint and representative man of the new "religion" (he "stands among partial men for the complete man"), and the recognition of the creative imagination as man's divine faculty.

For the Puritans, "a religious heart inevitably translated itself into the formulae of theology; to them the conception of private experience was real, but not of private expression—wherein they differed from modern poets." Although Edwards might have disagreed, Allen Tate has argued that the best poetry is written when the control of the intellectual and religious order of an age is breaking down. Then, says Mr. Tate, the poet—who knows the elements of this order as part of his heritage without being able any longer to accept them unquestioningly—is forced to examine that heritage in terms of his own experience. The shattering of the tradition frees yet directs the energies of the imagination, and the result is magnificent poetry. If Mr. Tate is correct, Emily Dickinson came at the auspicious moment and to precisely the right place. Nurtured in the conservative Connecticut Valley, she not only came to distrust its theology but was personally incapable of logical, not to say theological, thought. System and argument, like the austere New England winter, were too hard and frigid for her, but now, at the crucial period of thaw, she came upon the warm, swelling, swirling notions of the Romantic poet-prophets. In Margaret Fuller's energetic words from the manifesto of the first issue of The Dial, Emily Dickinson was merely responding to

> the strong current of thought and feeling, which, for a few years past, has led many sincere persons in New England to make new demands on literature, and to reprobate that rigor of our conventions of religion and education, which is turning us to stone, which renounces hope, which

looks only backward, which . . . holds nothing so much in horror as new views and the dreams of youth.

II

The testimony of Emily Fowler Ford, one of Emily Dickinson's closest girlhood friends, indicates that as early as the mid-1840's, before the poet had met Benjamin Newton or Henry Vaughan Emmons, the two girls were reading Byron, Lowell, Emerson, Motherwell, and Margaret Fuller's translation of *Günerode*, and Emily Dickinson was particularly "steeped" in Emerson's *Essays*.

In 1847 a series of lectures on the history of literature delivered at Amherst College by a man named John Lord was reported to be scandalously "pantheistic" and "transcendental." When Professor William Tyler, a neighbor and friend of the Dickinsons, wrote scornfully of the tone of the proceedings, his correspondent replied: "I picture to myself all the grave Prof's of Am. assembled at a transcendental poetical lecture, and I am taken in a very humorous state of mind to say the least . . . Miss Emily should not be absent." Of course, this may not have been our Miss Emily, but the possibility is too intriguing not to mention, especially since Emily would almost certainly have heard the substance of the lectures, even if she herself were not there.

Among Emily's Amherst friends Leonard Humphrey was interested in Wordsworth and Carlyle, and George Gould delivered a prize speech during Commencement Week, 1848, on "Carlyle's 'Dream of Jean Richter.'" Emily's acquaintance with Dr. Josiah G. Holland dates from the early fifties; and Holland, like Higginson later, was a genteel liberal who was interested in "Women in Literature" and had written an article on the subject for the *Springfield Republican*. He stood for a personal "creedless, churchless, ministerless Christianity," and hailed Emerson's thought as "a chain of brilliant ideas strung as thickly as Wethersfield onions when packed for export." In 1881 Emily warmly recalled to Mrs. Holland that when she had first heard her husband pray, she had thought that she felt "a different God" who was a friend.

Emily gave some idea of Emerson's influence upon her own thought in her comments on the *Poems, Representative Men*, and the Holmes biography, and in several allusions to his "immortal" poems. Emerson spoke in Amherst in 1855 on "A Plea for the Scholar," in 1857 on "The Beautiful in Rural Life," in 1879 on "Superlative or Mental Temperance," and led off a course of lectures in 1865 with "Social Aims." That he met with small crowds and little enthusiasm, even as late as his lecture of 1879 (by which time he was something of a national monument), indicates the extent to which Emily's interest outran that of her Amherst neighbors. Although there is no evidence that she attended any of these lectures, she must have listened from a distance, and after the 1857 visit, when Emerson stayed at the house next door with Austin and Sue, she wrote breathlessly to her sister-in-law: "It must have been as if he had come from where dreams are born!" In her last years she copied out several scraps of Emerson's verse. This was a special tribute, for she rarely copied the words of other poets, even her favorites; and the attribution to Emerson of the anonymously published "Success" (the only poem of hers to appear in print outside of a newspaper during her lifetime) must have amused and delighted her. She wrote of the severe shock which Emerson's death dealt her in April 1882. Since the Reverend Wadsworth had died just a few weeks before, death had struck down within a single month the men who symbolized and supported the two sides of her divided spirit.

For Emily Dickinson's indebtedness to Thoreau we have fewer hard facts to point to than in the case of Emerson, but circumstantial evidence intimates a great deal (though the influence here was somewhat later and so less directly formative than that of Emerson). The Dickinson library copies of *Letters to Various Persons* and *A Week on the Concord and Merrimack* and the two copies of *Walden* are dated from the middle sixties, but she might have read any of them earlier. Besides, she must have read the essays which appeared in the pages of the *Atlantic* during 1862: "Walking," "Autumnal Tints," "Wild Apples," and others. And her remark to Sue and Austin on a seaside vacation in 1865—"Was the Sea cordial? Kiss him for Thoreau"—shows that she knew the recently issued *Cape Cod*. Her writing is filled with scattered remarks which suggest Thoreau's influence: " 'My Country, 'tis of Thee,' has always meant the Woods—to me—'Sweet Land of Liberty,' I trust is your own—"; "The fire-bells are oftener now, almost, than the church-bells. Thoreau would wonder which did the most harm." There is, too, the charming anecdote of the lady who, having been "recently introduced in the family by marriage," was brought for the first time to Edward Dickinson's house to meet her new relatives. When by chance she "quoted some sentence from Thoreau's writings, Miss Dickinson, recognizing it, hastened to press her hand as she said, 'From this time we are acquainted;' and this was the beginning of a friendship that lasted till the death of the poetess." Emily must have felt a deep kinship with Thoreau for a passing reference to provoke so spontaneous and wholehearted a response to a stranger.

As for other Transcendentalists, she read some of Theodore Parker and later O. B. Frothingham's biography of Parker; and she knew enough about William Ellery Channing to use a verse of his as the basis for a poem of her own (P 1234, III.858). But since specific information is so meager, the full extent of her knowledge of what was going on in Concord can best be suggested through her own words. Curiously enough it is the conclusion of a comic valentine which indicates how clearly she had absorbed, as early as 1850, the essential features of Transcendentalism—the optimism, the emphasis on experimentation and originality, the sense of social purpose, the metaphysical and mystical speculations, the pulse of rhythm and imagery:

> But the world is sleeping in ignorance and error, sir, and we must be crowing cocks, and singing larks, and a rising sun to awake her; or else we'll pull society up by the roots, and plant it in a different place. We'll build Alms-houses, and transcendental State prisons, and scaffolds—we will blow out the sun, and the moon, and encourage invention. Alpha shall kiss Omega—we will ride up the hill of glory—Hallelujah, all hail!

The shock of Transcendentalism had been registered on the American consciousness even as far as Amherst; Brook Farm and *The Dial* were experiments now defunct, but they were events of such import that henceforth New England could not think without taking into account what they had stood for. In *The Blithedale Romance* (1852) Hawthorne would tell of Hollingsworth's schemes for penal reform; in *Walden* (1854) Thoreau would "brag as lustily as chanticleer in the morning . . . if only to wake my neighbors up," for "only that day dawns to which we are awake. There is more day to dawn. The sun is but a morning-star." Emily Dickinson's words of 1850 had already caught much of the imagery and fanfare.

III

The early letters of Emily's correspondence record the development of her imagination and her growing sense of poetic mission. From the first she welcomed the opportunity for "improving" a situation. In her earliest extant letter, written in 1842 when she was twelve, she told Austin of sleeping alone and imagining deliciously dire perils, then went on to describe Austin's hens which "will be so large that you cannot perceive them with the naked Eye when you get home," and narrated the theft of an egg by "a skonk . . . or else a hen In the shape of a skonk and I dont know which." These capricious childhood fantasies are not remarkable in themselves, except to indicate the play of fancy which she was soon to apply to increasingly serious purpose.

At about the time when she was discovering some of the new writers, she indulgently warned Abiah Root about the enchainment of the free spirit; and after loosing a flutter of metaphors on another occasion she paused to intone to her professing friend in sly mockery:

> Now my dear friend, let me tell you that these last thoughts are fictions— vain imaginations to lead astray foolish young women. They are flowers of

speech, they both *make*, and *tell* deliberate falsehoods, avoid them as the snake . . . Honestly tho', a snake bite is a serious matter, and there can't be too much said, or done about it . . . *I* love those little green ones that slide around by your shoes in the grass—and make it rustle with their elbows— they are rather my favorites on the whole, but I would'nt influence *you* for the world!

With a wave of the hand she had charmed the venomous serpent into a harmless grass snake, which was, after all, her favorite sort of reptile. The nimble feat of verbal prestidigitation was to admit the sins of fancy and then absolve them through the fancy's ingenuity.

In April 1850 (the year Emily received Emerson's *Poems* from Benjamin Newton) she wrote Jane Humphrey a long letter which, underneath all the inarticulate confusion, bespoke a special sense of dedication. The importance of the passage to the emergence of the poet—it may even be roughly analogous to the moment of consecration in Wordsworth's *Prelude*—merits its quotation in full:

I would whisper to you in the evening of many, and curious things—and by the lamps eternal read your thoughts and response in your face, and find out what you thought about me, and what I have done, and am doing . . . I have dared to do strange things—bold things, and have asked no advice from any—I have heeded beautiful tempters, yet do not think I am wrong . . . Oh Jennie, it would relieve me to . . . confess what *you only* shall know, an experience bitter, and sweet, but the sweet did so beguile me—and life has had an aim, and the world has been too precious for your poor—and striving sister! The winter was all one dream, and the spring has not yet waked me, I would *always* sleep, and dream, and it never should turn to morning, so long as night is so blessed. What do you weave from all these threads . . . I hope belief is not wicked, and assurance, and perfect trust—. . . do you dream from all this what I mean? Nobody *thinks* of the joy, nobody *guesses* it, to all appearance old things are engrossing, and new ones are not revealed, but there *now* is nothing old, things are budding, and springing, and singing, and you rather think you are in a green grove, and it's branches that go, and come.

Twice she asks the momentous question: what do you make of all this? Momentous indeed was the implication of the painful transition to a sweet new life and a renewed world. Perhaps it was a dream, as it seemed at first, but then the dream of joyous vision was better than hopeless reality. Excitement, mingled with reticence, blurred the point in a whirl of words, but even in her most intimate moments she would refer only obliquely to that "attitude toward the Universe, so precisely my own," for which she had relinquished the Christian "Vision of John at Patmos."

Now she was bold enough to appropriate to herself the title of poet. In 1851 she spoke of "the fancy that we are the only poets, and everyone else is *prose.*" A few months later, while the rest of the family was at church, she conducted her own service for Sue in her heart and only regretted the lack of things "which I may poetize" for "this sweet Sabbath of our's." In 1853 she good-naturedly chided Austin, her "Brother Pegasus," for writing verses, because as a poet in her own right she was reluctant to share the laurels with him. To the Hollands she identified herself with the village poet in Longfellow's *Kavanagh.* A sermon (given by Professor E. A. Park of the Andover Theological Seminary) on "the importance of Aesthetic in connection with Religious and Moral Culture" brought this exclamation: "I never heard anything like it, and dont expect to again . . . " By 1854 Sue's persistence about her sister-in-law's unregenerate state pressed too hard, but in her wounded repy Emily would not compromise her new calling: "Sue—you can go or stay—There is but one alternative . . . I have lived by this. It is the lingering emblem of the Heaven I once dreamed . . . " If in Sue's eyes she had abandoned Christ for Satan, it was too bad; her decision was unalterable, and, as if to emphasize her new role, she finished the letter with a poem. Most frequently now her signature read "Emilie," which some critics have taken as the mask of the child-poet (in the Blake-Wordsworth-Emerson tradition) but which might just as well be read as the sign of the new poet enjoying the embellishment of verbal curlicues.

During the fifties the letters began to mention and display a concern for style. The struggle for stylistic effects grew out of the necessity to make a language adequate to the more ambitious descriptions of nature that she was attempting. They are often keenly perceived and crisply phrased, and even the exuberant excesses are interesting as a novice's explorations of the resources of her medium. To Sue in Maryland she mused: the moon "looks like a fairy tonight, sailing around the sky in a little silver gondola with stars for gondoliers. I asked her to let me ride a little while ago—and told her I would *get out* when she got as far as Baltimore, but she only smiled to herself and went sailing on." The autumn countryside which she dispatched to the city-bound Austin is more finely realized:

> I have tried to delay the frosts, I have coaxed the fading flowers, I thought I
> *could* detain a few of the crimson leaves until you had smiled upon them, but
> their companions call them and they cannot stay away—you will find the
> blue hills, Austin, with the autumnal shadows silently sleeping on them,
> and there will be a glory lingering round the day, so you'll know autumn has
> been here, and the *setting sun* will tell you . . . The earth looks like some poor
> old lady who by dint of pains had bloomed e'en till *now*, yet in a forgetful
> moment a few silver hairs from out her cap come stealing, and she tucks
> them back so hastily and thinks nobody *sees*.

At the end of this message to her Brother Pegasus she set down (unobtrusively as rhymed prose) the first serious poem sent in a letter. In 1852 we find this imagistic scene: "the shy litle birds would say chirrup, chirrup in the tall cherry trees, and if our dresses rustled, hop frightened away; and there used to be some farmer cutting down a tree in the woods, and you and I, sitting there, could hear his sharp ax ring." In 1856 her cousin John Graves received a prose lyric whose landscape and logic are now completely imaginative: "Ah John— Gone? Then I lift the lid to my box of Phantoms, and lay another in, unto the Resurrection—Then will I gather in *Paradise*, the blossoms fallen here, and on the shores of the sea of Light, seek my missing sands."

By 1858, after some years of apprenticeship, she felt sufficiently sure of her sight and insight and of her technique to begin recopying verses and preserving them in bound packets. The letters and the rapidly expanding body of poems displayed increasing control of theme, image, and diction. Under the stress of emotional crisis she composed more than five hundred poems in 1862 and 1863. Nor were they all written to relieve the pressure of pain; there is in the nature poetry a deepening wonder at the awesome beauty of the world. The verse of these years includes nature poems, poems of states of feeling, poems about poetry and the poet, poems about love, death, and immortality—in short, all the major patterns of theme and imagery. By the early sixties the design of Emily Dickinson's art was set; the rest of her poetic life was an elaboration and a perfection.

IV

The critic can cull the poems and letters for a catalogue of transcendental "doctrines" which the poet had, for the moment at any rate, espoused. If Emerson referred to the world as "a divine dream, from which we may presently awake," Dickinson said: "Reality is a dream from which but a portion of mankind have yet waked . . . " If Emerson urged self-knowledge and self-reliance, Dickinson exhorted her poetic persona:

> Soto! Explore thyself!
> Therein thyself shalt find
> The "Undiscovered Continent"—
> No Settler had the Mind.
> (P 832, II.631)

And:

> Lad of Athens, faithful be
> To Thyself,
> And Mystery—
> All the rest is Perjury—
> (P 1768, III.1183)

If Emerson perceived the correspondence which made the world the emblematic "web of God," Dickinson saw things as "trembling Emblems" and felt the movements of an unseen Weaver. If Emerson's position rested on the divine faculty of Intuition, Dickinson claimed "Glee intuitive" as "the gift of God."

Anyone who has given Emerson and Dickinson a thorough reading can indulge in the game of finding more cases in point, but such analogues could be misleading if they are insisted upon too rigidly, because the words of a lyric poet like Emily Dickinson express not philosophic generalizations but the measure of a particular moment. On the other hand, the critic cannot resign himself to an aimless chronological reading of almost 1800 lyrics. He must try to perceive in the shifting record of successive moments the salient recurrences, relations, and patterns without reducing the poet's mind to an abstraction. And so we must watch Emily approach Emerson by a dark and circuitous path.

Wherever Emily Dickinson's mental processes may have led, they began with an intolerable sense of emptiness which drove her to project as concrete evidence of her incompleteness the loss of childhood, father, mother, lover. She could list childhood and the dead among the "Things that never can come back"; she could even enumerate the things lost with childhood. But in all honesty she had to add: "But is that all I have lost—memory drapes her Lips." These losses—genuine and heartfelt—were at least definable and hence bearable, but what seemed excruciating was the fact that almost the first act of the mind was an awareness of isolation. Edwards would have attributed this knowledge to original sin, and Emerson to the separation of the object from the Oversoul. But Emily Dickinson's was a characteristically personal response: all she knew was that she had to manage somehow from day to day, eating and sleeping and speaking and acting in the hollowness of the void:

> A loss of something ever felt I—
> The first that I could recollect
> Bereft I was—of what I knew not
> (P 959, II.694)

The poem does not specify what was lost; all she could say was that she was bereft of something in and of herself, something so private that it belonged to her as an individual and would make her, as she was not now, a whole person.

> I cannot buy it—'tis not sold—
> There is no other in the World—
> Mine was the only one
> (P 840, II.635)

Before anything—faith, love, happiness—were possible, before she could give or take or act, the unknown factor had somehow to be found:

> If I could find it Anywhere
> I would not mind the journey there
> Though it took all my store
> (P 840, II.636)

So hers was a quest through an interior waste land, trackless and guideless, without even the name of the missing treasure. She could call it what she would—friend, lover, mother, father, "Golden Fleece," God—but these names could never contain the dark immensity of "Missing All." Life began with "Missing All"; and its trek through time seemed a dreary repetition of losses, of missing in turn each of the things most dear, until "Parting is all we know of heaven, / And all we need of hell." In this private hell the lonely mourner "walked among the children."

Even Satan, however, soon found that hell had its own compensations—the stimulus to yearn and struggle and resist. And in her own way Emily Dickinson came to draw sustenance from the substance of her sorrow. "I always try to think in any disappointment that had I been gratified, it had been sadder still, and I weave from such suppositions, *at times*, considerable consolation; consolation upside down as I am pleased to call it." "Consolation upside down" gave way sometimes to a brighter possibility: "To miss you, Sue, is power"; "Possession—has a sweeter chink/Upon a Miser's Bar." Nor was she seeking solace in futile paradox; she was stating, flatly, and deliberately, her recognition of the only grounds on which life without delusion was possible: "The stimulus of Loss makes most Possession mean."

How could loss be power beyond possession? Because loss made us desire, made us project an object for our desire, made us strain urgently toward it. What we lacked we wanted, and if we lacked all, we wanted all. Fulfillment was static, like eternity; but desire was a process, and was therefore the prerequisite and condition of human life. At times, even, desire found response; for a moment we glimpsed what we wanted to see, grasped what we wanted to hold. Afterward, these fleeting moments of fulfillment provided the stimulus for the continuation of the process. Although we know that possession "is past the instant/We achieve the Joy," we can accept life for the memory of past moments, the ecstasy of the present, the anticipation of the future:

> Satisfaction—is the Agent
> Of Satiety—
> Want—a quiet Comissary
> For Infinity.
> (P 1036, II.735)

In other words, man's littleness was, in a strange way, the condition for his greatness, and his limitations pointed him toward infinity. Edwards would have regarded this thesis as untenable, and Emerson would have found it morbid. There is something peculiarly modern about it. Nietzsche defined the tragic sense as the assertion of the will to live in the face of death and the inexhaustible joy which that assertion releases. Yeats wrote in his autobiography, "We begin to live when we have conceived of life as tragedy." In his version of *Women of Trachis* Ezra Pound had the dying and thwarted Herakles exclaim: "what/ SPLENDOUR, IT ALL COHERES." In *The Myth of Sisyphus* Albert Camus rejects suicide and chooses life despite its absurdity. Emily Dickinson, who spoke of "Confident Despair," would have understood these expressions of tragic joy. It was knowledge of "this brief Tragedy of Flesh" that made life precious; it was acceptance of loss and defeat that made an unexpected moment of vision into "that bright tragic thing."

For this reason "Life never loses it's startlingness, however assailed," or—to state the idea in personal terms—"Who never lost, are unprepared / A Coronet to find!" The crown's shining and full circle did descend on us, if only in momentary glory, and life was not only possible but beautiful as long as there were times when the void was filled with abundance. In "Burnt Norton" T. S. Eliot restated the moment for a waste-land century, but it is very much the same event:

> Dry the pool, dry concrete, brown edged,
> And the pool was filled with water out of sunlight,
> And the lotos rose, quietly, quietly,
> The surface glittered out of heart of light, . . .
> Then a cloud passed, and the pool was empty.

If many of the Romantic prophets did not share her experience of darkness, they confirmed and defined for her the experience of overwhelming brightness. At its most sublime intensity, the momentary incandescence consumed the categories of human Understanding and held all in its illumination. In Emerson's words, with the movements of Reason, "there is the incoming or the receding of God: that is all we can affirm; and we can show neither how nor why." In Dickinson's image the manifestation was "a Blossom of the Brain," "the Spirit fructified." The cessation of such epiphanies would be "the Funeral of God," for each of these sublime moments was indeed "a cordial interview / With God"—not, she told her nephew Ned, the unseen Jehovah in epaulettes but another Eleusinian Deity who revealed Himself in an overpowering efflux of life. Heaven vested itself for each man, and for the sake of those incarnations one could endure the residue of life and "entertain Despair." For Thoreau they had the same vitalizing function:

> Within the circuit of this plodding life,
> There enter moments of an azure hue,
> Untarnished fair as is the violet

> So by God's cheap economy made rich
> To go upon my winter's task again.

So vital was the illumination that Emily tried time and again to make
stubborn words render some sense of the glory: it was God's intrusion through
which He was known and through which He confounded "Time's possibility"; it was "Eternity—obtained—in Time"; it was "Reversed Divinity,"
which, falling like a thunderbolt, transfixed mortality "in a moment of
Deathlessness." The quatrain below suggests metrically the moment's uncertain approach which reaches climactic force in the last leaping phrase:

> 'Tis this—invites—appalls—endows—
> Flits—glimmers—proves—dissolves—
> Returns—suggests—convicts—enchants—
> Then—flings in Paradise—
>
> (P 673, II.520)

For most of the Romantics, however transcendental, Nature served as
intermediary between self and Deity, as the meeting place of the new
"religion." Among Emily Dickinson's earliest poems there is a splendid
evocation of a very special summer's day (P 122, I.88), and many such poems
followed over the years. At the beginning of her correspondence with
Higginson, when she was trying to make him understand her "vision," she
spoke in one letter alone of the "noiseless noise in the Orchard," of the
stopping of breath "in the core of the Woods," of the sight of the chestnut tree
that made the skies blossom for her, and finally of the wood visited by Angels.
During her childhood her religious elders had forbidden her to enter the
woods because of the venomous snake and the poisonous flowers (remember
her warning to Abiah Root about the snake and the flowers of the imagination), but on later investigation despite their warnings she had found in
Nature only an angelic visitation.

Nature was precious because it was the material medium through
which God or the Life Spirit touched man and through which man touched
Him or It. Several poems invent images for the indefinable fusion of matter
and spirit:

> 'Tis Compound Vision—
> Light—enabling Light—
> The Finite—furnished
> With the Infinite—
> Convex—and Concave Witness—
> Back—toward Time—
> And forward—
> Toward the God of Him—
>
> (P 906, II.666)

Elsewhere she wrote that the ear could not hear without the "Vital Word" that "came all the way from Life to me," nor could the eye see without divine light. During these visitations dust and Deity, time and eternity, were one, like Eliot's moment neither in time nor out of time, neither flesh nor fleshless.

Man was by no means impotent in the process. Did not his openness, his striving for self-transcendence, indicate something in himself that answered to Spirit? Light, she said, enabled Light; for God to show Himself, we must be able to see. In these supreme moments our cringing souls, covert in the void, did emerge, did in turn show ourselves, did move and expand, so that we ourselves became microscopic incarnations, like "Holy Ghosts in Cages." For the soul exists only in the body, and the body acts only under the soul's impulsion. Or, in poetic imagery:

> The Music in the Violin
> Does not emerge alone
> But Arm in Arm with Touch, yet Touch
> Alone—is not a Tune—
> The Spirit lurks within the Flesh
> Like Tides within the Sea
> That make the Water live, estranged
> What would the Either be?
> (P 1576, III. 1086)

Nevertheless, like all occurrences in the material order, these "sumptuous moments" went as inexplicably as they came: "Not of detention is Fruition," or, as Frost was to say, "Nothing gold can stay." Despite his ebullient optimism, even Emerson had to admit that in the present state of things Reason's grasp was only momentary: "Like a bird which alights nowhere, but hops perpetually from bough to bough, is the Power which abides in no man and no woman, but for a moment speaks from this one, and for another moment from that one." Emily Dickinson endeavored mightily to accept joy's brevity as part of the process which impelled life to further inspiration. In the following poem the verses, seesawing back and forth in syntax and sound, suggest the oscillation from loss to recovery, from resonant correspondence back to hollow isolation:

> Image of Light, Adieu—
> Thanks for the interview—
> So long—so short—
> Preceptor of the whole—
> Coeval Cardinal—
> Impart—Depart—
> (P 1556, III. 1072)

In the whole span of the New England tradition, from Bradford and

Winthrop and Edwards to Emerson and Dickinson and later to Eliot and Frost, individual experience finally focused and rested upon the pivotal moments of revelation and insight—the moments of divine manifestation and human vision. This union—however insecure—in which the individual lost himself in totality is the sole end of that Augustinian strain of piety which Perry Miller saw as the bright heart of Puritanism. "Without it individual life was a burden; with it living became richness and joy." But while Christians see regeneration as the moment of grace, "other people have found other names for the experience: to lovers it is love, to mystics it is ecstasy, to poets inspiration." Edwards called men to the "Great Awakening"; Emerson smiled in the calm assurance of Reason's ever-expanding sway; and in *Four Quartets* Eliot—that Puritan misplaced in the Midwest, who moved through Boston back to orthodoxy in the Church that his forebears had abandoned—composed a masterful meditation on "the still point of the turning world." But Emily Dickinson, somewhat after Emerson and before Eliot, could not arrive at the peace and assurance that they found at the ends of divergent paths. In the face of conflicting evidences her problem, like Frost's, was "what to make of a diminished thing," and her response, like his, was "to get now and then elated." For a poet she was; and, in some senses of the words, a lover and a mystic as well. What remains, therefore, is to see what she made of and with her fitful vision.

V

If transcendence comes only to individuals and only in time and space, these moments of personal revelation must be made to shape the totality of meaning and of experience. The conquering of time through time of which Eliot spoke was possible only if the instant's revelation-vision was fixed in a world of flux, drawing time and space into perspective around itself and defining the design of faith. The center of light projects the encircling design on all things, and sustains the design through time and perhaps (who knows?) through eternity. If Christian theology no longer provided viable terms to formulate the design, the new "religion" would have to create a new vision; if the discarding of heaven left only earth as the arena of experience, the poet-priest would have to refashion the perception of the here and now.

In "New Views of Christianity, Society, and the Church," Orestes Brownson insisted that he was beginning the process of redefinition within the existing ecclesiastical organization, but the force of his thought carried him and others far beyond. He defined the religious dilemma of the nineteenth century in terms of the interaction of Materialism and Spiritualism. In the intensity of its genesis Christianity had fused the two modes of thinking and living into a dynamic unity. The Middle Ages had erred in an inordinate Spiritualism which scourged the flesh, fanatically blinded to its inherent goodness and beauty. The Protestant reaction swung wrongheadedly to Materialism, so that the only spiritual elements in religion since the Reformation were clinging vestiges of the medieval Church. Now that these had gradually fallen away, the last and supreme expression of Protestant Materialism was the Unitarians' gross and bloated complacency. Christianity could survive, Brownson concluded, only with a resurgence of the primal energy which would again join both orders—matter and spirit, nature and heaven, body and soul—into an organic whole.

In "A Discourse of Matters Pertaining to Religion" Theodore Parker invoked the same dialectic with slightly different labels and pushed the argument further—in fact, out of the Christian context. According to Parker, Naturalism made a substantial distinction between creation and Creator; it envisioned man in Nature, with God "but *transiently* present and active" at the moment of creation, "not *immanently* present and active" from instant to instant. Without God's immanence man could know only naturally through his human intellect; and the Naturalist train of argument soon propelled man into "the Doubt of Hume, the Selfishness of Paley, the coarse materialism of Hobbes," and the rationalism of the Deists and the Unitarians. Supernaturalism also conceived creation as separate from God but insisted that man could know only through God's special intervention and express commands; and this train of argument soon debased man into the superstition of miracles, sacraments, churches, heaven, and hell. However, Parker's argument ran, there was a third approach—Spiritualism, or the Natural-Religious View—which superseded both these partial and divisive views; it eliminated the materiality of the one and the necromancy of the other. Its great synthesis recognized the "connection between God and the soul, as between light and the eye, sound and the ear, food and the palate, truth and the intellect, beauty and the imagination." The authority of the Natural-Religious View, therefore, rested on the "religious consciousness" of "free and conscious men," and its revelation was the perception of the glorious coherence of all things in the immanent Godhead.

Thoreau eliminated the clumsy labels and abstractions of Brownson and Parker to catch the smack and sting of the concrete experience: "I see, smell, taste, hear, feel, that everlasting Something to which we are allied, at once our maker, our abode, our destiny, our very Selves . . . "; "I explore, too, with pleasure, the sources of the myriad sounds which crowd the summer noon, and which seem the very grain and stuff of which eternity is made." His celebration of "a natural Sabbath" was the prayer "for no higher heaven than the pure senses can furnish, a *purely* sensuous life." For "may we not *see*

God? . . . Is not Nature, rightly read, that of which she is commonly taken to be the symbol merely? . . . What is it, then, to educate but to develop these divine germs called the senses?" When the senses operated freely, heaven took place all around us, and multiplicity blended into the one divine articulation of Nature.

There was in Emily Dickinson a similar inclination of mind and heart. Whether or not she derived it from reading Brownson and Parker and Thoreau, her response to her own religious dilemma had much in common with theirs. In a letter to the Hollands she had expressed her love of " 'time and sense'—and fading things, and things that do *not* fade." It was hard to love time and sense, unless she could somehow transmute fading things into unfading permanence. She could sometimes hope for, sometimes believe in, heaven, and then she accepted earth as a preparation for immortality. But so uncertain a trust was no basis for a life's experience.

The stirrings of a new trust are suggested in these lines:

> The worthlessness of Earthly things
> The Ditty * is that Nature Sings—
> And then—enforces their delight
> Till Synods** are inordinate—
> (P 1373, III.947)

    * Alternate word: Sermon   ** Alternate phrase: Zion is

Viewed rightly, the crumbling impermanence of things was lost in the incandescence which illuminated them as it consumed them to ashes. Overpowered by splendor, "I'm half tempted to take my seat in that Paradise of which the good man writes, and begin forever and ever *now*, so wondrous does it seem." Since her vision of nature lay beyond and above the temptation to heaven, she could claim to be luckier than God Himself: "If God had been here this summer, and seen the things that *I* have seen—I guess that He would think His Paradise superfluous." Often Heaven seemed "a fictitious Country": merely a name for "what I cannot reach," a designation for the furthest extension of experience to an unknown but intuited absolute. Eternity, therefore, was here, not there, if one were but worthy of the vision, and the vision of Heaven below came to replace that of "Papa above." Though "the time to live is frugal," it is sufficient, for "each of us has the skill of life." That is, since each "gives or takes heaven in corporeal person," we can see Nature as Heaven and Heaven in Nature simply by being true to our best selves.

Weighing earth against a doubtful "Heaven to come," she summed up her choice with Yankee shrewdness in an aphorism that reads like Franklin pronouncing through Emerson: "A Savior in a Nut, is sweeter to the grasp than ponderous Prospectives." In the same vein she adapted another folk adage, using Poor Richard's pragmatism to ponder the choice between the temporal world and celestial eternity:

> I cannot help esteem
>
> The "Bird within the Hand"
> Superior to the one
> The "Bush" may yield me
> Or may not
> Too late to choose again.
> (P 1012, II. 726)

As a matter of fact, the old terms of distinction might audaciously be reversed: "To be human is more than to be divine, for when Christ was divine, he was uncontented till he had been human." So she would not be the proud wren who vainly sought "a home too high" but rather the lark who

> is not ashamed
> To build upon the ground
> Her modest house—
>
> Yet who of all the throng
> Dancing around the sun
> Does so rejoice?
> (P 143, I. 102–3)

The assumption underlying her moments of exultation was not so much that earth as earth was superior to heaven but that earth was heaven, that indeed as Emerson and Thoreau had said, "the 'Supernatural,' was only the Natural, disclosed." In the following poem the structure dramatically conveys the meaning. The statement of the first line—concise, declarative—stands out from the subsequent verses, grammatically tangled and blurred by the recurrence of negatives:

> The Fact that Earth is Heaven—
> Whether Heaven is Heaven or not
> If not an Affidavit
> Of that specific Spot
> Not only must confirm us
> That it is not for us
> But that it would affront us
> To dwell in such a place—
> (P 1408, III. 977)

"The Fact that Earth is Heaven"; in other poems "Universe" and "Firmament" and "Deity" become interchangeable alternatives. In her favorite metaphor of house and home—suggesting, as always, that odd Dickinson combination of coziness and awe—she called Nature a haunted house, a mystic house, God's house: the lost Father in Heaven found in His neighborhood lodgings.

The vision of the earth-heaven conferred, at least for those moments, a total acceptance of the natural order of time and process. "Time," cried Emily, "why Time was all I wanted!" With the great Romantic poets she celebrated the mysterious and vital process of growth in which self realized itself in cosmic unity. Time was preferable to eternity, "for the one is still, but the other moves." Immortality was an "ablative estate" which carried us from the dynamic drama of experience, and death's encroachment, which alone kept life from being perfect (that is, from being eternity), nonetheless provided the pressure which made life the more intensely experienced, the more frugally felt. The process—for Dickinson as for Wordsworth, Shelley, Keats, Emerson, and Thoreau—made the world "Fairer though Fading." Besides, the individual process contained and revealed the pattern: to Thoreau's "The revolution of the seasons—is a great and steady flow," Emily added: "Changelessness is Nature's change." So with the acceptance of change and death, the circle of the seasons could become for each of us the unwinding disclosure of heaven. Matter and Spirit, concrete and universal, are the same:

> "Nature" is what we see—
> The Hill—the Afternoon—
> Squirrel—Eclipse—the Bumble bee—
> Nay—Nature is Heaven—
> Nature is what we hear—
> The Bobolink—the Sea—
> Thunder—the Cricket—
> Nay—Nature is Harmony—
> (P 668, II.515)

The force which swept through the world, animating matter into heaven, is sometimes symbolized in the spontaneous harmony of bird-song, but more often in the breath of the wind. Emerson spoke of "the currents of the Universal Being," and Thoreau wrote, "In enthusiasm we undulate to the divine spiritus—as the lake to the wind." In Emily Dickinson's world, too, the wind was the Spiritus Sanctus, unseen but felt in all its operations: "The Wind didn't come from the Orchard—today— / Further than that—"; or, "A Murmur in the Trees—to note— / Not loud enough—for Wind—"; or:

> Exhiliration is the Breeze
> That lifts us from the Ground
> And leaves us in another place
> Whose statement is not found—
> (P 1118, II.786)

The culmination of the wind's sweep is a sudden and momentary breathless-
ness: "When Winds take Forests in their Paws— / The Universe—is still."
Suspended in stillness, we open eyes and heart, and we see and know. The
event was thus double: outward and inward, revelation and vision, "The
Capsule of the Wind / The Capsule of the Mind."

Those climactic capsule moments are most often symbolized in
"Lightning—and the Sun—." In Emerson's phrase, revelation traveled "like
a thunderbolt to the centre," and repeatedly in Dickinson poems the lightning, striking to the center with light so bright as to be borne for only a flashing
second, illuminated all the landscape for her stunned and reeling consciousness. Sometimes she softened the remembrance of the impact by domesticat-
ing the lightning image to "yellow feet" or "electric Mocassin" or "a yellow
Fork / From Tables in the sky," but she had felt, in ravished awe, the
slamming, blinding force. Thunder-stricken like Ahab, but shaken to life and
not to death, she saw things "Not yet suspected—but for Flash / And
Click—and Suddenness"; and so she "would not exchange the Bolt / For all
the rest of Life." Considered in their fullness, these spots of time seemed
"torrid Noons," and noon became a major image for their concentric
radiance:

> You'll know it—as you know 'tis Noon—
> By Glory—
> As you do the Sun—
> By Glory—
>
> (P 420, I.326)

Even when Emily Dickinson tried to conjure up a conception of
heaven as it was or would be, she could imagine only the natural order
extended through time and space. "Forever—is composed of Nows": "not a
different time," but a perfected time, an Arcadian Golden Age where "Sun
constructs perpetual Noon," where "perfect Seasons wait," where "Consciousness—is Noon."

> A Nature be
> Where Saints, and our plain going Neighbor
> Keep May!
>
> (P 977, II.706)

On the other hand the peerless moments revealed earth as Eden
before the Fall—Nature perfected to Paradise. If heaven is Arcadia, Eden is
heaven. An early poem tells a charming parable about a lost, frost-bitten
Puritan flower (a floral variant of the image of herself as a little girl locked out
in the cold) who found an unfallen Eden aglow with summer:

> As if some little Arctic flower
> Upon the polar hem—

> Went wandering down the Latitudes
> Until it puzzled came
> To continents of summer—
> To firmaments of sun—
> To strange, bright crowds of flowers—
> And birds, of foreign tongue!
> I say, As if this little flower
> To Eden, wandered in—
> What then? Why nothing,
> Only, your inference therefrom!
>
> (P 180, I. 132)

One inference is that under the thrust of that "bright" strain of the Romantic spirit of which Wordsworth and Scott are good examples in England, and Bryant, Emerson, and Whitman in America, Emily Dickinson was able to break open the dark inner void to a shining world outside in which, paradoxically, she could both lose and fulfill herself. We dwell in Eden every day, she said, would we but open our eyes, for "Paradise is of the option," is "always eligible." "Not—'Revelation'—'tis—that waits, / But our unfurnished eyes." To the poet's eyes " 'Eden' a'nt so lonesome / As New England used to be!"

Once again it is very easy to underestimate the complexity of Emily Dickinson's mind by fastening too exclusively on one aspect of it. Although her rhetorical question "With the Kingdom of Heaven on his knee, could Mr Emerson hesitate?" is a transcendentalist assertion, Mr. Emerson himself spoke in statements, not questions; and he would have shied away from the Christian connotation of "Kingdom of Heaven" and preferred an allusion to Hamatreya or Brahma or the Kingdom of Pan ("the patient Pan," "the eternal Pan"). Although Emily's prayer "In the name of the Bee— / And of the Butterfly— / And of the Breeze—Amen!" suggests the immanent Deity of Parker's Natural-Religious view, it is expressed in a parody of the Christian formula whose playfulness is utterly serious. Emily recognized the complicated motive: when we have lost something precious, we hasten to compensate by fashioning its image elsewhere, perhaps within ourselves, perhaps in Nature.

> And a Suspicion, like a Finger
> Touches my Forehead now and then
> That I am looking oppositely
> For the site of the Kingdom of Heaven—
>
> (P 959, II.695)

Emily Dickinson could not say as wholeheartedly as Frost's protagonist in A Masque of Mercy (whose mother "was left over from the Brook Farm venture"): "I say I'd rather be lost in the woods / Than found in church."

Unsatisfied by Emerson's pagan paradise, she had to invest the new-found Eden through image and metaphor with the import of the Christian faith which she had rejected. So she came to speak of creative energy as an inexplicable force much like Edwards' "indwelling vital principle" of grace— in fact, precisely a "Conversion of the Mind / Like Sanctifying in the Soul." Christening by water in the country church was superseded by a new baptism, in which the poet freely gave herself to the call of a full natural existence. Thereafter natural ecstasy corresponded to God's grace, and even the impermanence of ecstasy was transformed into the renunciation which was a sign of justification and election. The only commandment was to "Consider the Lilies" each ordained day, for Nature was the sacrament unto sanctification and spring the miracle of redemption and resurrection. The process of "sacramental" experience constituted, in Thoreauvian terms, the "natural Sabbath" of heaven at home:

> Some keep the Sabbath going to Church—
> I keep it, staying at Home—
>
> So instead of getting to Heaven, at last—
> I'm going, all along.
>
> (P 324, I. 254–55)

Here again Emily Dickinson circles back to her point of departure. If she had her Sabbath in Nature, it was still in some sense a Sabbath, as it was not for Thoreau. Moreover, at the same time that the poems constructed a new Sabbath in a romantic Eden, the term "old-fashioned" began to take on warm and comfortable associations. She often claimed to be old-fashioned; she dressed and looked old-fashioned; with another turn of the fancy she could even dress Eden up in New England garb: "Eden is that old-fashioned House"; in fact, "Nature is 'old-fashioned,' perhaps a Puritan." She could not resolve the paradox (or was it a contradiction?) logically or intellectually. Its origin, if not its resolution, lay in her emotional character. By yoking together two sets of associations she attempted to reconcile metaphorically her divided consciousness.

In reality, of course, a mutable earth could not really be heaven—if there were such a place. In the imagery of the poems noon declines into twilight and dawn only follows night. She might say, "That a pansy is transitive, is its only pang. This, precluding that, is indeed divine"; but she knew that the pang was real and fatal. In the grip of ecstasy she might accept the life-process, but still she was left with the compulsion to escape a "rotatory" life and the "ceaseless flight of the seasons." The transforming experience was the momentous interview—the "*separated* hour . . . more pure and true than *ordinary* hours," the "supreme italic" that punctuated life's course. But, suspended between italics, she could only relive earlier bliss in memory or anticipate bliss to come:

> Looking back is best that is left
> Or if it be—before—
> Retrospection is Prospect's half,
> Sometimes, almost more.
>   (P 995, II. 720)

Unable to rest, Emily Dickinson cast herself before and after. Prospect and retrospect became major themes in her poetry: in the desperate race with time they enabled her to keep in sight the emblazoned signposts that marked the journey; they solaced her in the empty stretches that intervened.

Emily Dickinson hoped that she had discarded the Calvinist God for another Deity who was friend instead of foe, but she found that her relation to Him was in many respects unchanged. He remained the unknown Jove-Jehovah, hurling lightning-bolts and leaving a stricken "little girl" to make what she could of the experience. If He lent no abiding stay, she would have to provide of herself, and turn once again to her own creative resources. Poetry had to do more than "pile like Thunder to it's close / Then crumble grand away." She would have to make its image catch and keep the blinding flash.

Emerson had already ponderously pronounced in the verses which preface the essay on "Art":

> 'Tis the privilege of Art
> Thus to play its cheerful part,
> Man in earth to acclimate
> And bend the exile to his fate,
> And, moulded of one element
> With the days and firmament,
> Teach him on these stairs to climb
> And live on even terms with Time;
> Whilst upper life the slender rill
> Of human life doth overfill.

Emily Dickinson also came, though less sanguinely, to conceive of art as the mediator between time and eternity. Isolating certain things from the flux, "We hasten to adorn" and use them, in order to construct marmoreal art; thereby "We—temples build"—not public temples but private shrines for the meeting of spirit and Spiritus. As an artist she made permanent the momentary acts of consciousness despite time's inexorable wheel. She might say that she lived in an Eden of unfading seasons and perpetual noon, but such a world existed only in her saying it—that is, only in the transcendent ordering of art. Over the last century and a half, poets have come to rely increasingly on this redeeming and immortalizing function of art: Wordsworth recollected and recorded in tranquillity, and Keats aspired to the nightingale's song and the moving stillness of the urn.

Faced with the increasing difficulty of coming to terms with personal experience within the safety of received religion, Emily Dickinson like many modern poets affirmed her supreme (and religious) dedication to comprehending her experience through the intense concentration of artistic expression. For Yeats the choice between religion and art was the "perfection of the life" or the perfection "of the work." In "Vacillation" he wrote:

> I—though heart might find relief
> Did I become a Christian man and choose for my belief
> What seems most welcome in the tomb—play a predestined part.
> Homer is my example and his unchristened heart.

For Yeats the part was not a rejection of heaven but a commitment to transmuting time's torments into "the artifice of eternity." For her own reasons Emily Dickinson rejected the comforts of Christianity and felt compelled to choose instead the life of the conscious artist. Only in conscious experience—if anywhere—could she find herself; and only in the perfection of art—if anywhere—would she escape the temporal wheel on which self turned. Born in Congregational Amherst half a century before Yeats, she could not transport herself to Byzantium any more easily than to Emerson's Eden. Still she lived for her own poetry and said to herself and to her neighbors: "Who has not found the Heaven—below— / Will fail of it above—."

VI

In the history of the New England spirit Emily Dickinson occupies a pivotal place. Puritan orthodoxy had reached its culmination as a religious and social order in the mid-seventeenth century and a century later had found its most magnificent exponent in Jonathan Edwards, after the order itself had begun to pull apart. By the 1850's Emerson had reinvigorated the New England spirit, but only by isolating certain aspects of Edwards' thought and combining and infusing them with the vitality of Transcendentalism. Nevertheless, by so doing Emerson brought about a further disintegration of the great Puritan synthesis, a separation of the heart from the head, just as Benjamin Franklin, Charles Chauncy, and Andrews Norton represented a separation of the head from the heart. For all his Calvinism—or rather precisely because of his acceptance of Calvinism with his mind and heart—Edwards was a more complete person than any of these men.

Emily Dickinson points to the end of the tradition not because she represents, as Emerson does, a splintering off of part of that tradition, but because she embodies in her life and poetry the painful divisions that sundered the New England mind. Emerson was essentially a serene soul, as she was essentially a tormented one. He could be happy because out of selected fragments he had made a shining new faith—shorn now of sin and dogma and devils. To reliance on the intuitive vision of the man-god in a sinless Eden he gave thumping assent with all the eloquent enthusiasm of the poet-preacher. But as Emily Dickinson realized—along with Hawthorne and Melville—he had had to close his mind and heart to much of the complex reality in order to achieve this serenity.

There is no indication that Emily Dickinson was acquainted with the writings of Jonathan Edwards; but from the remarks she made he was associated in her mind with the faith of the fathers. Since what remained of New England Protestantism seemed to her intellectually preposterous and emotionally spurious, she heeded Emerson's call to the poet's rather than the Christian's vocation. With Wordsworth and Emerson and Whitman, she sought to find herself by losing herself, to lose herself by opening "an original relation to the universe." For dazzling moments she and the world were transfigured into divinity, but the difficulty lay in holding the transfiguration in a sustaining vision. In a late poem she weighed "Orpheus' Sermon" against the preacher's, or Emerson's sermon against Edwards', and aligned herself again with Emerson and the "warbling teller." Nevertheless, her unshakable conception of reality and awareness of the human condition were derived not so much from Emerson as from the "old-fashioned" Puritans:

> Paradise is that old mansion
> Many owned before—
> Occupied by each an instant
> Then reversed the Door—
> Bliss is frugal of her Leases
> Adam taught her Thrift
> Bankrupt once through his excesses—
> (P 1119, II.787)

These seven lines of an unfinished poem rehearse all the major elements of the Puritan "vision": the initial harmony of the universe; man's violation of that harmony and his consequent alienation; the possibility of reunion and its fulfillment in visionary instants; the bankruptcy of life without vision.

In Dickinson's poetry there is a determined rigor of sight and mind which is largely lacking in Emerson: a flinty honesty which would spare her nothing, which wished (in Thoreau's words) "to live deliberately, to front only the essential facts of life," to know the abyss as well as the empyrean. There is a complexity of sensibility that brings us back to Bradford, Taylor, and Edwards and is found among the Transcendentalists perhaps only at times in Thoreau. Yet in Emily Dickinson this double consciousness finds resolution neither in Emerson's and Thoreau's belief in heaven here nor in Edwards' faith in heaven hereafter. The complexity of her mind is not the complexity of harmony but that of dissonance. Her peculiar burden was to be a Romantic poet with a Calvinist's sense of things; to know transitory ecstasy in a world tragically fallen and doomed. Her poems display a range and variety of emotional experience which far surpass that of Edwards, Emerson, Thoreau, or Whitman, but the work of all these men has a wholeness, a consistency, and finally a repose which hers lacks. She could be possessed only by the experience of the immediate moment, and so her art expressed itself in short lyrics each of which incarnated a moment. As a result her poetry emerged not in a consistent and overmastering design but in an intricate pattern of individual and contrasting fragments.

In Emily Dickinson the opposing tendencies that divided the New England mind met at cross-purposes, and after her the tendencies were to diverge again. One line of development would lead to T. S. Eliot, who was able in mid-twentieth century to hold timeless moments amid the stretching wastes of time by subsuming them both again in the Christian vision. For Eliot, perfection of the life and perfection of the work converged once more to a single center; mind and heart and art moved with one purpose; his beginning and his end were the Alpha and the Omega. That he could pursue his purpose, however, only away from his native shores signalized, in the one direction, the all-but-final collapse of the New England tradition. Of those who stayed at home, Robinson Jeffers' Calvinist sensibility could find root only in the brute beauty of the wilderness on the opposite coast. Of those who stayed in New England, Robert Frost exemplifies in many respects another line of development that proceeded from Emily Dickinson. In Frost's poetry—"Bereft," for example—man is alone in an indifferent universe without Edwards' grace or Emerson's Reason or Jeffers' pantheism; he sees "neither out far nor in deep"; from nature (no longer with a capital N) he receives either no response, as in "The Most of It," or at best an indecipherable hint that might be something or nothing, as in "For Once, Then, Something." In a chaos without objective absolutes Frost draws his materials from experience and imposes his own order in "the figure a poem makes"; perfection of the work provides "a momentary stay against confusion." Robert Lowell, the most distinguished of the younger New England poets, would readily agree: obsessed by a dead tradition and a shattered world, he sought refuge in Catholicism for a time; now he sifts the pieces through his mind, constructing blazing cries of loss and failure.

In the long list of those who saw "New Englandly," Emily Dickinson occupied a critical position. She came after the fatal cleavage that split the Puritan mind between 1740 and 1840, and in her, for the last time, the dislocated elements came together to struggle for articulation, if not for readjustment, before they diverged, by Henry Adams' law of acceleration, to dissipate their last energies. The astonishing and characteristic thing about Emily Dickinson is that at the crosspoint of the X she could have written both these quatrains about earth and heaven:

> In thy long Paradise of Light
> No moment will there be
> When I shall long for Earthly Play
> And mortal Company—
> (P 1145, II.803)

> God is indeed a jealous God—
> He cannot bear to see
> That we had rather not with Him
> But with each other play.
> (P 1719, III.1159)

DAVID PORTER

The Early Achievement

W e can be sure that the essential body
of Emily Dickinson's fully realized poetic expression will grow as the canon
receives renewed critical attention. Her occasional pieces of undistinguished
intent and her periodic reversions to adolescent versifying will recede to the
periphery of her art, and we shall rediscover those neglected but brilliant
pools in which are distilled her bold experimentation and her mature artistry.
Many are to be found here in the work of the early years when Emily Dickinson repeatedly realized the furthest extent of her artistic capabilities. Eminent critics have remarked on a few of these early poems, but we recognize
now that in more than two dozen prior to the flood years of 1862 and after,
she had mined the richest depths of her creative resources. In these works
we discern the distinctive qualities of her creative mind: an audaciousness
born of irrepressible candor, a startling sensitivity that was yet sufficiently
controlled to be refracted through the instrument of irony and wit, a tragic
understanding not to be compromised by the promise of heaven or the
onslaught of despair, a latent nervous energy the more remarkable for its
disciplined release. We discern, too, the distinctive qualities of her art: its
bold disregard of conventional shapeliness, the surprise of its novel verbal
strategies, its seizure of the significant image, its disconcerting integrity in
psychological disclosures, its firm control of powerful emotion.

Like filings in a magnetic field, those early poems which assert her
genius define the emotional contours of the central theme of aspiration. In
them she savors the distance between desire and its goal. Where specific
poems have a dramatic immediacy as performance, the speaker, in one or the
other attitude of her divergent roles or in an attitude constituted of both, is

distinct and impressive. In several of these compositions of highest achievement, the metrical base provides occasion for the irony, and the central
metaphorical construct of motion and stasis orders the perceptions. Throughout, instances of rhyme variation and stylistic mannerism that we now
recognize as Emily Dickinson's unique mode of expression charge the poems
with urgency, create the feelings of spontaneity and sincerity, and make us
constantly aware of the immanence of the creative personality.

In diverse ways, each element contributes to the concision and
accompanying complexity of her expression, and ultimately to that fine
interior control she exercises over the emotional vitality within her poems.
Indeed, in her finest poems the emotional experience reaches an intensity
that necessarily reveals at the same time the stylistic control which prevents
those feelings from lapsing into intemperance. Her success in confining the
centrifugal pressures of emotions within an aesthetic framework represents
perhaps her highest achievement as an artist. That achievement of control
which would not stifle the intensity she intended to express undoubtedly
posed her most challenging problem. The questing condition and the recurrent recognition that mortality forever denies ideal fulfillment are states
inherently subject to the extremes of emotion. Yet, even though for Emily
Dickinson the emotions mediated her experience, her art allowed her to
order those potentially destructive psychic responses.

The principal method by which she resolved this problem of control is
her absolute distillation of expression, which provides not only a formal
control but so closely circumscribes emotions that they cannot trail off into
self-indulgence. This ability of extreme condensation attests also to her
powers of psychological insight, for with the greatest economy of terms she
could reach directly to the core of a particular feeling. This habit of the
elliptic expression, however, sometimes fragments her compositions. The
early works provide numerous examples of the precise and piercing expression, yet these fragments of genius sometimes constitute the single
effective element of otherwise unsuccessful poems. Foreshadowings of her
consummate artistry reside in these brilliant expressions which typify her
poetic mode.

A complete gathering of her markedly felicitous and distinctly Dickinsonian phrases would be an extensive one, for early in her career the ability
to compact articulation in deceptively simple terms is fully developed.
Among her reflections on death, for example, she distills in two lines the
recognition of the inevitability of death:

> Good night, because we must,
> How intricate the dust!
>
> (P–114)

In rebellious pose, she concentrates in political metaphor the recognition of the uncommitted state of her soul, declaring that

> Imps in eager Caucus
> Raffle for my Soul!
> (P–139)

She imaginatively constructs in homely metaphor the experience of death in the absence of any guiding faith:

> Dying! Dying in the night!
> Wont somebody bring the light
> So I can see which way to go
> Into the everlasting snow?
> (P–158)

Early, too, she was capable of pressing her reflections on the precise moment of death into remarkably concise expressions. She seems repeatedly to have applied herself to formulating an answer to the problem posed in the line which begins an otherwise unsuccessful poem: "She died—*this* was the way she died" (P–150). Fixing upon the image of the open eyes glazed in death, she defines that condition as

> . . . but our rapt attention
> To Immortality.
> (P–7)

She precisely objectifies the abstract terms by picturing the final physical convulsion:

> A throe upon the features—
> A hurry in the breath—
> An extasy of parting
> Denominated "Death."
> (P–71)

The qualities of utter finality and motionlessness she describes succinctly as

> The quiet nonchalance of death—
> No Daybreak—can bestir.
> (P–194)

Defined irreverently in the terms of commerce, death is

> . . . just the price of *Breath*—
> With but the "Discount" of the *Grave*—
> Termed by the *Brokers*—*"Death"*!
> (P–234)

Death personified is a frighteningly efficient workman. He is:

> Industrious! Laconic!
> Punctual! Sedate!
> Bold as a Brigand!
> (P–153)

Like the frost's, his work is irreversible, and so the gestures of grief the mourner offers

> Were useless as next morning's sun—
> Where midnight frosts—had lain!
> (P–205)

The lifeless body, dispossessed even of gender in its new state, yet becomes of greatest worth when lost. Its value grows

> Vast—in it's fading ratio
> To our penurious eyes!
> (P–88)

Emily Dickinson's obsessive recognition of the absolute disjunction which death causes demanded the creation of a new word for the condition of the dead, who exist

> . . . while we stare,
> In Leagueless Opportunity,
> O'ertakeless, as the Air.
> (P–282)

Her scrutiny of nature, like her scrutiny of the moment of death, also evoked brilliant expressions. That close investigation of the things of this world, she implies in the much-quoted quatrain defining the utility of faith, is what sustains one who does not accept the specious comfort of strong belief:

> "Faith" is a fine invention
> When Gentlemen can see—
> But *Microscopes* are prudent
> In an Emergency.
> (P–185)

The recurrent mysteriousness of the changing seasons is one quality that engages the imagination, evading rational comprehension:

> If Summer were *an Axiom*—
> What sorcery had *Snow?*
> (P–191)

And in other lines she asserts her habitual regard for the familiar seasonal signs:

Without the Snow's Tableau
Winter, were lie—to me.
(P–285)

Images of summer she selected and rendered in expressive metaphors. She speaks of "An axe shrill singing in the woods" (P–140) and of "Butterflies . . . On their passage Cashmere" (P–86). Early summer is the time when nature takes up its characteristic music, when·

Lethargic pools resume the whirr
Of last year's sundered tune!
(P–64)

The summer snake's darting motion through the grass, the precise movement of which is the only visible sign of him, strikes immediate fear in the observer:

Did but a snake bisect the brake
My life had forfeit been.
(P–11)

Emily Dickinson's visionary apprehension of the ideal afterlife is objectified in the personification of nature. The dancing on that "remoter green" is

As if the stars some summer night
Should swing their cups of Chrysolite—
And revel till the day.
(P–24)

The "Western Mystery" of the sunset with its continually changing cloud patterns and exotic colors on the horizon she describes metaphorically as a wharf standing by nature's celestial ships from the Orient:

Night after Night
Her purple traffic
Strews the landing with Opal Bales.
(P–266)

Her rendering of the emotion of great exultation is by way of the apt metaphor of church bells proclaiming military victory:

. . . Bells keep saying 'Victory'
From steeples in my soul!
(P–103)

The opposite, the condition of incredible torment confined within a single body, is neatly conveyed in the combined metaphors of the small boring tool (gimlet) and the predatory panther, as well as in the implicit suggestion that at such times one's body seems to be a single receptive nerve:

> . . . Gimblets—among the nerve—
> Mangle daintier—terribler—
> Like a Panther in the Glove.
>   (P–244)

For the finely managed, intrinsic control of despair she employs a military figure. Psychic confrontation with the killing forces of desperation is a kind of heroism; those people engaged in that inner struggle, she says, are

> . . . *gallanter*, I know
> Who charge within the bosom
> The Cavalry of Wo.
>   (P–126)

The precarious balance between the contrary ideals of spiritual chasteness and absolute selflessness is negotiated in the simple image of the snowflake. Addressing her lover, the speaker pleads that he

> . . . hallow just the snow
> Intact, in Everlasting flake—
> Oh, Caviler, for you!
>   (P–275)

Remembrance of an earlier love returns vividly in the reading of the preserved love letters with their

> . . . faded syllables
> That quickened us like Wine!
>   (P–169)

Death of the lover may seem to eradicate those past experiences, however,

> . . . as if no plight
> Had printed yesterday,
> In tender—solemn Alphabet.
>   (P–263)

Finally, Emily Dickinson in her early career was able to declare sharply and with great economy the attitude of disdain for public recognition. Her choice of the simile of the lowly frog conveys that tone with simple directness:

> How dreary—to be—Somebody!
> How public—like a Frog—
> To tell your name   the livelong June—
> To an admiring Bog!
>   (P–288)

These varied examples of her fresh and arresting technique, however, are little more than dissociated fragments of her genius. The poems in which this artistry is sustained are the superior achievements and, indeed, are the ultimate products of those early attempts at refining an authentic voice. In drawing attention below to the early works of thorough artistry, many of which are discussed [elsewhere], I have necessarily limited my remarks to those elements which constitute the principle effectiveness in the individual poems.

Of the works embodying the subject of death, at least ten are superior renditons: the earliest is "There's something quieter than sleep" (P–45). Its impact issues from the frugal but suggestive imagery of the dead body and the conventions of mourning, and from the dramatic situation constructed about the three "characters"—the corpse, the mourners, and the speaker. Each has a distinct role, and the contrasts in their three responses to death produce a complex tension. The corpse is inert, yet the focal point of interest; the mourners busily make the conventional gestures of grief over "the early dead," while the speaker frankly confesses she understands neither the fact of death nor the mourners' reaction to it. The central perception, wonderfully understated, is that even in its absolute simplicity death defies comprehension:

> It has a simple gravity
> I do not understand!

Since the speaker cannot cope rationally with the fact of death, as the other mourners seem able to do, she evades it with the laconic but telling observation that the birds have migrated. As readers, we come with almost embarrassing suddenness upon an intimate nervousness that discloses the mind's effort to cohere in the face of final mysteries.

"I never lost as much but twice" (P–49) stands among those poems which convey an emotional intensity seemingly out of all proportion to the magnitude of the statement. Its success is in the stark rendering of the gamut of emotional responses to bereavement. The feelings compounded are those of grief, of bitterness, of indecision, and resignation. This range is effectively expressed through the metaphors of crime and commerce, each of which gives way abruptly to the final humility implied in the paternal address.

> Burglar! Banker—Father!
> I am poor once more!

In briefest possible compass (compare "Lycidas," "In Memoriam," for example) the poet has presented dramatically the transformation of the speaker's attitude from outrage and defiance to humble acquiescence.

"Some things that fly there be" (P–89), . . . a central document of Emily Dickinson's theme, concentrates its force in the symbols, in the direct fusion of object and idea, which together pose the riddle of time and eternity. In "Went up a year this evening!" (P–93) . . . the miracle of the dead rising up is dramatically rendered. The force of the poem resides in the artful combination of fear and wonderment as responses to the spectacle of death. The poet successfully avoids conventional solemnity, creating the more authentic emotion the more effectively by inducing it obliquely. In "I'm 'wife'—I've finished that" (P–199), she expresses a similar awe to dramatize the experience of achieving maturity through crucial experience. The recognition of new status is effectively conveyed in the terms of coronation and the sacrament of marriage. The integrity of the perception locates the pain-pleasure paradox that crucial and irrevocable alteration of one's condition, even to a more desirable state, involves contrary feelings; that whatever now is gained is necessarily at the price of commensurate loss.

Another early poem of considerable skill is "If your Nerve, deny you" (P–292). It presents with cutting wit the dilemma of the mortal state, where spirit and flesh are attracted to polar ends. To the nerves the ideal state is absolute inertia, and this is to be accomplished only in the grave:

> That's a steady posture—
> Never any bend.

The ideal state of the soul, however, is freedom to fly up in resurrection. This basic material of life's tragedy is skillfully distanced from a sentimental handling by a careful measure of humor:

> If your Nerve, deny you—
> Go above your Nerve—
> He can lean against the Grave,
> If he fear to swerve—
>
> That's a steady posture—
> Never any bend
> Held of those Brass arms—
> Best Giant made—
>
> If your Soul seesaw—
> Lift the Flesh door—
> The Poltroon wants Oxygen—
> Nothing more.

The rhyme pattern frames the argument, providing exact harmony in the opening and closing stanzas where the ideal teleology of the flesh and spirit is stated. In the central stanza, however, which recognizes that death is the only resolution and which describes the frightful prison of the grave, the suspended rhyme is properly disconcerting. It provides an audible quality for the less than ideal manner by which the body can avoid anguish.

"One dignity delays for all" (P–98) has been treated in detail [elsewhere]. It is enough here to reiterate that its artistry is manifested principally in the sustained identity between the imagery of a coronation and a funeral, and in the superb irony which underlies the statement the poem makes. Life's only dignity may well reside, the poem implies, in the ritual observance of life's end. The apparent consolation for death, consequently, is finally overwhelmed by the surging condemnation of life. "I like a look of Agony" (P–241) strikes us by the way it works out justification for the shocking callousness of the opening line. The poem's residual attitude is not cynicism but rather simple candor in the recognition that death is the ultimate novelty and cannot be feigned. The cruel opening is immediately retrieved by the second line, and then justified in the third and fourth lines:

> I like a look of Agony,
> Because I know it's true—
> Men do not sham Convulsion,
> Nor simulate, a Throe.

In the poem as a whole, death finds its precise definition by the homely details of its physical appearance. Less well known is "That after Horror—that 'twas us" (P–286). It recreates the speaker's reaction to a near-confrontation with death. The metaphor of drowning and the novel imagery of the dispassionate mask of death provide effective body, ironically, to "The very profile of the Thought" which, the speaker says, "Puts Recollection numb."

> That after Horror—that 'twas us—
> That passed the mouldering Pier—
> Just as the Granite Crumb let go—
> Our Savior, by a Hair—
> A second more, had dropped too deep
> For Fisherman to plumb—
> The very profile of the Thought
> Puts Recollection numb—
> The possibility—to pass
> Without a Moment's Bell—
> Into Conjecture's presence—
> Is like a Face of Steel—
> That suddenly looks into our's
> With a metallic grin—
> The Cordiality of Death—
> Who drills his Welcome in.

The helpless near-victims and the grisly figure of death perform against the background of the ideal implied by the common meter pattern; the horror is intensified by the contrast. We recognize the same effect in the more horrendous nursery rhymes where gruesome tales are the more macabre for rocking along in jumping rhythm.

Perhaps her most artful metaphorical excursion in the early period is to be found in the poem "A Clock stopped" (P–287). The figure of man as a clock puppet conveys the satirical recognition that man lives his "Dial life" according to the gestures of a clock face. The tragic knowledge is that the force is inhuman, with power neither to create nor restore the life it tyrannizes. The poem once again proclaims the absolute change that death effects: when man dies into another life, into a scheme of timelessness, no skill of this earth can call him back from "Degreeless Noon," through the "Decades of Arrogance" to this "Dial life" again:

> A Clock stopped—
> Not the Mantel's—
> Geneva's farthest skill
> Cant put the puppet bowing—
> That just now dangled still—
>
> An awe came on the Trinket!
> The Figures hunched, with pain—
> Then quivered out of Decimals—
> Into Degreeless Noon—
>
> It will not stir for Doctor's—
> This Pendulum of snow—
> The Shopman importunes it—
> While cool—concernless No—
>
> Nods from the Gilded pointers—
> Nods from the Seconds slim—
> Decades of Arrogance between
> The Dial life—
> And Him.

This poem slays with stunning directness the cozy dream of recapturing what is lost to time by turning back the clock. Out of that cliché Emily Dickinson compounded a telling commentary on man's routine of life, the drama of his death, and the nature of the immensity of that change.

Her obsessive concern with the moment when the activity of this life dies into soundless inactivity engendered the well-known early poem "Safe in their Alabaster Chambers." (For analysis I use the superior version [P–216; *Poems*, I, 154] which the poet enclosed in her first letter to Higginson.) The work is yet another treatment of the subject of death, of the aspiration of the dead for immortality, and of the riddle of those that resting, rise. It possesses the characteristic emphasis on motion and stasis which informs so much of her poetry. Here the contrast is clearly drawn, providing the structure for the work. Indeed, the mature artistry of the poet is evident in the severe imagery of the stillness of the tomb in contrast to the incessant motion in the universe outside. The effective force of the poem arises from this contrast and from the brilliant closing simile in which the motion in the second stanza is arrested in the snow image, which in turn directs the reader back again to the cold repose of the tomb with which the poem opens. Promise and denial, forever inseparable, are symbolized by the bright satin beneath the impassable stone:

> Safe in their Alabaster Chambers—
> Untouched by Morning—
> And untouched by noon—
> Sleep the meek members of the Resurrection,
> Rafter of Satin—and Roof of Stone—
>
> Grand go the Years,
> In the Crescent above them—
> Worlds scoop their Arcs—
> And Firmaments—row—
> Diadems—drop—
> And Doges—surrender—
> Soundless as Dots,
> On a Disc of Snow.

The intrinsic control of movement within the poem yet allows an element of abiding tension created by the residual skepticism and uneasiness. For though the cycle of life is completed within the poem there is no assurance that the dead will indeed rise up to their supposed reward. They are the opposite of "grand" (as the world goes); they are "untouched" as yet by immortality. The discomfiture is sounded in the rhyme scheme, for in the opening stanza which describes the tomb where resurrection is as yet unachieved, the rhyme is only approximate. In contrast, the resolving function of the image of snow at the end is reinforced by the exact rhyme. Having encountered the apparent resolution, however, the reader is directed back by both sound and image correspondence to the the opening stanza. He is turned back, that is, to the tension at the beginning. In the brief compass of thirteen lines the poet distills life and death, gathers the one into the other, leaving unresolved the promise of immortality. Elsewhere she describes this tension as

> ... Gravity—and Expectation—and Fear—
> A tremor just, that All's not sure.
>
> (P–408)

Other early poems of superior achievement cluster about the idea that the worth of an experience is ultimately best measured by those who are denied gratification in it. The central paradox is that in equal ratio to the suffering caused by denial one receives an increased comprehension. "Our lives are Swiss" (P–80) is a succinct rendering of this conception and perhaps one of the best-known examples from her early work. A less well-known early poem of mature skill is also addressed to this subject. Though the work, "If *He dissolve*—then—there is *nothing—more*" (P–236), ... is weakened by the conventional imagery at its close, the opening is nowhere in her canon surpassed for its intense rendering of the experience of separation. The loss of the lover is *"Eclipse—at Midnight," "Sunset—at Easter,"* and *"Blindness—on the Dawn."* The metaphors are wide-ranging and consequently imply the magnitude of the grief. "I've known a Heaven, like a Tent" (P–243) and "Unto like Story—Trouble has enticed me" (P–295) are also early achievements of a high order. Each has been discussed [elsewhere]. The effective force in the first poem is created in large part through the sustained and novel metaphors for lost faith—the fleeing tent and the staring gesture. The art of the second poem is evidenced principally in the tight control the speaker has over her centrifugal emotions. The discipline of emotion dramatized within the poem is reflected in the compactness of the expression. Like the speaker's emotions, the poet's close articulation is "Drilled bright." The best known of the poems about compensation is undoubtedly "Success is counted sweetest" (P–67). It is also one of her finest works from the early years. The value of fulfillment, the poem declares, is understood fully only by those who are denied it. The argument is superbly rendered in the metaphor with which the poem closes: it is only the dead ear, paradoxically, that hears most clearly the music of triumph.

The group of early poems of mature artistry which focus on nature as spectacle and as symbol of the aspirer's goal includes poems already discussed: "There's a certain Slant of light" (P–258), "On this long storm the Rainbow rose" (P–194), and "An awful Tempest mashed the air" (P–198). The skill in these poems lies principally in the choice of imagery and in the way familiar experience is recreated in novel perspective. "These are the days when Birds come back" (P–130) succeeds in its creation of the devotional tone; we are engaged in the dramatic transformation of the speaker's attitude from her initial awareness of the deception of nature (in its Indian summer days) to her final capitulation when the emotional pressures of desire triumph over reason, and she humbly seeks to participate in the "Sacrament of summer days." In this general subject area, too, is the much-anthologized "I taste a liquor never brewed" (P–214). The whole sense of the poem is that in nature one may find the stimulants for intemperate joy. The engaging qualities of this poem are not, of course, in the hackneyed notion that nature is the aliment of happiness. Rather, those qualities issue from Emily Dickinson's wit in appropriating nature imagery to the underlying metaphor of inebriation. The ultimate triumph of her virtuoso performance in this poem is that she sings the scandalous behavior of the speaker (perhaps a bumblebee, but very unlike Emerson's) in the stately rhythms of the common meter of hymnody.

The remaining early works in which we discover Emily Dickinson's profoundest skill are brilliant studies in the psychology of emotional discipline. "A *Wounded* Deer—leaps highest" (P–165), "I can wade Grief"

(P–252), "'Hope' is the thing with feathers" (P–254), and "One Year ago—jots what?" (P–296) have been discussed [elsewhere] in this study. In general, their effectiveness derives from exact imagery, from highly concentrated expression, and from their communication of emotional complexity. On the experience of psychic breakdown, perhaps no poetic expression surpasses the aptness of metaphor or the psychological authenticity of the progression of mental collapse as the rightly famous "I felt a Funeral, in my Brain" (P–280). In addition, certain of her finest early works deal conversely with the stoical ideal of controlled emotions and of the power to be possessed from pain. Though "I have never seen 'Volcanoes'" (P–175) is one of these superior poems, it has had little critical regard. Its effectiveness springs from the sustained and perfectly appropriate adoption of the volcano metaphor to embody the idea of intense emotions under deliberate control:

> I have never seen 'Volcanoes'—
> But, when Travellers tell
> How those old—phlegmatic mountains
> Usually so still—
>
> Bear within—appalling Ordnance,
> Fire, and smoke, and gun,
> Taking Villages for breakfast,
> And appalling Men—
>
> If the stillness is Volcanic
> In the human face
> When upon a pain Titanic
> Features keep their place—
>
> If at length, the smouldering anguish
> Will not overcome—
> And the palpitating Vineyard
> In the dust, be thrown?
>
> If some loving Antiquary,
> On Resumption Morn,
> Will not cry with joy "Pompeii"!
> To the Hills return!

The extended comparison in the geological-emotional analogue moves deftly toward the climactic, assured attitude epitomized in the final heretical viewpoint. The speaker declares triumphantly that if God (the "loving Antiquary") won't allow even on Judgment Day the wished-for purgation of pent-up anguish, then through eternity she is capable of concealing the pain. While the poem's apparent goal has been to render a final and divinely sanctioned emotional eruption, its profounder purpose has been to characterize the triumph of the stoical self.

A similar sort of heresy animates "I got so I could hear his name" (P–293), another early work of consummate artistry. By the fourth stanza, having by painfully slow degrees and great effort become sufficiently detached from the anguishing experience of separation from a loved one, the speaker is able to contemplate an attempt for comfort in prayer, even though it is an unfamiliar gesture. We see how the soul's agony is made vivid by the imagery of physical pain:

> I got so I could hear his name—
> Without—Tremendous gain—
> That Stop-sensation—on my Soul—
> And Thunder—in the Room—
>
> I got so I could walk across
> That Angle in the floor,
> Where he turned so, and I turned—how—
> And all our Sinew tore—
>
> I got so I could stir the Box—
> In which his letters grew
> Without that forcing, in my breath—
> At Staples—driven through—
>
> Could dimly recollect a Grace—
> I think, they call it "God"—
> Renowned to ease Extremity—
> When Formula, had failed—
>
> And shape my Hands—
> Petition's way,
> Tho' ignorant of a word
> That Ordination—utters.

Having so effectively brought emotional disturbance under control, the speaker in the final stanza rejects the thought of pleading for divine aid, for, she believes, though she prays to the ultimate power, if that power has not also known despair it can offer comfort only in some disinterested and ineffectual way. The ultimate power may consider her misery trivial, but to her that "minute affair" of anguish is so enormous it excludes any sort of interruption, including (she says finally) even the offering up of prayer:

> My Business, with the Cloud,
> If any Power behind it, be,
> Not subject to Despair—
> It care, in some remoter way,
> For so minute affair
> As Misery—
> Itself, too great, for interrupting—more.

Reading the first line of this last excerpt as if it ended with a period clarifies the meaning. The fusion of agonizing experiences, mental and physical, the sharp metaphorical depiction of pain, and the articulation of how the person is ravished by the experience of loss—how first the physical senses respond, then the emotions, then the mind, as each is in turn called back to activity from paralysis—are highly effective. The vision is a tragic one: even if God is attentive to individual anguish, He is effectually indifferent.

In this poem, as in the other works referred to in this chapter, Emily Dickinson's genius clearly had guided her expression beyond the level of conventional sentiment and emotional cliché to the level of mature poetry. In the years from 1850 to 1862 she succeeded in refining genuine and effective expressions of feeling from a clutter of commonplace ideas and syntaxes. Perhaps the principal reason for her early success is that she addressed herself again and again to a single theme. The repeated application not only deepened her psychological insight, but allowed her opportunities to pursue a variety of attitudes and to refine her expression. That refinement is evidenced in a wide range of elements, but most obviously perhaps in her imagery and in her prosodic variations on the hymn patterns that provided her metrical base. The development of irony she was able to maintain effectively through the speaker's vigorously secular attitude and through meaningful manipulations of sound correspondences.

But ultimately the totality of her art in the early years is greater than the sum of the individual elements that go into its makeup. Her expressive skills combined to effect a concision, a specific gravity, as it were, not often encountered in English poetry. Her elliptic expression is all the more remarkable for embodying the complexity which it does. That complexity and the intensity of the feeling with which she informs her best works from this period are, in turn, the more remarkable for being under firm control. Long before she wrote to Higginson to inquire if her poetry "breathed," Emily Dickinson had reached on several occasions that high level of lyric expression at which extraordinary emotional impulses are matched and dominated by even more extraordinary discipline. Beyond this accomplishment, she had by 1862 developed her unique ability to dissociate feelings from the limitations of specific causal experiences. Her poems exist independent of the confining facts of exterior experience, and become thereby increasingly universal. She distilled the essential psychic responses to experience—those feelings that are communicable most fully intact. That she displayed this consummate artistry in a substantial body of early work, and that in an even greater number of poems she successfully experimented in usages outside the poetic conventions of her time, provides irrefutable testimony to the judgment that she composed with purpose and conviction. Her assurance of her poetic capability is evidenced most profoundly by these early performances, which fulfill the artistic promise in her response to Higginson's "Letter to a Young Contributor" and in the poems she enclosed.

ROBERT WEISBUCH

The Necessary Veil:
A Quest Fiction

Hope never knew Horizon — . . . Moving on in the Dark like
Loaded Boats at Night, though there is no Course, there is
Boundlessness —

—from L 871

Dickinson's bardic pronouncements
are countered by her confessions of failure and suffering; her belief that each
earthly moment contains a potential paradise is countered by her belief that
this heaven is always lost as time runs on. Just so, the poems of the regulation
fiction are countered by the poems of epistemological quest. In the regulation
fiction, God (and again I will insist that we not identify Dickinson's God-
term completely with the God of orthodox Christians, but define it simply
as the prime source of meaning and power) is within as well as abroad, always
threatening to overflow the grooves of sense. In the quest fiction, God is not
only separate from the first-person speaker; he is hidden and possibly absent,
the power behind the cloud "If any Power behind it, be" (293). The quester
need not fear involuntary transport and the mind's abundance of wild power
in this fiction, but involuntary stoppage and the mind's limitations.

We can exemplify the crucial differences between these two fictions
by recalling the image of the "hair." In the regulation fiction, the hair
symbolizes the delicate balance which the persona must maintain between
his temporal and eternal self; he seesaws giddily upon it. In the quest fiction,
the hair remains in the same position, but it has become an absolute barrier.
It prevents the persona of "I had not minded—Walls—" from reaching the

---

object of her desire, an object which may be considered as either a departed lover or a godlike personification of self-completion, or both. Were the barrier a wall and all the universe a rock, the persona proclaims, "I'd tunnel—till my Groove / Pushed sudden 'thro to his—." It is the barrier's insubstantiality, as an invisible law of life, which makes such a tunneling impossible:

> But 'tis a single Hair—
> A filament—a law—
> A Cobweb—wove in Adamant—
> A Battlement—of Straw—
>
> A limit like the Veil—
> Unto the Lady's face—
> But every Mesh—a Citadel—
> And Dragons—in the Crease—
>
> (398)

This hair, like the "Forest of the Dead" in "Our Journey had advanced—," signifies the limit of the mind's knowledge. It establishes a territory for the unknown and protects that territory with the dragons of Spenserian romance. So near and yet so far, the great mystery tantalizes but remains ungraspable. The quester, however persistent, never will bypass this hair; it dooms him, as another poem expresses it, to inhabit only "The Suburbs of a Secret" (1245). He will never penetrate the inner city. How can one penetrate a hair?

If the regulation fiction, with its self-frightened insistence on the boundless possibilities of the self, illustrates Dickinson's relation to (and her reaction against) Emersonian Transcendentalism, these poems of frustrated quest may be considered Dickinson's puritan fiction, her humble vision of a profoundly dependent self striving to reach the object of her faith. That goal is never achieved, not in the life of this consciousness; yet the crux of this fiction, the event of this quest which most deserves explanation, is Dickinson's transformation of a tragic-seeming vision of limitation and necessity into a hope-filled vision of opportunity and will.

To begin our own quest toward this explanation, we first must wade the turgid waters of philosophical debate. It is widely held, especially among her most ardent admirers, that Dickinson is naive in philosophical matters—this, always with the addendum that formal philosophy has little to do with poetic expression. Such a generalization is too vague to mean anything, though in one respect it is itself hopelessly naive. H. J. C. Grierson insists that Plato, "despite his condemnation of poets, effected that inter-relation of philosophy and poetry which has characterized every great romantic movement." The nineteenth-century romantics, with the exception of Coleridge, may not have studied every document of the epistemological debate which began with Descartes. Nonetheless, its resolution in the German idealism of Kant permeated the romantic air. Most simply put, this debate concerns the relationship of the human agent and his scene, the world, and the specific issue of whether mind or matter is prior and creative. Such a statement of the problem, with its either/or formulation, simply annoys Dickinson. She responds to it with a pair of hilariously contradictory poems, obviously designed to dismiss the question. The first asserts that the effect of an oriole's song depends on its hearer's state of mind. It concludes:

> The "Tune is in the Tree—"
> The Skeptic—showeth me—
> "No Sir! In Thee!"
>
> (526)

The second proceeds from an assumption exactly opposite: "Split the Lark— and you'll find the Music— / Bulb after Bulb, in Silver rolled—" (861). Not only do the poems cancel each other, but each expresses such an extreme and simplistic view that it deliberately parodies itself and argues for the opposite view. Dickinson cannot take seriously the all-or-nothing question of whether the internal or the external is the source of the other. In the regulation fiction, the problem is that they can combine to become all too real; and, as we have seen, Dickinson's poetic techniques generally put the question aside to examine things-as-they-are, a procedure which anticipates modern phenomenology.

Yet, characteristically, Dickinson is willing to consider the question, and even to worry it over and over again, once it is formulated less dogmatically. I do not wish to picture Dickinson poring over the *Critique of Pure Reason*, but she shares Kant's sense of the futility of the prior debate and reaches toward the same conclusions. Bertrand Russell neatly summarizes Kant's resolution:

> According to Kant, the outer world causes only the matter of sensation, but our own mental apparatus orders this matter in space and time, and supplies the concepts by means of which we understand experience. Things in themselves, which are the causes of our sensations, are unknowable; they are not in space and time, they are not substances, nor can they be described by any of those other general concepts which Kant calls "categories." Space and time are subjective, they are part of our apparatus of perception.

As Kenneth Burke notes, human perception becomes "a questionnaire with a set of blanket questions to be filled in differently in the case of each object, but with the whole set of questions requiring some kind of answer in every case." Our perceptual grid of time and space prohibits a pure knowledge of absolute realities yet that grid is a trustworthy human reality which allows for a relationship to things-in-themselves. Dickinson expresses this very notion in a poem which thoroughly disproves the opinion that she is philosophically naive:

> Perception of an object costs
> Precise the Object's loss—
> Perception in itself a Gain
> Replying to its Price—
>
> The Object Absolute—is nought—
> Perception sets it fair
> And then upbraids a Perfectness
> That situates so far—
>
> (1071)

Denis Donoghue believes that in this poem "the dualism of subject and object is, in a flash, consumed," but the poem expresses no such facile merger. Rather, dualism is replaced by an idea of imperfect, partial relatedness. As soon as the absolute *Object* is perceived, it becomes a mere object. Gain and price: human perception is necessary for any comprehension of the real, but through it we lose any hope of knowing the real in its raw, unreduced state. As a final irony, only by the act of our limited perception do we learn how limited it is, how far the real is situated outside the mind's circumference.

The limited gift of the perceptual grid provides us a "why" for the quest poems: why the quest is doomed to failure until death, when, it is hoped, the subject-object opposition *will* be consumed in a flash; and why the quest nonetheless is worth the undertaking, as a preparation for perfection. In this life, mind is larger than matter but smaller than matter's underlying reality. "The Brain—is wider than the Sky—," begins a poem which seems to claim all for consciousness; the brain is also "deeper than the sea—." Nature, as appearance, is easily enclosed within circumference. The final stanza begins in the same vein (vain), but at the last moment enacts a quicksilver reversal:

> The Brain is just the weight of God—
> For—Heft them—Pound for Pound—
> And they will differ—if they do—
> As Syllable from Sound—
>
> (632)

We must take that qualifying "if they do" ironically. The difference of weight between "Syllable" and "Sound" is at once minute and absolute, the difference of a hair. It is the difference between the thing itself and its imperfect, itemized explanation. It is the difference, say, between paraphrase and poetry, poetry and thought. The brain is not quite and not at all the weightless weight of God.

Dickinson's achievement in the quest fiction is to accept the mind's limitations without flinching, and to make the best of those limitations by recasting the role of the quester. Dickinson's poetic quester is heroic not because he succeeds in reaching his goal but because he is motivated to devote himself to this ungraspable goal. He is special only because he can intuit that which he, no more than another man, can rationally comprehend. This awareness is the function of Dickinson's sixth sense; the quester alone possesses "The Ear / Susceptive" to "Reportless Measures" (1048). This sixth sense is fiercely opposed to analysis, for "Too much of Proof affronts Belief" (1228) and emphasizes the mind's limits in spite of itself. "By intuition, Mightiest Things / Assert themselves—and not by terms—" (420). These intuitions become "The Pierless Bridge" of an inferential faith, "Supporting what We see / Unto the Scene that We do not—" (915) and interpreting "Apprehensions" as "God's introductions" (797).

But to infer a far reality is not to own it or know it satisfactorily, as we saw in Dickinson's poems on evanescences:

> Their Graspless manners—mock us—
> Until the Cheated Eye
> Shuts arrogantly—in the Grave—
> Another way—to see—
>
> (627)

Could we presume the pier "behind the Veil" to which the bridge of faith leads,

> The Bridge would cease to be
> To Our far, vacillating Feet
> A first Necessity.
>
> (915)

At best, the poetic quester is actively walking that bridge. To change metaphors, he is within a cocoon, no longer a caterpillar crawling from appearance to appearance, but not yet a butterfly able to soar to a final reality:

> My Cocoon tightens—Colors tease—
> I'm feeling for the Air—
> A dim capacity for Wings
> Demeans the Dress I wear—
>
> So I must baffle at the Hint
> And cipher at the Sign
> And make much blunder, if at last
> I take the clue divine—
>
> (1099)

The image of the cocoon, a three-dimensional circumference, serves both as a preventing veil and as a promise that the veil will finally be rent.

The cocoon, with its implication of a gradual metamorphosis, eases the quest fiction's terrible message, that the "divine" is achieved only by

death, if then. More often, Dickinson fleshes out the poet's middlemost
position in the person of the stranded quester. Throughout his life, he
remains at the edge of the "Forest of the Dead," where advance is impossible
and "Retreat—was out of Hope—" (615). At most, as in "Tho' I get home,
how late—how late—," he can only prophesy his delayed, postmortem
victory. Dickinson's quest is a long, arduous journey which must conclude in
disappointment:

> Three rivers and the Hill are passed—
> Two deserts and the sea!
> Now Death usurps my Premium
> And gets the look at Thee.
>
> (1664)

The quester is stopped at the boundary of life and language; this is the point at
which the voices of "I felt a Funeral" and "I heard a Fly buzz" can say no more.
"The lonesome for they know not What" are never envisioned possessing the
"What" they have lost "ever since—the purple Moat / They strive to
climb—in vain—" (262). The sunset sky cannot be climbed. The final
reality, like the dead loved one in the early stages of the typology of death, is
beyond the grasp of the living mourner. The same model persists even when
the sought goal is not outside the quester, but within. In "Each Life Converges to some Centre—," Dickinson comforts herself with the belief that
there "Exists in every Human Nature / A Goal—." But the question of
achieving the goal of self-fulfilment in this life is cause for grief:

> To reach
> Were hopeless, as the Rainbow's Raiment
> To touch— . . .
>
> (680)

However "converged" the center becomes, it will seem as diffuse as the
prismatic rainbow. The "real ME" here becomes an unexplored and forbidden territory, sadly contradicting the regulation fiction's idea of a real self that
is all too available.

It would seem sufficiently frustrating that the quester cannot achieve
his goal. Yet, in addition, the quester lacks an exact idea of that goal: "Our
Port a secret / Our Perchance a Gale" (1656), the gale of real or figural death.
Even when the barrier suddenly and mysteriously disappears, the goal refuses
to present itself:

> I saw no Way—The Heavens were stitched—
> I felt the Columns close—
> The Earth reversed her Hemispheres—
> I touched the Universe—

> And back it slid—and I alone—
> A Speck upon a Ball—
> Went out upon Circumference—
> Beyond the Dip of Bell—
>
> (378)

Even when life opens up to hurl the quester out upon the circumference of his globed mind, out beyond his limitations, the quest is not yet completed and the goal is not yet known. The quester's middlemost position, his extreme alienation from both the mundane and the spiritual, the before and after, is simply redefined.

When Dickinson compares her questing self to "the Seed / That wrestles in the Ground," hoping to push through hard-packed soil but unsure of how this penetration will be achieved or what the achievement will mean, "The Hour, and the Clime— / Each Circumstance unknown," we must agree with her conclusion: "What Constancy must be achieved / Before it see the Sun!" (1255). This is a quest which demands utmost patience and the daring of a faith unsure of its object. Amazingly, many, even most, of these poems of quest are avowals of purpose rather than plaints of frustration. Such plaints do surface occasionally. It is a bitter reassurance that "I shall know why—when Time is over— / And I have ceased to wonder why—." When Christ explains "each separate anguish / In the fair schoolroom of the sky," Dickinson implies that the explanation will be a large bit tardy: "I shall forget the drop of Anguish / That scalds me now—that scalds me now!" (193). This exclamatory repetition shrieks that present harms cannot be satisfied by postponed cures. The hidden God's "fond Ambush" is a pleasant joke only if he does not carry it too far:

> Should the glee—glaze—
> In Death's—stiff—stare—
>
> Would not the fun
> Look too expensive!
> Would not the jest—
> Have crawled too far!
>
> (338)

If the goal is hidden and unknown, who is to say that it exists at all? And if it does not exist, then the quester himself ceases to exist as a hero and becomes a self-deluded fraud:

> Finding is the first Act
> The second, loss,
> Third, Expedition for
> The "Golden Fleece"

> Fourth, no Discovery—
> Fifth, no Crew—
> Finally, no Golden Fleece—
> Jason—sham—too.
>
> (870)

In such cryptic and emphatic language, Dickinson can call into question the worth of her quester, the persona by which, as I shall show, she justifies her own mode of living. Yet I would see these poems of doubt in the same light as those poems of the regulation fiction which momentarily disown "transport" for the low comforts of the "Daily mind." In the quest fiction, recalcitrance comes to be defined as impatience and despair, and it must be eschewed for the travails of quest. "Out of sight? What of that?" Dickinson demands of her fears. "Better 'tis to fail—there— / Than debate—here—" (703). The quest fiction's ethic is, in part, a recapitulation of Dickinson's idea that a value must struggle to exist:

> What merit had the Goal—
> Except there intervene
> Faint Doubt—and far Competitor—
> To jeopardize the Gain?...
>
> (550)

But since the "far Competitor," death, will not only jeopardize but win the gain, the ethic must extend itself to justify hopelessness:

> The Service without Hope—
> Is tenderest, I think—
> Because 'tis unsustained
> By stint—Rewarded Work—
>
> Has impetus of Gain—
> And impetus of Goal—
> There is no Diligence like that
> That knows not an Until—
>
> (779)

The greatest diligence is to push forward the quest in spite of the strong suspicion that it is endless and fruitless. Success is irrelevant. Dickinson's quest fiction enacts a momentous change in the history of romance, a new emphasis on the hero's act of questing over against his successful completion of the quest. This theme has appeared so often in modern works that it has lost some of its moral surprise for us; the disruption of a convention becomes a convention in turn. But in Dickinson's poems of hopeless yet noble quest, as in Browning's "Childe Roland," we rediscover the passion, the thrill of discovery, that accompanies the restructuring of a narrative pattern at the moment of its disruption.

Dickinson is redefining values through an ethic which somewhat resembles the "purposiveness without purpose" by which Kant defines beauty. Dickinson's ethic, like Kant's formulation, is, in W. K. Wimsatt's apt words, "not a teleology toward a nameable further end." But whereas the purposive purposelessness of beauty for Kant consists in "a highly satisfactory fitting of experience precisely to our own faculty of experiencing, to the progress of our knowledge," Dickinson's "tenderest Service" consists in an invigorating and unsatisfying imbalance between imaginative desire and "our faculty of experiencing" which it outruns, again "to the progress of our knowledge." Dickinson's idea of beauty, her impossible quest, includes tragedy as an assumption and thus, on its own terms, becomes invincible to it. In its doomed failure, the quest fiction is profoundly comic.

A far more pragmatic belief couples with this Sisyphus-like heroism to cheer the quester. Richard Wilbur names this belief, in Dickinson's own phrase, "sumptuous destitution." It is the law that "once an object has been magnified by desire, it cannot be wholly possessed by appetite," and further that "food, or victory, or any other good thing is best comprehended by the eye of desire from the vantage of privation." The idea runs through hundreds of poems, as a fruitful investigation and enlargement of a statement credited by Dickinson to Charlotte Brontë: " 'Life is so constructed that the event does not, cannot, match the expectation' " (L 442). Dickinson has this principle connect and subordinate topics as she constantly reimages it: "Dominion lasts until obtained" (1257); "The moment that a Plot is plumbed / Prospective is extinct—" (1417); "How destitute is he / Whose Gold is firm" (1477); and even "Anger as soon as fed is dead— / 'Tis starving makes it fat—" (1509). "Sumptuous destitution" serves as a retrospective explanation for many of Dickinson's poetic habits. Its inverted formulation indirectly explains Dickinson's technique of making common phenomena strange:

> I had a daily Bliss
> I half indifferent viewed
> Till sudden I perceived it stir—. . .

To make the common strange so that it "Increased beyond my utmost scope" (1057) is to get it right. The inherent value of the ungraspable also explains Dickinson's constant interest in death and the formulation of the separation-death typology in particular. And it is in this idea of sumptuous destitution that the fictions of regulation and quest combine. The regulation fiction's approval of dread may be interpreted in terms of the quest's approval of impossible desire:

> Expectation—is Contentment—
> Gain—Satiety—

> But Satiety—Conviction
> Of Necessity
>
> Of an Austere trait in Pleasure—
> Good, without alarm
> Is a too established Fortune—
> Danger—deepens Sum—
>
> (807)

Thus, paradoxically, the regulation fiction's "transport" may be found in the quest fiction's unfulfilled "expectation," the very frustration of transport.

Though the principle of sumptuous destitution affords these new perspectives on a range of Dickinson's poetic concerns, its major effect is on the quest fiction in itself. Its demand for the imagination to outrace reality transforms the quest's failure into a self-willed predicament. The forbidding hair may be erected not by a God who wishes to remain hidden but by the self's "Sweep Skepticism of the Heart," which

> Invites and then retards the Truth
> Lest Certainty be sere
> Compared with the delicious throe
> Of transport thrilled with Fear—
>
> (1413)

The quester here chooses to be balked, to become passive. The Veil becomes the lady's own, and she refuses to lift it "Lest Interview—annual a want / That Image—satisfies—" (421). The will's denial of itself is nonetheless an act of will. Because "It's finer—not to know—," Dickinson tells God to keep his secret:

> I would not—if I could,
> Know what the Sapphire Fellows, do,
> In your new-fashioned world!
>
> (191)

Once again, we view Dickinson in the act of converting a law of necessity into a necessary choice and working that conversion in such a way that it is no mere rationalization. Once again, the voice of the lowly sufferer modulates into the voice of the divine bard: "Consummation is the hurry of fools, but Expectation the Elixir of the Gods—" (L, p. 922).

The necessary veil does not replace the veil of necessity, except in the progression of our argument. In the poetry itself, the quest as deliberately self-doomed simply alternates with the quest as doomed by life, another example of Dickinson's agile ability to allow two conflicting visions their appropriate moments of insight. Yet this prismatic effect of the poetry is itself an aesthetic borne of the principle of nonattainment. When Dickinson asks the Moon "Which is the best—the Moon or the Crescent," the Moon refuses

to choose. "That is best which is not—Achieve it— / You efface the Sheen"
and "Transport's decomposition follows— / He is Prism born" (1315).

II

If Dickinson "Invites and then Retards" any number of truths, the possibility
of self-willed incompletion nonetheless has mighty effects. For one, it creates
a renunciatory ideal which we can state in positive terms as the maintenance
of the ego's freedom. The quest fiction's psychological ethic is simple and
terrible: do not tie your entire self to any earthly object, for that would be to
worship a false God:

> Enchantment's Perihelion
> Mistaken oft has been
> For the Authentic orbit
> Of its Anterior Sun.
>   (1299)

We must not attribute ideal qualities to real entities, for disappointment must
follow and that disappointment will cause us to discard both the imagined
ideal and the reality which cannot measure up:

> Taking up the fair Ideal,
> Just to cast her down
> When a fracture—we discover—
> Or a splintered Crown—
> Makes the Heavens portable—
> And the Gods—a lie—...

The "Heavens" are not "portable." We are here and they are there, beyond
our reach. Keep the realms separate, Dickinson advises; cherish the ideal as a
nonreality

> Till the broken creatures—
> We adorned—for whole—
> Stains—all washed—
> Transfigured—mended—
> Meet us—with a smile—
>   (428)

It is only "the hurry of fools," exemplified by the poor persona of "My Life had
stood," which can prevent a final, postmortem marriage of the real and its
ideal mate.

No lover, no friend, no worldly ambition deserves dominion over the
soul. A failure to recognize Dickinson's insistence on this point has created
countless difficulties for interpreters of her poetry and her life. The chief
victim, perhaps, has been this poem:

> The Soul selects her own Society—
> Then—shuts the Door—
> To her divine Majority—
> Present no more—
>
> Unmoved—she notes the Chariots—pausing—
> At her low Gate—
> Unmoved—an Emperor be kneeling
> Upon her Mat—
>
> I've known her—from an ample nation—
> Choose One—
> Then—close the Valves of her attention—
> Like Stone—
>
> (303)

This is the poem invariably invoked when a biographer wishes to nominate a new candidate as Dickinson's secret lover, the "One" chosen by Dickinson's feminine soul before she closes "the valves of her attention." But if we read the poem without the intention of pimping, we see that the second stanza rules out worldly suitors, emperors, and their chariots. The chosen "one" is a "what," not a "who," unnamed because its only name is "Mystery"; as a Grecian bard Dickinson writes,

> Lad of Athens, faithful be
> To Thyself,
> And Mystery—
> All the rest is Perjury—
> (1768)

The soul must attend to itself and its furthest goal; everything in between is perjury. Less censoriously, Dickinson tells Higginson, "To live is so startling, it leaves but little room for other occupations though Friends if possible are an event more fair" (L 381). More fair, perhaps, but less essential: "The Missing All—prevented Me / From missing minor Things" (985).

Only in contrast does the quest fiction's psychological ideal relate to Freud's more familiar theory of the ego. J. H. Van den Berg, in a wild though engaging attack on Freud, demands that we recognize the pessimism of Freud's models, especially his model of the object-seeking libido:

> What prompts the libido to leave the inner self? In 1914 Freud asked himself this question—the essential question of his psychology, and the essential question of the psychology of the twentieth century. His answer ended the process of interiorization. It is: the libido leaves the inner self when the inner self has become too full. In order to prevent it from being torn, the I has to aim itself on objects outside the self; ". . . ultimately man must begin to love in order not to get ill." So that is what it is. Objects are of importance

only in an extreme urgency. Human beings, too. The grief over their death is the sighing of a too far distended covering, the groaning of an over-filled inner self.

Van den Berg wishes to see the ego's object-finding as ugly, and he locates this ugliness in the "interiorization" begun by Rousseau and concluded by Freud. The idea of object-finding (and even the actuality, for Van den Berg is one of those scholars who assumes that the psyche changes every few years, with each new cognitive theory) is blamed on romanticism and its "interioriza-tion" (for which, in truth, romanticism is not a cause but an antidote). Dickinson would agree that object-finding is ugly, but not because it is the function of an overstuffed selfhood. She denies herself object-finding so that the self's circumference can expand continually as it takes account of that mystery which it cannot, or will not, wholly contain. The self is never "over-filled" because it is constantly expanding. It is not worried about ego-affiliations because, in one sense, the self is a "Nobody":

> I'm Nobody! Who are you?
> Are you—Nobody—Too?
> Then there's a pair of us?
> Don't tell! They'd advertise—you know!
>
> How dreary—to be—Somebody!
> How public—like a Frog—
> To tell one's name—the livelong June—
> To an admiring Bog!
>
> (288)

For Dickinson, the simple desire for a private life contains, by implication, the life-principle of a protean ego, free to identify with its moving thoughts as they move forward (not to) the mystery behind the veil. She will sacrifice fame for immortality since "One's—Money—One's—the Mine—" (406); again, this is the difference between "Syllable" and "Sound." Dickinson's persona forsakes the frog-like certainty of a public Somebody to become a voyaging epistemology, voyaging in the hope of finally achieving the status of a Somebody at the Source, an Everybody-Everything with yet—chief para-dox of hope—an individual identity, the carpetbag of the ego. It is, essen-tially, an isolated quest; "Growth of Man—like Growth of Nature— / Gravitates within—" by "the solitary prowess / Of a Silent Life—" (750), though "friends if possible are an event more fair." This very growth, borne of longing, will substitute for social relations as a source of present joy. It is a joy "edible to longing, / But ablative to show"; if Freudian anxiety is a dis-ease without an object, the quester's joy is "The joy that has no stem nor core, / Nor seed that we can sow" (1744).

Dickinson names this quest "the White Exploit" (922). The "White" is a symbol for the ego's pure devotion to the Ultimate. It is a borrowing of Mary's "blameless mystery" (271), a denotation of chosen "Tribulation" (325), a substitution of low joys by "that White Sustenance— / Despair—" (640), and a futile portrayal of "This limitless Hyperbole / Each one of us shall be—" (1482). In her maturity, Dickinson identified with her fictional quester by constantly wearing the white robes which symbolized both the nature and the unattainable object of the quester's faith. We should not be surprised by this direct transference of a poetic idea to Dickinson's life. Romantic poetics, with its avowal of sincerity, makes demands on the poet's life which an aesthetic stressing impersonal craftsmanship might find absurd. Romantic poets, Harold Bloom writes, "provide both a map of the mind and a profound faith that the map can be put to a saving use." In Dickinson's phrasing, "For Pattern is the Mind bestowed"; by "imitating her" our lives will "Exhibit worthier" (1223).

Dickinson's pattern is in her poems, and they are a more reliable map to her life than the abstract psychological theories frequently and ruthlessly applied to her. Her isolation (which, in any case, was not so complete as her early biographers believed—as witnessed by the *Letters*, friends were frequently "possible") and her resultant failure to marry cease to vex us once we comprehend the quest's renunciatory ethic. In fact, the real problem becomes Dickinson's three apparent lapses, including her two verifiable romances. The first, with the Philadelphia clergyman Charles Wadsworth, is well characterized by Albert Gelpi as "an affair that could not exist beyond the confines of her mind"; it was, in other words, an infatuation, carried on by Emily before she became Dickinson, the writer of poems. The second, an affair conducted by Dickinson when she was fifty with the elderly widower Judge Otis P. Lord, was very real, and as delightful as it was strangely tardy. Millicent Todd Bingham reports that Susan, Emily's sister-in-law, remarked to her mother when her mother called one day, "You will not allow your husband to go there, I hope! . . . I went in there one day, and in the drawing room I found Emily reclining in the arms of a man."

We find an explanation even for this late lapse in the poems. Dickinson's romance is the result of a minor rebellion against her own principles, against sumptuous destitution and the ego's freedom as a "Nobody." "I was always told that conjecture surpassed Discovery, but it must have been spoken in caricature, for it is not true," Dickinson tells Higginson in a letter written either just before or just after Lord's first visit (L 459). She then concludes the letter with a poem which directly turns on "I'm Nobody!" by praising "The long sigh of the Frog" as an ideal. Earlier and more seriously, in "Renunciation—is a piercing Virtue—," Dickinson lauds "The letting go / A

Presence—for an Expectation—." But as the poem continues, a doubt concerning this characteristic recommendation is cast in the form of a further definition:

> Renunciation—is the Choosing
> Against itself—
> Itself to justify—
> Unto itself—
> When larger function—
> Make that appear—
> Smaller—that Covered Vision—Here—
>
> (745)

To paraphrase these badly crabbed lines, renunciation must renounce itself at the appropriate time. Dickinson is aware that her "White Exploit" may have a neurotic component; she wishes to assure herself that, when the time is ripe, she can accept an ending to her quest. In the poem, the ripe time is after time, not "Here." But in her last years, this fear that her isolation was an escape may well have aided Lord in his courting.

Yet the quest fiction even influences Dickinson's rebellion against it. Apparently, Lord proposed marriage; perhaps he proposed something less honorable. In any case, she answers him in the language of sumptuous destitution: "Dont you know you are happiest while I withhold and not confer—dont you know that 'No' is the wildest word we consign to Language?" (L 562); and again, with some irony, "I have a strong surmise that moments we have *not* known are tenderest to you" (L 750). Still, when Dickinson informs Judge Lord of "The withdrawal of the Fuel of Rapture" (L 842), we cheer the renunciation. Perhaps it is unfortunate that Dickinson formulated libidinal love and the quest as an either/or. Perhaps she broke her own rule of recognizing the real and the ideal as separate in leading her life according to a bodiless ideal. But with "thoughts—and just two Hearts—," with love, that is, "Immortality—can be almost— / Not quite—Content—" (495). Dickinson deserves a less qualified contentment; she deserves the destiny patterned for her by her mind.

The third threat to Dickinson's poetic quest is of a different nature. It is the poetry itself. At times, poetry seems enough. In "I reckon—when I count at all—," Dickinson "reckons" poets, the sun, summer, and "the heaven of God":

> But, looking back—the First so seems
> To Comprehend the Whole—
> The Others look a needless Show—
> So I write—Poets—All—

The "Further Heaven" may be as beautiful as the heaven the poets prepare

"For those who worship Them," but "It is too difficult a Grace— / To justify the Dream—" (569). Fine as it is, this is nonetheless a poem of fatigue and impatience, part of that minor complaint of recalcitrance which gives the major affirmation of quest such force. Elsewhere Dickinson will write, "No message is the utmost message, for what we tell is done" (L, p. 913). Poetry is part of the "done" which the imagination must outrace. It is "when I cannot make the Force, / Or mould it into Word" that Dickinson knows she is "From mathematics further off / Than from Eternity" (1668). The mind is bestowed to pattern the life, not to replace the goal. Surely it was the poetic imagination to which a teenaged Dickinson referred when, shortly after she had refused to stand for an orthodox Christ and sometime before she had begun to compose actual poems, she wrote to her friend Jane Humphrey of "a long, big shining fibre which hides the others—and which will fade away into Heaven while you hold it, and from there come back to me" (L 35). Poetry was to be Dickinson's thread to heaven, not the heaven itself.

Yet poetry as the mind's continual thrust toward the ungraspable, as questing rather than completed vision, could replace the goal of a final heaven; the ideal of imaginative desire could persist even within a mediated eternity. True, in poems which describe the difficulties of an arduous quest the goal is desirable simply as an end to questing; and in a poem like "Renunciation—is a piercing Virtue—," Dickinson schools herself to be ready to accept the goal when it presents itself. The goal, so far as its nature may be assumed, is assumed to be an equatorial "Zone" of sublime rest, "Whose Sun constructs perpetual Noon / Whose perfect Seasons wait—" (1056). It is "a safer place" from which we "look down some day, and see the crooked steps we came" (L 263). But when Dickinson contemplated that vision of eternity in itself, she must have been dissatisfied. In life, one continually pushes desire beyond the barrier of the accessible:

> I find my feet have further Goals—
> I smile upon the Aims
> That felt so ample—Yesterday—
> Today's—have vaster claims—...
>
> (563)

One is constantly outgrowing his prior desires and fashioning new ones which will provide an ample fit. Will not an unchanging eternity go against the belief that "Utmost is relative" (1291), that "Desire's perfect Goal" is by definition "Within its reach, though yet ungrasped" (1430)? Though "Hope never knew Horizon" (L 871), will not this static eternity replace expectation with an inferior contentment? It is with some fear that Dickinson asks, "Unto the Whole—how add?" (1341). She cannot specify an answer, but she can affirm that "Immortality contented / Were Anomaly" (1036). In "Each Life

Converges to some Centre—," the poem in which the "Centre" can be reached in life no more than the rainbow can be touched, Dickinson can prophesy that eternity will not provide access to the "Centre" but will "enable the endeavoring / Again" (680). She can see the immortal self as a "limitless Hyperbole," limitless and more dynamic and desirous than ever before. Eternity need not epitomize completion, but endlessness:

> As if the Sea should part
> And show a further Sea—
> And that—a further—and the Three
> But a presumption be—
>
> Of Periods of Seas—
> Unvisited of Shores—
> Themselves the Verge of Seas to be—
> Eternity—is Those—
>
> (695)

Eternity will bear a newer goal surpassing it as it surpasses life, and that new goal will bear yet another surpassing it. On and further on, to the endless end, Dickinson's quester will voyage forever.

III

The poet always frustrates the man of order who demands perfect consistency. Dickinson's mind is no jigsaw; the fictions of regulation and quest will not "fit." They will rub against each other briefly, as in this prose fragment: "Paradise is no journey because it is within—but for that very cause though—it is the most Arduous of Journeys—because as the Servant Conscientiously says at the Door We are always—out—" (L, p. 926). But in the regulation fiction, where heaven is always available, the self's absence is a sure sign of self-abnegation; while in the quest fiction, where heaven is always absent or, if present, thrown further on, this absence is a boast of questing courage. We said earlier that Dickinson always confronts the same world, whether as an all-sufficient God or a never-sufficient votary. But that choice is basic and the dual answers argue for a division of belief, a division in no way regrettable since it creates a prismatic spectrum of visionary colors.

 Nonetheless, we can go some way in defining the one light which the fictions split. Both fictions value a continual dynamism of the spirit. Dickinson will not attend church because "instead of getting to Heaven, at last— / I'm going, all along" (324). Whether the self is flung from the common to the wild unknown, or actively flings out a wild vision which she then quests toward, she is always inviting and retarding truth:

Escaping backward to perceive
The Sea upon our place—
Escaping forward, to confront
His glittering Embrace

Retreating up, a Billow's height
Retreating blinded down
Our undermining feet to meet
Instructs to the Divine.

(867)

Dickinson is always retreating forward, escaping from one danger to find herself another. In both fictions, skepticism and fear somehow strengthen faith, for this is a poet who believes that "Faith is *Doubt*" (L 912). "Peril as a Possession / 'Tis Good to bear" (1678), and both fictions value a dynamism fired by dread. Vitalizing peril is the only possession this poet finally will "own."

We cannot see Emily Dickinson safely home. The bridge of faith has no pier. We must leave her as she rushes toward and rushes past that point in existence "Beyond the Dip of Bell," where syllable grows into silence and the language ends.

SHARON CAMERON

"A Loaded Gun":
The Dialectic of Rage

The storyteller ... is the man who could let the wick of his life be consumed completely by the gentle flame of his story.

— WALTER BENJAMIN

All men are heroes
By the simple act of dying
And the heroes are our teachers.

— NICANOR PARRA

Stories are time- and space-bound phenomena, structured by plots that, as Aristotle pointed out, have beginnings, middles, and ends. The narrator does not tell his character's story all at once; incident or event (indeed, like language itself) reveals its meaning gradually, in slow and often painful unraveling. In that time, certain confrontations occur. Perhaps the most central of these takes place between the individual character and the demands of the world to which he must accommodate himself. Stories are the working out of such accommodations, and we value them partly for their insistence that the world's demands, albeit difficult, can be complied with. The fair lady must guess Rumpelstiltskin's name to be saved from his demands; Sir Gawain confront the Green Knight; Dorothea Brooke win freedom from Casaubon, Don Quixote from his illusion, and for each of these imperatives only a limited time is allotted. Most stories show characters coming to the world's terms or suffering because they have failed to do so. In this respect, stories are astonishingly moral. Stories

From *Lyric Time*. Copyright © 1979 by The Johns Hopkins University Press, Baltimore/London.

both enact chronology and insist that it is chronology that has the power to save us. Time will sanction reversals, permit insights, provide space for action, or so we are assured.

Such generalizations about stories, which I must leave, for the moment, incomplete, lead me directly to my subject, which is not stories at all but rather poems, and specifically a group of Dickinson poems that retreat from the telling of stories; from chronology; and sometimes even from coherence. These poems, like those which "name" experience by exempting themselves from it, are patterned by their refusal to make the sort of accommodations described above; they seek a way out of time, a reprieve from it. As such, they raise questions not only about themselves but also about lyric poems as we are going to want to distinguish them from narratives or stories proper. My concerns in the following pages then, will be twofold: first, with a specific group of Dickinson's poems, and second, with the insights they shed on lyric poetry generally.

The Dickinson poems about which I shall be speaking tell a story predicated on a dialectic: this life versus the next; the pleasures of love and sexuality versus a more chaste and bodiless devotion; the demands of the self versus their capitulation to the world's otherness. The dialectic, as my examples suggest, is based on sacrifice (and on protest at its necessity), and it therefore appears to fit into my description of the way in which stories reveal the world as schooling individual expectations. The conflict in the poems, put simply, seems to be between forces of sexuality and forces of death; the poems schematize experience for the explicit purpose of preventing the convergence of sexuality and death, of avoiding the acknowledgment that the two join each other in time, and that the self comes to its end at their meeting. A third voice, intervening in the dialectic, which takes its passion from the knowledge of sexuality and its vengeance from the knowledge of death, is often one of rage.

Rage is a way of preventing the convergence of sexuality and death, albeit momentarily and albeit in full and painful awareness that the two can be kept apart only conceptually and only one step removed from experience. This third voice (the one breaking into the established dialectic in order to complicate it) is a complex one, for its existence, its presence, effects the stopping of time by framing the dilemma in words that exempt themselves from the very process against which they rage and to which they must inevitably return. Thus, if we were to chart the three voices, the two dialectical ones would appear along the same linear plane, although distanced from each other. The third, disruptive, voice would place itself erratically above that linear progression, in defiance of it. Its position in relation to the two dialectical points against which it was lodging its protest would of course determine the specific nature of the poem.

Often protest in the poems I shall discuss takes the form of a speaker's recoil from the eminence of her own insights. When the refusal to know is an unconscious one, Dickinson loses control over her subject, and seems afflicted by the same paralyzing despair that prohibits coherence as her speakers are. If, to simplify matters, we look first at a poem not structured explicitly by the triad of voices but one in which, nonetheless, the subject matter invites distraction, we will see the disruptive consequences of knowledge that dares not scrutinize itself:

> I got so I could hear his name—
> Without—Tremendous gain—
> That Stop-sensation—on my Soul—
> And Thunder—in the Room—
>
> I got so I could walk across
> That Angle in the floor,
> Where he turned so, and I turned—how—
> And all our Sinew tore—
>
> I got so I could stir the Box—
> In which his letters grew
> Without that forcing, in my breath—
> As Staples—driven through—
>
> Could dimly recollect a Grace—
> I think, they call it "God"—
> Renowned to ease Extremity—
> When Formula, had failed—
>
> And shape my Hands—
> Petition's way,
> Tho' ignorant of a word
> That Ordination—utters—
>
> My Business, with the Cloud,
> If any Power behind it, be,
> Not subject to Despair—
> It care, in some remoter way,
>
> For so minute affair
> As Misery—
> Itself, too vast, for interrupting—more—
>   (P 293)

The first three stanzas, with their fusion of agonizing physical and emotional pain, are clear enough. The remembered transport of agony, the marriage of excruciation and ecstasy, the subsequent mastery of emotion—and the speaker's distancing of all of these in the past tense—lead us to expect a peripety. Control recollected may be control that has suffered a collapse; and the stress on the past-tense nature of the control at the beginning of the initial stanzas suggests that the space between the stanzas, to which the speaker's mind temporarily reverts, is occupied by a less manageable present that will eventually overwhelm even memory. But instead of the collapse of control with which the poem tantalizes us, we get a distraction from it: an appeal to God that becomes a way of avoiding feeling, and the poem ends not with passion, as we might expect, but rather with passion defended against. For passion would need to acknowledge directly the attendant circumstance of its loss, the "him" whose most palpable fact is absence.

Thus in the last stanza, confounded by the requirements of the present, utterance is most in disarray. There the speaker seems to be suggesting she would have commerce with a cloud *if* she could be sure a God were behind it, and, in addition (for "be" in the stanza functions as the verb for two subjunctives), that, could she determine such a power were not itself subject to despair, she would cease petitioning it for relief from an affliction that, failing to understand experientially, it could not mitigate. As my paraphrase suggests, the pronoun referent, like the reason for speech itself, is a matter of confusion. Though "It [would] care" refers grammatically to the cloud, the pronoun would be a less enigmatic "He" if the speaker had any confidence in the power behind it. But although the fifth stanza claims to invoke a God, it is clear by the last stanza that the speaker does not know to whom she is talking, does not know whether she wishes to be talking, and ignorance finally gives way to the acknowledgment that, in such a state, no more can or must be said. For the breaking off of utterance comes at a point when "more" would be an affront not only to God, who may or may not be attending from a distance, but also to the speaker, who acknowledges, albeit covertly, that she has herself become distanced from her subject.

Indeed, what begins as the endurance of great feeling turns into blasphemy on two counts, first with respect to the earthly lover and second with respect to the God who displaces him, for the poem's initial line suggests a pun on "taking His name in vain." To take it in vain is to take it without comprehending its significance, and this the speaker does initially when his name (the lover's) fails to tap the current of meaning, and later when His name (God's) becomes a denomination so remote in significance that it can barely be summoned, and, once recalled, is attributed to someone else ("I think, they call it 'God'—").

Though the reduction of the experience is attributed to God, "remote[ness]" is a psychological remedy, not the divine cause. Put briefly, God is a way out, an object of simple projection. To the extent that Dickinson fails to know this and does not, I maintain, intend it, we have a complex hermeneutic situation here. Meaning breaks off, dissolves, goes under, at the moment when it is perceived as too painful, and that fact is attended by the rhythmic transformations in the last three stanzas; full rhyme disappears, the common particular meter established in the first three stanzas gives way to variation, as does the regular four-stress line. Such rhythmic change also counterpoints the paraphrasable sense of the lines. The message of the words (their meaning insofar as it can be figured) is "God does not understand and hence cannot care." The rhythmic message of the last three stanzas, however, is "I myself no longer wish to understand and therefore, of course, you must not either." Such a proposition may be arguable, but it makes experiential sense. It is, in fact, the only explanation that makes sense of the abrupt and rather elaborate confusions with which the poem concludes. Agony—in fact all meaning—goes dead on the speaker when she summons distance from her experience and, in so doing, relinquishes it. The poem, though not, I suspect, intentionally, is about what it is like to trivialize feeling because, as is, feeling has become unendurable. Better to make it nothing than to die from it.

The disjunction between the two parts of "I got so I could take his name" is revelatory of narrative breakdown, not of controlled narrative transformation. The speaker is not in possession of her story, or rather she is in possession of two stories, the bringing together of which points to a fundamental ambivalence and an attendant obfuscation of meaning. As a consequence of the ambivalence, meaning becomes symptomatic, breaks out into gesture where it cannot be fully comprehended and where it often expresses feelings that seem antithetical to the earlier intention of its speaker or author—it is difficult to distinguish adequately between the two in such instances, since both are victims of the same confusion.

Stories are comprehensible because of the connections, implicit or otherwise, that exist between their respective elements. Freud saw health in such connection and in the intelligibility that connection implies. The severing of connection, the gaps in chronology, the faulty memory—it is these psychoanalysis claims to treat so that the end result is nothing less than a complete story that is, in Freud's words, "intelligible, coherent, unbroken." I bring this up here because Stephen Marcus's description of such a coherent story offers an important insight into the problematic aspects of Dickinson's poems when they resist knowledge:

> It is a story, or a fiction, not only because it has a narrative structure but also because the narrative account has been rendered in language, in conscious speech, and no longer exists in the deformed language of symptoms, the untranslated speech of the body. At the end—at the successful end—one has come into possession of one's own story. It is a final act of self-appropriation, the appropriation by oneself of one's own history. This is in part so because one's own story is in so large a measure a phenomenon of language, as psychoanalysis is in turn a demonstration of the degree to which language can go in the reading of all our experience.

Poetry, one might say, acknowledging the substitution, is a demonstration of the degree to which language can go in the reading of all our experience. When it fails, erupts into gesture, becomes "untranslatable," or when its rhythmic manifestations grow so distracting as to convey a separate meaning of their own, we may want to ask why devastation is preferable to coherence, how knowledge threatens the self so that it forgets its own story or falters in the telling of it.

Recognizing that the poems often resist cognitive enclosure, we may want to seek another way of understanding them, or we may modify our conception of what a successful poetic statement is. Jerome McGann, writing of Swinburne's poetry, speaks of poetic speech that conveys "its most moving insights at a level below or beyond the limits of customary discourse." McGann continues, "Swinburne deliberately puts meaning beyond the grasp of the cognitive faculties by creating immensely difficult poetic systems or relations; and . . . he simultaneously presents those systems as perfected enclosures which, though they do not define a comprehensive meaning, represent the fact and the idea of wholeness." While Dickinson's and Swinburne's poetry lie distant from each other in almost every respect, McGann's description could well apply to the poems about which I shall be speaking. Like "I got so I could hear his name," the poems that present the triad of voices are problematic ones. In them, it is easy enough for the reader to follow the story established by the dialectic. What is not so easy to interpret is the disruptive third voice, which often finds direct language inadequate.

In the first group of poems I shall consider, we will be dealing with that third voice, the one that interrupts a poem's conclusion and, in so doing, hints at a story other than the one propounded by the ostensible narrative. In the second group of poems, the third voice makes its appearance earlier and more openly by breaking into the center of the narrative and suggesting an outright criticism of the story, which it then revises. In the first instance, disruption of the story renders meaning ambiguous; in the second instance, disruption becomes meaning.

Both groups pose questions about how voice or presence (terms that I shall use synonymously) exists in contradistinction to action, consequence, and even story, and in both groups voice seems to fight against coherence, because it assumes coherence means consequence and consequence, death. Speech in the poems, then, is not the end of, or a response to, emotion, but rather its eruption, and this defense against completion (which, as we shall see, is in fact a defense against death) is exactly opposite to the one employed by the definitional poems. There we observed meaning to be trivialized, winnowed from its own complexity. In the following poems, however, we are dazzled by the confusions of complexity, by multiple meanings often contradictory. The profusion of meaning, the simultaneous posing of its antitheses, does not arise from the dialectic, as we might expect, but rather from the conversation between the dialectic and the third voice, which wishes to subvert it. The dramatic manifestations of such speech indicate that these utterances are neither tranquil nor recollected. Caught in the moment, they draw the reader into the net of their own irresolutions, and, if he does not look sharp he, or his comprehension at any rate, perishes there.

II

"Repetition and recollection are the same movement," Kierkegaard wrote, "only in opposite directions: for what is recollected has been, is repeated backwards, whereas repetition, properly so called, is recollected forwards." Kierkegaard continues: "When one does not possess the categories of recollection or of repetition, the whole of life is resolved into a void and empty noise." In possession of them, however, one takes the universe to task for failing to sanction the categories it has prescribed as requisite for meaning. The following poem is generated by the insight that this world must not be allowed to duplicate the next, lest the latter be found superfluous:

> I should have been too glad, I see—
> Too lifted—for the scant degree
> Of Life's penurious Round—
> My little Circuit would have shamed
> This new Circumference—have blamed—
> The homelier time behind.
>
> I should have been too saved—I see—
> Too rescued—Fear too dim to me
> That I could spell the Prayer
> I knew so perfect—yesterday—
> That Scalding One—Sabachthani—
> Recited fluent—here—
>
> Earth would have been too much—I see—
> And Heaven—not enough for me—
> I should have had the Joy
> Without the Fear—to justify—
> The Palm—without the Calvary—
> So Savior—Crucify—
>
> Defeat—whets Victory—they say—
> The Reefs—in old Gethsemane—
> Endear the Coast—beyond!
> 'Tis Beggars—Banquets—can define—
> 'Tis Parching—vitalizes Wine—
> "Faith" bleats—to understand!
>
> (P 313)

By the end of the poem it is manifestly clear that what "they say—" is different from what the speaker knows, for the concept of too much salvation is a horrifying, if not nonsensical, concept. Yet God, far from abjuring sameness, seems to require it: the pattern of the speaker's life must duplicate the Savior's lest the "little Circuit" of this life outclass the "new Circumference—" of the next. If there is a threat prompting the implicit denials, it is inherent in the thought that God does not permit "The Palm—without the Calvary—." Although we might regard the last line as continuous with the poem—considering it only proper for one of the flock to assert that faith must "bleat" its comprehension of God's demands for sacrifice—the quotation marks suggest that this member of the flock who tries to utter the truisms finds herself instead speechless with rage. Thus the implicit grammar of the last line is altered slightly by its juxtaposition to the rest of the poem. The speaker is not saying that faith would have to bleat in order to understand, but rather that faith shakes off human utterance and is roused to animal fury precisely because it cannot. The cry of outrage disrupts the complacent irony that had seemed to structure the initial dialectic, for since "Faith" is the designation for every assertion that has preceded it, at the moment we perceive quotation marks enclose it, the entire poem is suddenly cast into quotation marks.

Although the poem is about excess and the prohibitions against "too much—," it must itself be seen as an extravaganza of protest, enacting the very "too-muchness" that it claims has been prohibited. "Too glad," "too lifted," "too rescued," "too much"—the repetition defies (and not very subtly at that) the injunction against duplicating experience. The syntactic repetitions are equally attention getting ("I should have had the Joy," "My little Circuit would have shamed"); and also attention getting, all the choral expressions of insufficiency ("too dim," "not enough," "without the Calvary—"). Both the common particular meter and the rhyme scheme remain regular throughout, and the poem employs a number of exact rhymes with an insistent repetition that renders their presence didactic, even harsh. It is just the regularity or monotony of sound which seems charged with the fury that will explode at the poem's conclusion.

Thus far my analysis might suggest the poem is an example of what Booth would call "stable irony," the discrepancy between the content of the words and the tone of their delivery intimating that all is not what it says. But since the reader is overwhelmed by the resonances of verbal and syntactic repetition *before* he understands their significance, and since the poem will ultimately subvert implication entirely, we must distinguish it from a purely ironic statement in which there is a balanced discrepancy (accorded by the simultaneity of perception) between the content and tone that always remains implicit. Here, although the poem seems to move between the dialectical terms it has established—this world versus the next, defeat versus victory, the Palm versus Calvary, words of acceptance versus words of denial—there is neither balance nor distance. The speaker cannot echo the words Christ said in Gethsemane, "not as I will, but as Thou wilt"; she cannot echo any words at all. Insofar as fury is the foundation of the poem, it threatens to rupture the walls of each stanza and to dissolve, as it finally does, into the "bleat[ing]" of incomprehension. At that moment, there is only the fluency of rage, whose true language, as the poem's conclusion attests, leaves words in its wake.

The third voice, then, finds direct language inadequate. The inadequacy is exposed by the neat dialectics, for a dialectical understanding of experience here seems to be a way of simplifying it. Underlying the dialectic, inarticulate but fulsome in its power, is the generative force of rage, an alternative voice that concludes the poem by disrupting or redefining its established meaning. Such a conclusion suggests that even irony, which, in other circumstances, we might have trusted as a mirror for the truth, is an evasion of feeling. The ironic story, no less than the one "told straight," is subject to the revisions that passion cannot contain.

If the conclusion of "I should have been too glad, I see" is a readily comprehensible demonstration of the way in which rage grows louder than story until it finally submerges the latter, the conclusion of the following more troubled poem makes it necessary to observe that, although sense is to be found, it is not in the telling of the story:

> My Life had stood—a Loaded Gun—
> In Corners—till a Day
> The Owner passed—identified—
> And carried Me away—
>
> And now We roam in Sovereign Woods—
> And now We hunt the Doe—
> And every time I speak for Him—
> The Mountains straight reply—
>
> And do I smile, such cordial light
> Upon the Valley glow—
> It is as a Vesuvian face
> Had let its pleasure through—
>
> And when at Night—Our good Day done—
> I guard My Master's Head—
> 'Tis better than the Eider-Duck's
> Deep Pillow—to have shared—
>
> To foe of His—I'm deadly foe—
> None stir the second time—
> On whom I lay a Yellow Eye—
> Or an emphatic Thumb—

Though I than He—may longer live
He longer must—than I—
For I have but the power to kill,
Without—the power to die—
                                        (P 754)

I should like to offer two conventional paraphrases of the poem,
which I shall then suggest are inadequate. In the first, picked up by God, the
speaker becomes His marksman: the mountains resound with the echoes of
her shots; those bursts of gunfire are as "cordial" as the eruption of a volcano;
with the threat of more gunfire, she guards him at night, imagining her power
to be total. Alternatively, if "Owner" is a term that suggests a deity, "Master"
may suggest a lover (a theory prompted by the "Master" letters). In this
reading, the speaker receives identity when she is carried off by the earthly
lover whom she thereafter guards with murderous and possessive fury, anxious
to protect him from his enemies and preferring, it seems, to watch over his
bed than to share it with him; preferring, that is, violence to sexuality. But
the problem with the poem is that it makes sense neither as religious
allegory—the speaker's service to God does not involve the killing of the
unrighteous—nor as the depiction of an erotic relationship. For either
paraphrase, once it confronts the last stanza, faces its own inadequacy.

While the last stanza plays with the connections between life and
death in a joke of comparative terms, those terms fail to make sense when
applied literally to human beings (how could they have the power to kill
without the power to die?) and make such obvious sense when applied to the
inanimate gun (it goes without saying, and therefore it is unnecessary to say,
that guns can kill but not die) that something further seems intended. The
seepage of additional meaning, resonances of more complicated intention,
infect the experience of the whole poem so that on the first reading we reject a
superficial interpretation—the poem depicts neither the relationship between a man and his gun—nor one between a woman and her God or
between a woman and her lover. Meaning bearing down on us and, at the
same time, eluding us casts doubt on our ability to identify what we are
reading, and this mystification is partly a consequence of the way in which the
conceit draws attention to its own transparency. In stanza one, for example,
it is unclear whether we are to imagine the speaker as gun or as person, and
the revealing taint of human presence continues in stanza two, where the
echoes returned by the mountain might as easily be those of a voice as of a
gun. Likewise in the third stanza, the speaker's smile, however provisional,
conceivably takes place on a human countenance—the Vesuvian face that
admits, albeit reluctantly, of pleasure. In the next stanza, the implicit
alternatives of sexuality and death are clearly human alternatives. In the

next, the human parts of the body are so fused with, and completed by, the parts of the gun, that our attention is drawn to the speaker's thumb rather than to the hammer it cocks.

The fusion of gun and person, force and identity, possessor and possessed defines the central problematic features of the poem as well as the central problematic dilemmas of its speaker. The central trope—life as a loaded gun belonging to someone else that, when claimed, goes off—once it is figured, still leaves many questions unanswered, the most crucial of which is: What imaginable relationship can be explained by such violence? I shall begin to address these questions by suggesting that "identity" in the poem is conceived of as violence, just as life is apparently conceived of as rage. The poem is thus the speaker's acknowledgment that coming to life involves accepting the power and the inescapable burden of doing violence wherever one is and to whomever one encounters. But that interpretation, if it is a true one, is also terrifying, for violence turned upon the world can be returned by it. It is to guard herself against this return that the speaker imagines herself immortal. For the most foolproof protection from violence against the self is the denial of death. Although my interpretation may sound extreme, it is prompted by the enigmatic last stanza, which makes a shambles out of any conventional interpretation of what precedes it. In the stanza, the focus shifts to the speaker's scrutiny of her own fury, and suggests, as we might have suspected, that this was the real subject after all. The speaker–gun is viewed as the agent of death and not (as the person for whom it stands would be) the object of it. Or, in other terms: fury grown larger than life disassociates itself in terror from the one who feels it and fantasizes its own immortality. The problem with the poem, then, is not that it is devoid of meaning but rather that it is overwhelmed by it (a problem exactly opposite to the one we witnessed in the definitional poems, though related to it, because both are prompted by the same retreat from both partiality and ending). Its phenomena surpass, seem larger than, their explanations. This fact suggests that any explanation will be inadequate, and it therefore draws our attention away from explanation and toward something else.

A similar distraction occurs in the following poem of anonymous authorship, believed to have been written in England around 1784:

> There was a man of double deed
> Who sowed his garden full of seed.
> When the seed began to grow
> 'Twas like a garden full of snow,
> When the snow began to melt
> 'Twas like a ship without a belt,
> When the ship began to sail

> 'Twas like a bird without a tail,
> When the bird began to fly
> 'Twas like an eagle in the sky,
> When the sky began to roar
> 'Twas like a lion at the door,
> When the door began to crack
> 'Twas like a stick across my back,
> When my back began to smart
> 'Twas like a penknife in my heart,
> And when my heart began to bleed
> 'Twas death and death and death indeed.

Although the poem employs a rigid logical structure—the pairing of life and death images, one of which generates, by association, the first term of the next pair (as "melt" suggests "ship," "sail"/"bird," "roar"/"lion," etc.)—the connections that link the images and seem to anticipate their own conclusions are themselves thrown off balance by the shock of death, for which no anticipation can prepare the speaker. Hence, as we read, our experience is not primarily one of the logical relation between incidents, for, like the speaker, we are diverted from logic by the swiftness with which it flashes by us.

In "The Man of Double Deed," as in "My Life had stood a Loaded Gun," it is death that breaks out of the metaphor or allegory at the poem's conclusion. Metaphor and allegory collapse and give way to a more inescapable reality—death "indeed," which in the one poem is recognized as inevitable and in the other is defended against as impossible. In both poems, however, there is a rapid progression toward terror. That progression is set in motion by forces that are as incomprehensible as they are sudden, triggered in the one case by the "Owner's" appearance and, in the other, by the planting of a seed that bears not fruit but snow. The release of power—in each case destructive: power to kill, power to be killed—corresponds to and becomes no less than the speaker's identity. Who each speaker is, then, is presented strictly in terms of the force that annihilates him or by which he annihilates others. All the storytelling conventions ("This happened, then this, then this") are a thin disguise for the deeper story, which is elegantly simple in its assertion that human life gains its identity when it encounters death. Death "indeed" snaps the conventions of the ordinary and raises man to the dimensions of the hero. The real connections, the likenesses that shoot us through a dizzying sequence of events whose specific content matters less than our inability to order or perceive its shape, inform us that the only defining experience that does not admit of ambiguity is death. Putting an end to experience, death also reveals its shape. It specifies who we are. Despite Shakespeare's adage about cowards who die a thousand deaths, it is those experiences which prefigure death by imitating it that also prepare us for it. Our concern with that preparation is a partial explanation for why we read. For when we read, at least when we read novels, what we read are completed stories: stories whose characters have come in touch with their own ends, or who perceive a stopping point to incident that implies a closure akin to death.

Death makes incident finite and one can best order or assert meaning over that which has both a beginning and an end. At the moment of death, therefore, experience not only becomes knowable, it also assumes transmittable form. Commenting upon the relationship between a storyteller's power and his knowledge of a character's death, Walter Benjamin writes, "Death is the sanction of everything that the story can tell. . . . In other words, it is natural history to which [the teller's] stories refer." Benjamin elaborates:

> "A man who dies at the age of thirty-five . . . is at every point of his life a man who dies at the age of thirty-five." Nothing is more dubious than this sentence—but for the sole reason that the tense is wrong. A man . . . who died at thirty-five will appear to *remembrance* at every point in his life as a man who dies at the age of thirty-five. In other words, the statement that makes no sense for real life becomes indisputable for remembered life. The nature of the character in a novel cannot be presented any better than is done in this statement, which says that the "meaning" of his life is revealed only in his death. . . . The novel is significant, therefore, not because it presents someone else's fate to us, perhaps didactically, but because this stranger's fate by virtue of the flame which consumes it yields us the warmth which we never draw from our own fate. What draws the reader to the novel is the hope of warming his shivering life with a death he reads about.

Only autobiographical novels, as Scholes and Kellogg remind us, cannot find their resolution in the protagonist's death and must substitute a stasis of insight for a stasis of action. Indeed, this is also true for the lyric, which casts off its knowledge of remembered life, driving past and future apart and away with the wedge of the eternal now. Thus one crucial difference between most lyric poems and most novels is that the former do not ordinarily yield the representation of completed lives. Epic poems do so—Adam's expulsion from paradise is perhaps the greatest story of the first end. Narrative poems can do so—Browning's "Childe Roland to the Dark Tower Came" not only posits an end for its protagonist, it is also obsessed by the proper interpretation of that end. But lyric poems catch their speakers in isolated moments and off guard. Insofar as they record a history, it is not the history of a life but rather of a moment. In fact, as the following assertions are meant to imply, the lyric's premise of temporality bears obvious similarities to the temporal assumptions of the poems discussed in these two chapters, though Dickinson's exaggeration of that premise may distort it past all recognition.

Concerned neither with ends nor with beginnings, concerned with etiologies only on occasion and sometimes, then, by chance, the context of the experience narrated in a lyric will need to be reconstructed from the particularities of the moment. It is its speaker's words that matter, not her past or future. For the configuration the lyric speaker presents is usually a static one; not because nothing happens in it but rather because what does happen is arrested, framed, and taken out of the flux of history. One might almost go so far as to say that in lyric poems history gets sacrificed to presence, as if the two were somehow incompatible. Hence poems often begin in the middle of an action ("I struck the board and cry'd, No more") or in direct address ("Batter my heart, three person'd God"), with an injunction ("Do not go gentle into that good night") or a complaint about a specific relationship ("They flee from me that sometime did mee seek"). No matter how expansive or elaborately philosophical their implications, they frequently withhold physical geography, or if one exists, it seems shockingly limited ("I walk through the long schoolroom questioning"). Experience, then, is unitary in these worlds and it is incidental, although the incident is curiously independent of both time and place. Lyric poems insist that coherence be made of isolated moments because there is no direct experience of an alternative. They suggest, too, that meaning resides neither in historical connection nor in the connection between one temporal event and another. Meaning is consciousness carved out of the recognition of its own limitations. They insist that meaning depends upon the severing of incident from context, as if only isolation could guarantee coherence. The lyric's own presence on a page, surrounded as it is by nothing, is a graphic representation of that belief. If there is a victory in the form of the lyric—the stunning articulation of the isolated moment—despair underlies it. It is despair of the possibility of complete stories, of stories whose conclusions are known, and consequently it is despair of complete knowledge. In its glorification of the revelatory moment, the lyric makes a triumph of such despair.

To return now to "The Man of Double Deed" and "My Life had stood a Loaded Gun," with which we began, it is clear that those poems do tell stories and that the stories they tell are concerned with the way in which death confers both knowledge and power. In "The Man of Double Deed," death can be neither anticipated nor known; it can only be experienced, and before it is experienced, the life of the poem comes to a halt. In the Dickinson poem even the anticipation of death is denied the speaker, though what could put an end to violence (violence turned against the self) would also explain it. Without a foreseeable end, with the fantasy of immortality, there is also no interpretation. The poem thus plays with the idea of death as explanation and concludes by despairing of both death and explanation. Its power is a direct consequence of the explosion that hovers over the individual incident each stanza narrates, and provides a counterstrain to it. One final, parallel example, Marvell's "The Mower's Song," may help to illustrate how the threat of violence (here, the fact of violence) dominates, as an obsession dominates, and actually obscures the progressions in each stanza:

I

My Mind was once the true survey
Of all these Medows fresh and gay;
And in the greenness of the Grass
Did see its Hopes as in a Glass;
When *Juliana* came, and She
    What I do to the Grass, does to my Thoughts and Me.

II

But these, while I with Sorrow pine,
Grew more luxuriant still and fine;
That not one Blade of Grass you spy'd,
But had a Flower on either side;
When *Juliana* came, and She
    What I do to the Grass, does to my Thoughts and Me.

III

Unthankful Medows, could you so
A fellowship so true forego,
And in your gawdy May-games meet,
While I lay trodden under feet?
When *Juliana* came, and She
    What I do to the Grass, does to my Thoughts and Me.

IV

But what you in Compassion ought,
Shall now by my Revenge be wrought:
And Flow'rs, and Grass, and I and all,
Will in one common Ruine fall.
For *Juliana* comes, and She
    What I do to the Grass, does to my Thoughts and Me.

V

And thus, ye Medows, which have been
Companions of my thoughts more green,
Shall now the Heraldry become
With which I shall adorn my Tomb;
For *Juliana* comes, and She
    What I do to the Grass, does to my Thoughts and Me.

The refrain of Marvell's poem, like the concluding stanza of Dickinson's poem, brings the narrative up short with omnipresent and present-tense violence. It is as if conception can tolerate nothing further than violence that shifts curiously enough from past to present tense, in both poems, and defies historical connections by reversing them: "*Juliana* came" but now she "comes." In "My Life had stood a Loaded Gun," the distinction between the pluperfect and the present tense is somewhat less abrupt, but the insistence upon the recurrent present baffles progression in a similar manner: the story we first thought past tense, first thought over, cannot, does not know how to, conclude. Thus the act of annihilation that is promised and prophesied in every stanza of both poems never comes to pass or never ceases coming to pass. "None stir the second time—," but the fact that the killing must be repeated, albeit with a different object, suggests that violence is never done until life itself is done.

Different as the traditions are that shaped Marvell's and Dickinson's poems, and easy to understand as "The Mower's Song" is in comparison, the source of their magic is similar. The "Owner" in Dickinson's poem reveals no presence; all that we know of him is contained in the speaker's response. Although Juliana in "The Mower's Song" is a more conventional figure (the cruel lady of courtly love), she bears analogies to the "Owner" in that she is not so much an individual as a force: she appears precipitously, cuts down life as the mower cuts grass, disorders the natural world and transforms it into a decorative heraldry for his tomb. Though in the poem's beginning Marvell's speaker is victim rather than murderer, the fourth stanza makes clear how thoroughly "Revenge" dissolves the distinction between those terms and how ineffective either posture is against the mysterious otherness of the world. For threaten as he may, Juliana still "comes," and murder as Dickinson's speaker will, she is nonetheless "Without—the power to die—." The real otherness, then, in both poems (represented by Juliana in one and by the "Owner" in the other) is the world, in whose service one engages one's powers. It is against the world or for it (the distinction barely seems to matter) that one does battle, a world whose identity is, at best, shadowy and is, at most, a projection of the force against which, or for which, one fights, and whose power is finally inexorable.

"My Life had stood a Loaded Gun," like "The Mower's Song" and "The Man of Double Deed," is a story that is both without an ending and cognizant of where that ending lies. Held up against the world's otherness and deriving identity in its service, the meaning of the speaker's experience remains hidden in the future of its defeat. The relationship between meaning and death, ending and interpretation—the hero who will not die in Dickinson's poem, and the one who will not stay dead in Marvell's—reminds us of Freud's assertion that the person asleep never dreams of his own death. For the speaker in these poems, as for Freud's dreamer, death is a reality that escapes completion. Huger than life and eventually overtaking it, it lurks meantime in the underlying rhythm of all action.

III

When death is the center to which "Each Life Converges" (P 680), the semiotic distractions it creates will be discernible below the surface of the poem's meaning and will erupt only at its conclusion, as we have seen in "My Life had stood a Loaded Gun." There death's static is perceived as an undercurrent, for the cause of the static is precisely death's failure to manifest itself. Always threatening exposure, it ceases to counter the signs of life only at that moment when it overwhelms them. With this explanation in mind, we can perhaps better understand why the apparent sense of "My Life had stood a Loaded Gun" is threatened by resonances or undertones that are not entirely audible. When, however, the situation is reversed so that death is viewed directly as so omnipresent and continuous a force that it suffers a rupture only brief enough to admit life, the disruptions will themselves break into the center of the space that has been cleared for them. "Human life," Geoffrey Hartman writes in "The Voice of the Shuttle," ". . . . is an indeterminate middle between overspecified poles always threatening to collapse it. The poles may be birth and death, father and mother, mother and wife, love and judgment, heaven and earth, first things and last things. Art narrates that middle region and charts it like a purgatory, for only if it exists can life exist." In the following poem, which provides a clear demonstration of Hartman's insight and an important definition of those poems I shall discuss in this section, the speaker is that middle term whose presence pushes eternity and immortality apart and, by so doing, creates the space of life:

> Behind Me—dips Eternity—
> Before Me—Immortality—
> Myself—the Term between—
> Death but the Drift of Eastern Gray,
> Dissolving into Dawn away,
> Before the West begin—
>
> 'Tis Kingdoms—afterward—they say—
> In perfect—pauseless Monarchy—
> Whose Prince—is Son of None—
> Himself—His Dateless Dynasty—
> Himself—Himself diversify—
> In Duplicate divine—
>
> 'Tis Miracle before Me—then—
> 'Tis Miracle behind—between—
> A Crescent in the Sea—
> With Midnight to the North of Her—
> And Midnight to the South of Her—
> And Maelstrom—in the Sky—
>
> (P 721)

"Eternity" and "Immortality" are literally out of this world. Free of both beginning and end ("Dateless") and unbroken by event ("pauseless"), they escape real characterization or comprehension. "Midnight" echoes "Midnight," "Miracle" "Miracle"; even dawn suggests death, so closely does it resemble twilight. Meaning stuck in the same groove becomes nonsense. Divinity duplicated is thus nothing but an absence, our world drained of all its meaning. For while the second stanza, which elaborates on "Immortality," might at first be mistaken for a reverential expression of dogma, the vacancy of the internal rhyme ("Son of None—") and the insistence on establishing these facts as suspect ("they say—") are clear indications of scorn. Were Christ humanly fathered, we might recognize Him. But perfection rules out both recognition and discrete identity. "Eternity" and "Immortality" seem like mirrors hung on opposite walls, with barely anything between. Except, as the last stanza insists, there is something between, which is the speaker's presence. Her existence disrupts order, is a movement rising out of the sea, shot upward, finally, in chaos ("Maelstrom—in the Sky—"). As Charles Anderson notes in his provocative comment on the poem, the east-west axis of eternity-immortality is entirely different from the referential poles of the speaker's life. In the concluding stanza, the switch in pronouns from the first to the third person suggests that even the speaker's vision of her own life has been redefined and objectified. As she presses against the poles of eternity and immortality with the force of life's disorder, we know that the price of her collapse, the disappearance of the middle term, is not only personal extinction but the omission of life itself, leaving mirrors that reflect the diversity of nothing.

The disruption in the poem, then, is literally the story the speaker has to tell about life. What can be chronicled, what, in other words, has both beginning and end, also has identity. But while the speaker in "My Life had stood a Loaded Gun" shies away from the knowledge that her story has an end (because she equates its end with her own annihilation), this speaker turns her attention elsewhere; here value is wedded to the fact of action as it can be seen to survive its origins and to shake off or, at any rate, stall, its consequences. Value is disruption and disorder: it lies in the volatile middle term.

It must by now be clear that the poems about which I have been speaking enact a tug of war between life and death. The equanimity with which the speaker in "Behind Me dips Eternity" holds at bay the surrounding forces that converge on her is, however, rare. Indeed, a poem like "Behind Me dips Eternity" is marked by its competence in managing the upstart forces of both life and death; even "Maelstrom—in the Sky—," as presented to us, is not especially threatening. But the quiescence of the middle term vanishes when we see it no longer in a definitional context, but now in active engagement with those forces that threaten its existence. In the following two poems, life is also represented as a disruption of stasis. But the disruption here seems more like an outbreak around which control keeps trying, unsuccessfully, to close:

> I tie my Hat—I crease my Shawl—
> Life's little duties do—precisely—
> As the very least
> Were infinite—to me—
>
> I put new Blossoms in the Glass—
> And throw the old—away—
> I push a petal from my Gown
> That anchored there—I weigh
> The time 'twill be till six o'clock
> I have so much to do—
> And yet—Existence—some way back—
> Stopped—struck—my ticking—through—
> We cannot put Ourself away
> As a completed Man
> Or Woman—When the Errand's done
> We came to Flesh—upon—
> There may be—Miles on Miles of Nought—
> Of action—sicker far—
> To simulate—is stinging work—
> To cover what we are
> From Science—and from Surgery—
> Too Telescopic Eyes
> To bear on us unshaded—
> For their—sake—not for Ours—
> 'Twould start them—
> We—could tremble—
> But since we got a Bomb—
> And held it in our Bosom—
> Nay—Hold it—it is calm—
>
> Therefore—we do life's labor—
> Though life's Reward—be done—
> With scrupulous exactness—
> To hold our Senses—on—

> (P 443)

Here, in two places, meaning disrupts both vacuous action and the sententia in which such action takes refuge: first, in the lines acknowledging that, if one were to admit it, life would be seen to have come to a dead halt:

> And yet—Existence—some way back—
> Stopped—struck—my ticking—through—

and second, in the suppositional statement that plays with the possibility of exploding the "Bomb [be]got[ten]" by the speaker's fury at life's loss of meaning:

> We—could tremble—
> But since we got a Bomb—
> And held it in our Bosom—
> Nay—Hold it—it is calm—

but steadies itself ("Nay—Hold it—"), rejecting such an explosion. For in order to "hold [her] Senses—on—" course or, more simply, "on" (intact), she thinks fury must tolerate repression.

From its similarity to other Dickinson poems in which the speaker's loss of love is not accompanied by the loss of her life, we can infer that "the Errand" she "came to Flesh—upon—" is both incarnation and carnal destination, the general effort to wrest meaning from experience and the more particular effort to gratify the desires of the flesh. The ticking of existence, the heart, stops not because death overtakes it, but rather because vengeance at the inevitability of loss overtakes it, transforming it into a bomb, as love suffers a metamorphosis into fury. Though the speaker asserts that there is nothing to help and everything to hide, that science and surgery would be "start[led]" by this transformation, it is for purposes of self-protection that calm is maintained, as the last stanza makes eloquently clear. For fury let loose would explode the very reason of the poem: it would blast holes in reason as the lines I have pointed to blast holes in the narrative. Here again, then, life is represented as fury coming to terms with sexuality, and both are subject to the efforts of repression.

If "I tie my Hat—I crease my shawl" makes an oblique acknowledgment of sexuality and its loss, the following poem rises to the occasion of explicit statement and finally to heresy, and the consequence is not rage but rather ecstasy. Although its catechism is one of renunciation, we must scrutinize the poem carefully to see how renunciation can be so resonant with the presence of what has been given up:

> I cannot live with You—
> It would be Life—
> And Life is over there—
> Behind the Shelf
>
> The Sexton keeps the Key to—
> Putting up
> Our Life—His Porcelain—
> Like a Cup—
>
> Discarded of the Housewife—
> Quaint—or Broke—

A newer Sevres pleases—
Old Ones crack—

I could not die—with You—
For One must wait
To shut the Other's Gaze down—
You—could not—

And I—Could I stand by
And see You—freeze—
Without my Right of Frost—
Death's privilege?

Nor could I rise—with You—
Because Your Face
Would put out Jesus'—
That New Grace

Glow plain—and foreign
On my homesick Eye—
Except that You than He
Shone closer by—

They'd judge Us—How—
For You—served Heaven—You know,
Or sought to—
I could not—

Because You saturated Sight—
And I had no more Eyes
For sordid excellence
As Paradise

And were You lost, I would be—
Though My Name
Rang loudest
On the Heavenly fame—

And were You—saved—
And I—condemned to be
Where You were not—
That self—were Hell to Me—

So We must meet apart—
You there—I—here—
With just the Door ajar
That Oceans are—and Prayer—
And that White Sustenance—
Despair—

(P 640)

With the exception of the second and third stanzas, which digress both from
the form of assertion established elsewhere and from the patterned recital of

facts, the poem is structured as a list of criteria that would make union impossible. In most stanzas we hear two voices: one that renounces the earthly lover and another that explains the need for renunciation, the foremost explanation being the imminence of a divine rival. But the comparison between earthly and divine, and the rhythm of statement and counterstatement established by the pairing, is broken into by the even stronger, more subversive force of sexual energy. The energy is, in part, revealed in the colloquial speech rhythms that disrupt the more formal and laconic litany of renunciation (I cannot live with You—/It would be Life—) in order to qualify it ("And I—Could I stand by/And see You—freeze—/Without my Right of Frost—"). The intimacy of address, with its tone of patient explanation and its scrupulous concern for accuracy ("For You—served Heaven— You know,/Or sought to—"), warms to its subject and becomes impassioned by it in its testimony of what finally keeps the lovers apart.

Interestingly enough, what prohibits union seems to be the fact that it has already occurred. The injunction, then, cannot be to avoid union but must be rather to guard against its repetition. For although "Because Your Face/Would put out Jesus'—" seems suppositional, two stanzas later the event is echoed, explained, and located not in the future at all, but rather in the past:

> Because You saturated Sight—
> And I had no more Eyes
> For sordid excellence
> As Paradise

The lines here are rich with the pride of acknowledged sexuality, and in their acknowledgment of supremacy they demote paradise from its conventionally unrivaled estate. The speaker is not only saying "I had no more eyes for *such* sordid excellence *as* Paradise," but also, more radically, "I had no more eyes *to see* sordid excellence *as* Paradise." The lover, in this latter interpretation, not only occupies vision but also, apparently, purifies it. Thus, while we are expecting the notion of paradise to be rivaled by love, we are not expecting it to be revised by it, and the revision constitutes much of the power of the lines. A similar transformation occurs two stanzas later where we expect to hear:

> And were You—saved—
> And I   condemned to be
> . . . [In] Hell

and what we hear instead is a new definition of Hell prompted not by God's judgment but rather by the lover's absence, and half-echoing Milton's "Myself am Hell":

> And were You—saved—
> And I—condemned to be
> Where You were not—
> That self—were Hell to Me—

To return to the earlier stanza, even the lover's excellence is seen as sordid because it is excessive. Indeed, it is precisely the absoluteness of the lover's excellence, his uncontested supremacy, against which the denomination "sordid" makes its puritanical outcry. For the excess of pleasure is the real force that drives the two lovers apart, notwithstanding the more superficial reasons reiterated by the closing stanzas, which are fashioned around all the external prohibitions against union: the difference in age (implied by the fifth and sixth stanzas), in religious status (implied by the eighth and eleventh stanzas), etc. Although the poem attempts to recover its composure, the stanzas I have spoken about remain too dazzling to be dismissed as containing just a number of good reasons for the lovers' separation. Even their syntactic introductions ("Because Your Face/Would put out Jesus'—," "Because You saturated Sight—"), with their direct announcement of explanation and their implicit accompaniment of passion, insist we consider their centrality.

Despite the "Door ajar," which leaves a distance commutable only by ocean or prayer, and which we might suppose would produce tension, there is a curious quiet to the concluding lines, and two extra lines to the stanza that seem to insist on the enlarging space between the two lovers. The resolution of tension is a consequence of the fact that the renunciation the speaker has predicted as inevitable has been accomplished. The sustenance she now lives on (she calls it "Despair—," but perhaps it is memory drained of detail) is "White" because it has been purified of presence and sexuality. The rhythms of "Oceans" and "Prayer" are calm, all the passion of life has slowed to them. Thus, while the voice of implicit sexuality is quelled utterly in the last stanza, the poem's conclusion offers a resolution, not of the passion, for which there is no resolution, but rather of the less problematic series of statements and counterstatements that have served to divert speaker and reader from passion's verbal enactment throughout the poem.

"To lose what we never owned might seem an eccentric Bereavement but Presumption has its Affliction as actually as Claim—," Dickinson wrote in L 429. But loss also legitimates the desire for possession by freeing desire from all illusion that its object will be granted, and a speaker then affirms her absolute claim to what has absolutely been denied her. As I suggested elsewhere, in such instances the bodily absence of both loss and immortality associates the two states as if in an identity, and utterance is charged with the task of the pouring of form into what has no form, shape into the hollows of absence. In the service of the reconstruction, memory can be so delusively persuasive that, like the speaker in the following poem, we are swayed into confusing it with actual presence:

> I live with Him—I see His face—
> I go no more away
> For Visiter—or Sundown—
> Death's single privacy
>
> The Only One—forestalling Mine—
> And that—by Right that He
> Presents a Claim invisible—
> No Wedlock—granted Me—
>
> I live with Him—I hear His Voice—
> I stand alive—Today—
> To witness to the Certainty
> Of Immortality—
>
> Taught Me—by Time—the lower Way
> Conviction—Every day—
> That Life like This—is stopless—
> Be Judgment—what it may—
>
> (P 463)

There is something incantatory about the poem's tone, which suggests that its meaning is positive, that immortality has been discovered in the presence of the earthly lover. But what makes the tone sound so positive is also what makes it sound suspicious. To "see His face—," to "hear His Voice—" is to know the lover by his absence, through memory or longing rather than in fact, for the insistent affirmations (his voice, his face) offer proofs that compensate in the absence of the whole. And as if to reveal the pain of such a memory, its perpetuity is designated by the word "stopless—," familiar to us from "It was not Death for I stood up," and customarily used by Dickinson to indicate despair. The poem, then, is structured to produce a reversal of what it first leads us to expect, and only on a second reading do we really see what is being said.

In the first stanza we are told that the speaker retreats with the memory of her absent lover in otherwise perfect isolation for, in context, "I live with Him—I see His face—" is the cry of vision estranged from presence. In the second stanza, the pronoun reference switches from the lover to death. Only death, the second stanza informs us, can exact a more imperious solitude; its demand is the only one powerful enough to "forestall" the speaker's vision by canceling her life. But the speaker's life, once canceled by the absence of the earthly lover, leaves little more for death to negate. Sufficient proof of endlessness, loss is the only certainty, the unconditional "given" of human existence. Any other judgment, even death itself, as the grammar of the last stanza reminds us, seems weak as an untested hypothesis. And, if proved, redundant.

"For fear of which hear this thou age unbred," Shakespeare wrote, flaunting the mortality of the friend. Dickinson, acquainted with a more harrowing vision of mortality, one whose consequences were inevitably only personal, faced time with less bravado. If "I tie my Hat I crease my Shawl," "I cannot live with You," and "I live with Him I see His face" all create worlds where vacancy postdates meaning, in the latter poems the speaker insists on its reconstruction. In this case, reconstruction is tantamount to memory— the invention of presence where not to have it would leave the world absent even of pain. The speaker here will not reduce the world to nothing. Only death can relieve the world of meaning; only death can wipe it clean like a slate. And after death? In another one of Dickinson's poems the speaker, anticipating a meeting with God, can only say half drolly and half in disappointment, "Savior—I've seen the face—before!" (P 461).

IV

Holding to one's course, and the evenness of rhythm therein implied, might be defined as the inability to feel, the pulse that refuses to quicken, or so Dickinson suggests in the following poem:

> Through the strait pass of suffering—
> The Martyrs—even—trod.
> Their feet—upon Temptation—
> Their faces—upon God—
>
> A stately—shriven—Company—
> Convulsion—playing round—
> Harmless—as streaks of Meteor—
> Upon a Planet's Bond—
>
> Their faith—the everlasting troth—
> Their Expectation—fair—
> The Needle—to the North Degree—
> Wades—so—thro' polar Air!
>
> (P 792)

Convulsion is "Harmless," however, only when not experienced. But what constitutes convulsion? What elements of sexuality and death and in what relationship? For it is these elements in combination that characterize every poem I have spoken about in this chapter. Only the martyrs in the above poem, seemingly not subject to the force of sexuality, give the illusion of escaping the force of death, for when sexuality is not even there to be overcome, life assumes death's shape. In poems other than this one, however, a choice has been made against sexuality and for death. The consequence of the choice, since it is an unwilling one, is rage that is speechless ("I should have been too glad I see") or subverted by ecstasy ("I cannot live with You") or explicitly repressed ("I tie my Hat I crease my Shawl"), or that escapes repression by protest ("I live with Him I see His face") or defines life as disorder ("Behind Me dips Eternity"), or that erupts openly into violence ("My Life had stood a Loaded Gun").

Insofar as rage constitutes a tear in the established fabric of the narrative, it exists in relation to that narrative very much as Todorov describes the supernatural's relationship to the narrative and with the same important "coincidence": "We see, finally, how the social and the literary functions coincide: in both cases, we are concerned with a transgression of the law. Whether it is in social life or in narrative, the intervention of the supernatural element always constitutes a break in the system of pre-established rules, and in doing so finds its justification." Like the supernatural, rage, too, is a transgression of the social, of the agreed-upon laws that ritualize life and sometimes render it immobile. Both contain outbreaks of sexuality that would not be sanctioned in the mainstream of the narrative or in the mainstream of social action out of which it is woven. "Sexual excesses will be more readily accepted by any censor if they are attributed to the devil," Todorov writes, and indeed the same claim might be made about the scape-goat function of rage. For rage is a kind of devil that bears the burden of all our disapprobation: it is that which, no less than primitive sexuality, we are socialized out of. And significantly it is what, when it overtakes us, we make responsible for all our expressions of will and desire. As Kent reminds us in *Lear*, "Anger hath a privilege." Rage is the great disclaimer, the feeling that puts us beyond ourselves, and in so doing puts us in touch with all the social and private dictates that vie against one another for the dominance of the self. Recognition becomes sanction at precisely that moment when the alternative is seen in its death-dealing context: existence "struck-through" and "stopped." At such a moment, speech itself is a protest against the status quo. The speaker elects words rather than silence, mediation rather than stasis, disruption rather than death.

Ultimately, of course, election is complicated by inadequate alternatives. In one of Dickinson's central utterances, the acknowledgment of inadequacy, of the poverty of both literal and imaginative terms, leads the speaker to a despair rich with the sense of life pressing against its own limitations:

> Title divine—is mine!
> The Wife—without the Sign!
> Acute Degree—conferred on me—
> Empress of Calvary!
> Royal—all but the Crown!

Betrothed—without the swoon
God sends us Women—
When you—hold—Garnet to Garnet—
Gold—to Gold—
Born—Bridalled—Shrouded—
In a Day—
Tri Victory—
"My Husband"—women say—
Stroking the Melody—
Is *this*—the way?

(P 1027)

My reading of the poem is hypothetical by default, for its syntax alone, not to mention the elliptical progressions and the rapid transformation of pronouns, insists upon respect for its difficulty. What we can ascertain is that the speaker is comparing the life of the heavenly bride to that of the earthly one. The woman exalted in the first half of the poem is royal by virtue of what she does not have. Without the sign or ring legitimating marriage and without the swoon of sexuality, this woman, seemingly self-elected, is dangerously close to Plath's "Lady Lazarus," who will also insist upon "Acute Degree—" and who will carry the claim of suffering one step further into hyperbole than Calvary. This miracle—a woman without the swoon, divine by virtue of its absence—makes us hunger for a more generous world where salvation is not had at the expense of life. It is the other world we think we are getting when we read of "the swoon/God sends us Women—/When you—hold—Garnet to Garnet—/Gold—to Gold—." But the transition is strangely enough no transition; deprivation is here not absent, it is simply of another order. "When you—hold—Garnet to Garnet—/Gold—to Gold—" (in the secular context of the earthly wedding ceremony), what you get is death ("Born—Bridalled—Shrouded—/In a Day—"). The shift in pronouns is a shift to the colloquial "you," almost as if in talking implicitly about sexuality the speaker had to cast attribution as far from herself as possible. But in the very process of distinguishing herself from the wealth of the earthly alternative, she temporarily allies herself with it, with the swoon "God sends us Women—." In the fusion and confusion of these lines, both options funnel to death, the contraction of the self into its own ashes. For the birth of the wife becomes the death of the woman. Upon such sacrifices, the gods themselves throw incense. The problem is that both alternatives require sacrifice.

Between the nothing that is the self and the nothing to which the self gets reduced when it capitulates to another, we see our options clearly. While it is true that the jewels in the poem suggest the blessing of the earthly wife, the lines, coming as they do in the middle of the poem (as a manifestation of its transition from divine to earthly), are a half-implied metaphor for the necessary complement of divine and earthly wife, for each by herself is inadequate. Thus although the lines tell us that garnet is held to garnet and gold to gold (each alternative able to assess only itself), the proximity of the lines requires us to see the colors (and the choices they represent) held against each other, as if the speaker's vision of impossibility momentarily enabled its transcendence.

"Stroking the Melody—" is perhaps a metaphor for the very impossibilities delimited by the poem. For the need to get a hold on sound, to imbue it with physical dimensions, reminds us that we have a metaphoric world to console us for the impoverishment of the physical world. Like Lear's desire to "sweeten the imagination" or to wipe the hand "of mortality," Dickinson's phrase suggests that simultaneous perception of loss and compensation that grips the mind at such moments of imaginative invention, as, in the process of calling wishes into being, the speaker inevitably acknowledges their status as wishes, not subject to fulfillment in reality. If only one could "sweeten the imagination" or "Strok[e] the Melody." So utterance grows out of desperation and registers violence at its fact.

Yet options exist because we must take them. We cannot, as Sartre pointed out, not choose. This recognition is the moment the poem records. For the speaker, from the vantage of Calvary, looks enviously at the earthly alternative and finds that it is nothing. Previously she thought she could imitate in name, if nothing else, the title of the earthly wife. Now it is apparent that the imitation is purposeless. She cold not have it if she wanted it, and if she had it, she sees now that she would not want it. Her title, then, like the earthly wife's is empty, the "Melody—" sought after but finally strained once it is acknowledged that any possession is by itself inadequate.

The problem of otherness perceived as death; the problem of otherness for lack of which there is death: the alternatives in these poems are stark ones. Yet the poems themselves are not stark, are, in fact, loaded with energy that is, as I have been suggesting, close to explosive. And it is the energy that needs accounting for, fed as it is by the fuel of sexuality on the one hand, and death on the other, by that combustible that ignites into rage. In the poems presence seems manifested *as* rage and, in particular, as rage at all that is temporal, all that has a history whose requirement is sacrifice and choice. If narrative is that thing which carries a story to its conclusion, presence disrupts the continuity of narrative by holding its moments apart so that its outrageous demands relax their grip on the speaker, as she scrutinizes at leisure and rejects at will the alternatives to which she must eventually capitulate, and this is quite different from the passive protest against temporality as we observed it in the definitional poems. We might say that here protest requires rage because only rage can provide a sufficient stronghold against each of the two terms that threaten to reclaim the speaker. Voice at cross-purposes with conflicting forces, coherence purchased at the expense of continuity, is a central phenomenon in all lyric poems, as I suggested earlier. What is important about the Dickinson poems that I have discussed is that we see the dynamics of this ordinarily hidden triad more explicitly and hence with greater clarity.

It is a commonplace, albeit a sophisticated one, that speech in poems exists across time and space, that a poem never happened or that it happens every time it is read. The commonplace becomes important when we acknowledge its consequences for annihilating process, for Yeats' vision of Byzantium or Keats' of the Grecian Urn. Yet these latter poems are conscious gestures, controlled rejections of the world replaced by the artful vision. The rejection of process is neither as conscious nor as stable in the Dickinson poems I have discussed. True, the world is envisioned as a dead-end, eternity and immortality, for all practical purposes, one and the same. Yet presence or voice breaks into and disrupts the dreaded sequence of moments that follow so rapidly on one another that their very movement blurs to the illusion of stasis. Voice cannot be in a poem except in contradistinction to action. Voice gives way, exhausts itself, at the recognition that it cannot make a difference, that it cannot *be*, except removed from time, also static. So prose wears a poem's guise at last.

If these poems counsel that we must return to what kills us, they also console us by revealing that reading, no less than speaking, offers us a reprieve. For when we read, we are no longer engaged in the world of action: we have set aside those concerns that drive us, willingly or not, to shape our own ends. Like the speaker in the poems, we have agreed that action requires reprieve—because it hurries by, fails to take adequate account of the self entangled in the web of its own inevitabilities. Voice (or as I have been calling it, presence) breaks through the linear sequence of events, disrupts it, offers a temporary escape by refusing the only alternatives, alternatives that are, at the same time, inadequate ones. Yet the temporary escape that is really no more or less than presence afforded the provisions that guarantee its existence—unbounded by event, free of both past and future—suffices, and in the next chapter we shall see how poems take the escape from temporality as their explicit subject (as they have not done in the utterances discussed in these last two chapters) and dare to dream themselves into the structure of the defiant death excursions.

We cannot change the story of our lives. We cannot undo or do again, and if we could, we would not always do better. Even the future takes its shape beyond us. All that we have to make good on is the space of the present. Freud suggested that to be in possession of a story is somehow to be reconciled to it. But no knowledge is sufficient to permit us to forgive the exigencies of a world whose demand for sacrifice is absolute. And, as comedy teaches, without forgiveness, there is no reconciliation. It is not knowledge that saves us but rather the recognition that salvation is a luxury our lives will not purchase. Salvation might mean that our lives could be shaped with the coherence of written stories, well authored and progressing with deliberation toward the promised end. In lieu of this, we accept the space left vacant by the abandoned idea of salvation. Like Keats's "Negative Capability," this space is liberated from the strictures of certainty, closure, and conclusion, all those inevitable first laws of action. Presence occurs at the moment when the self absents itself from the flow of action because comprehension of it requires a slowing and temporary halt of the momentum that, blurring past, present, and future, renders them indistinguishable. These occasions of presence gain the self the only immortality it will ever know, for in a very real sense they lie outside of time and do not "count" in (are not counted by) it. Thus, the absence of consequence that we might once have greeted with despair, we come finally to understand as a consolation. At a distance from experience, presence comes to know its own mind. It shakes off the imperatives of past and future, self and other, sexuality and death, by learning its responses to them and by learning, too, that action, however inexorable, cannot do away with response. Presence then is action's corollary. It is action's "other," and its wisdom consists in what it comes to know of experience once it has been freed of the compulsion for consequence. Purified of event, presence summons up all that is representative of untempered vision, what Yeats called "the foul rag-and-bone shop of the heart."

Yet though severed from experience, presence remains in touch with experience's dilemmas and in touch, too, with the fact that it must inevitably vacate its privileged position and rejoin the stream of action. As we shall see, even in the proleptic utterances, the speaker's freedom from this world prescribes the limits that return her to it. The hope is that once the self is returned to event, it will know better what to do in it. The poem is like a breathing space, a necessary "time out." The aside to oneself, the soliloquy to an audience, the rush of adrenalin in the actor the moment before the play begins, or simply the man alone pausing before his options—these are analogies. Ultimately, of course, the world will not wait. It catches the speaker up in its momentum again and exerts its authority to insist he make choices. As I have been suggesting, in Dickinson's poems, if choice involves the resolution of conflict, rage represents the refusal to choose. the splitting of impossible infinitives. Vitalized by this refusal, presence meets conflict head-on. Heroic in its "power to kill,/Without—the power to die—," presence is not yet weakened by the realization that immortality is an illusion. In its dissociation from action, its repudiation of necessity, lies strength, a redemptive counter to the dutiful complicity that characterizes our lives.

MARGARET HOMANS

Emily Dickinson and Poetic Identity

Dickinson thought of herself not just as a poet but as a woman poet. The first and most obvious evidence for this statement is that she searched for models among the famous women writers of her day, admiring George Eliot, the Brontës, and Elizabeth Barrett Browning in particular. This interest was more personal or biographical than it was literary, but this indicates no disparagement, since her poetry was scarcely influenced by literary men, either. In her letters she mourns the deaths of these great women as vehemently as she admires their work. She inquired insistently after the prospects for a biography of George Eliot in an exchange of letters with the Boston publisher Thomas Niles in April 1882. In March 1883 Niles sent her Mathilda Blind's *Life of George Eliot*, and in 1885 she received the first volume of Cross's *Life* from her literary correspondent Thomas Wentworth Higginson. After reading Blind's biography she commented, "A Doom of Fruit without the Bloom, like the Niger Fig," which echoes an earlier comment, made shortly after Eliot's death, indicating a range of biographical affinities between the two women:

> Now, *my* George Eliot. The gift of belief which her greatness denied her, I
> trust she receives in the childhood of the kingdom of heaven. As childhood
> is earth's confiding time, perhaps having no childhood, she lost her way to
> the early trust, and no later came.

She possessed portraits of Mrs. Browning and was even sent a picture of her grave, testifying to her friend's knowledge of her interest. She found A. Mary F. Robinson's biography of Emily Brontë "more electric far than anything since 'Jane Eyre' " (*L*, III, 775). Again alluding not to Brontë's own work but to what was written about her—Charlotte Brontë's 1850 Biographical Notice—Dickinson refers to Brontë as a person more than as a writer in the following comparison with her friend Mrs. Holland: she was

> humbled with wonder at your self-forgetting, . . . Reminded again of gigantic Emily Brontë, of whom her Charlotte said "Full of ruth for others, on herself she had no mercy."
>
> (L, III, 721)

In these comments she extends her sympathies to these women as suffering human beings, not as women, but she also considers them as women, and is aware of special difficulties that were perhaps similar to hers.

> That Mrs. Browning fainted, we need not read *Aurora Leigh* to know, when she lived with her English aunt; and George Sand "must make no noise in her grandmother's bedroom." Poor children! Women, now, queens, now!
>
> (L, II, 376)

She also uses womanhood specifically as a literary classification. In 1871 she wrote to Higginson, "Mrs Hunt's Poems are stronger than any written by Women since Mrs—Browning, with the exception of Mrs Lewes" (*L*, II, 491). She must be making a special point in referring to George Eliot as Mrs. Lewes and in using a dash to emphasize Elizabeth Barrett's marriage, but it is unclear whether this is a private reference to her metaphor of wife and bride for poetic power, or whether she is thinking of the difference marriage might make to a woman writer. In 1870 she held a curious exchange with Higginson about another married woman poet.

> You told me of Mrs Lowell's Poems.
> Would you tell me where I could find them or are they not for sight?
>
> (L, II, 480)

Maria White Lowell's poems were published in 1885, but Higginson had apparently been referring to her poems in a metaphoric sense, because in her next letter Dickinson says

> You told me Mrs. Lowell was Mr Lowell's "inspiration" What is inspiration?
>
> (L, II, 481)

Dickinson is incensed that, when she has a chance to read a woman's poetry, or, just as good, to learn of another woman poet as private as herself, Higginson, a self-proclaimed champion of women's rights, asks her to consider the poetess in her more acceptably feminine role as her husband's muse.

That Dickinson can compare reading Emily Brontë's life with reading

Jane Eyre indicates that she groups real and fictive biographies under the category of exemplary lives. When she turns from the lives to the works of these women writers, it is usually without reference to gender. Her comments on Eliot and Emily Brontë suggest affinities between their work and aspects of her own work that seem to have nothing to do with femininity. She characterizes Eliot as "she who Experienced Eternity in Time" (*L*, III, 689).

> "What do I think of *Middlemarch*?" What do I think of glory—except that in a few instances this "mortal has already put on immortality."
> George Eliot is one. The mysteries of human nature surpass the "mysteries of redemption," for the infinite we only suppose, while we see the finite.
>
> (*L*, II, 506)

Dickinson is perhaps expressing her surprise and delight that a novel can do what she expects of poetry; in any case it is Eliot's encompassing mind that she is considering, and not "Mrs Lewes." Several very late letters quote one "marvelous" stanza from Brontë's "No coward soul is mine," each time subsuming it to the expression of her own sentiment (*L*, III, 802–803, 844, 848). One of these quotations includes an illuminating misinterpretation. Writing in 1883 of the "sorrow of so many years" brought by the deaths of so many beloved friends and relatives, she says "As Emily Bronte to her Maker, I write to my Lost 'Every Existence would exist in thee—'" (*L*, III, 802–803). Dickinson must have known that Brontë was referring not to "her Maker" but to a more personally defined death, a conception much closer to Dickinson's own than Dickinson seems willing to acknowledge. She treats Brontë the poet as a rival and distances her, while at the same moment welcoming an affinity on the personal level.

Just as Dickinson compartmentalized her own interest in women writers, studies of her have tended to consider her femininity at the level of biography and to leave her femininity out of critical readings of her poems. Even though she seems to have been more openly conscious than Dorothy Wordsworth or Emily Brontë about the difficulties of being a woman and a poet, any treatment of her specifically as a woman poet runs the risk of being either confining or tangential, because she has too large and brilliant a body of poetry to be adequately interpreted from any single perspective. However, this chapter will argue that Dickinson derives her unique power from her particular way of understanding her femininity, and that her work is as complex and profuse as it is, at least in part, because she is able to put behind her problems of identity that make Dorothy and Brontë linger over the same themes and issues in poem after poem. For example, in the letter discussed above in which she quotes from Brontë, she telescopes Brontë's long and arduous struggle to center an external poetic power within herself, and although this telescoping may be unfair, it suggests what Dickinson views as a crucial difference between Brontë's concept of language and her own: for Brontë linguistic power is a single entity, which may or may not be possessed, but Dickinson goes on in the rest of the letter to sketch obliquely her concept of language's doubleness. The most recent and stunning of those deaths, that of her eight-year-old nephew Gilbert, has broken language into its components. Naming is difficult and self-conscious:

> Sweet sister.
> Was that what I used to call you? . . .
> The Physician says I have "Nervous prostration."
> Possibly I have—I do not know the Names of Sickness.

Her disease is unnameable because it is a disease of referents lost through the recent deaths. Gilbert's last words—" 'Open the Door, open the Door, they are waiting for me' "—have set her thinking about what is for her an ultimately missing referent, where just previously she has supplied one for Brontë. "*Who* were waiting for him, all we possess we would give to know. . . . All this and more, though *is* there more? More than Love and Death? Then tell me it's name!" She splits language to find genuine mysteries, and she finds in language's doubleness, paradoxically, a way around the hierarchizing dualism that impedes Dorothy Wordsworth and Brontë. In a letter to her friend Abiah Root written when she was nineteen, Dickinson tells an extravagant and amusing story about a cold, and then, in a gesture that distinguishes artist from anecdotist, she exposes her fictive strategy:

> Now my dear friend, let me tell you that these last thoughts are fictions—vain imaginations to lead astray foolish young women. They are flowers of speech, they both *make*, and *tell* deliberate falsehoods, avoid them as the snake, and turn aside as from the *Bottle* snake, and I don't *think* you will be harmed.
>
> (*L*, I, 88; 29 Jan. 1850)

Although this letter dates from well before Dickinson's first serious poetry, such self-consciousness establishes this and related passages as the proper place to begin an investigation of her sense of identity as a writer and as a woman. The writer here is logically, though never overtly, associated with the snake, since she is the inventor of the "vain imaginations," and in a postscript she refers to her story about the cold as "mistakes" and "sin." Her interlocutor, so innocent that she must be told that the story is a fiction, plays Eve to Dickinson's Satan. At the end of the passage the writer renounces her guise as a fiction-maker and turns abruptly to what she announces to be her sincerer feelings. Searching for a better topic she says, "Oh dear I don't know *what* it is! Love for the absent dont *sound* like it, but try it, and see how it goes." She signs the letter "Your very sincere, and *wicked* friend," as if to demarcate, retrospectively, two separable styles of address and of self.

These are sins in jest, of course, but the reader is provoked to take this language seriously because of the context in which it occurs. In a letter to her friend and former teacher Jane Humphrey, written only six days earlier, she uses the same language to describe her own life as genuinely wicked. Charitable works would provide an opportunity "for turning my back to this very sinful, and wicked world. Somehow or other I incline to other things—and Satan covers them up with flowers, and I reach out to pick them" (L, I, 82; 23 Jan. 1850). The letter to Abiah simply transfers the metaphor of flowers and falsehood to a less serious tenor. The origin of this fatal view of herself is her failure to become converted to the evangelical Christianity that most of her friends were then embracing. She herself views it as a failure: in the sad discussions of religion of this period and earlier she never expresses a doubt that Christianity has a patent on goodness and that in not accepting Christ it is she who is in the wrong. In 1846 she had, from her report, experienced a temporary conversion, and in describing its aftermath she uses the unequivocal language of true and false: "I had rambled too far to return & ever since my heart has been growing harder & more distant from the truth" (L, I, 31; 28 March 1846). If truth is a place, then her dislocation from it repeats the Fall:

> I think of the perfect happiness I experienced while I felt I was an heir of heaven as of a delightful dream, out of which the Evil one bid me wake & again return to the world & its pleasures. Would that I had not listened to his winning words! . . . I determined to devote my whole life to [God's] service & desired that all might taste of the stream of living water from which I cooled my thirst. But the world allured me & in an unguarded moment I listened to her syren voice.
>
> (L, I, 30)

Her transfer of religious metaphor to fiction-making later on is not fortuitous. Religious and literary concerns converge at the idea of truth. In the passage above, both orthodoxy and her fall are portrayed as fictive: one was a delightful dream, the other the product of winning words and a siren voice. Her insistence in these religious passages that there is such a thing as the truth may be a defense against her growing knowledge that there is no absolute truth or literal meaning. The Bible is said to be a true text, yet her own experience shows her how easily figurative language can deceive, and the Bible is figurative. That the satanic storyteller in the letter about the cold is a guise does not necessarily make the contrasting sincerity genuine. If she can speak in one invented style, all forms of address may be fictive. When she writes to her more religious friends, her apparently genuine self-depreciation may be as fictive as the most extravagant of her announced fantasies. She is writing to please her readers, and she may also be convinced of her own sincerity, writing to please herself as well. But she depicts such a worldly sinner and such a radical fall that it is hard to believe that she did not see, or even intend, the melodrama. The modern reader prefers to think that she saw the religious fervour of her day as a delusion, and in retrospect it is easy to doubt that she would ever have considered entrusting her mental faculties to the keeping of her saviour. But a parodic element is coextensive with whatever sincere religious sorrow she expresses; and to mean two opposing things at the same time would very likely debase the writer's faith in the possibility of a literal truth, whether secular or Christian.

A few months prior to the letter in which she invokes the language of the Fall, she jokingly identifies herself with Eve on the grounds that there is no account of her death in the Bible, and the Bible must be taken at its word. "I have lately come to the conclusion that I am Eve, alias Mrs. Adam. You know there is no account of her death in the Bible, and why am I not Eve?" (L, I, 24; 12 Jan. 1846). This is the kind of remark that is entirely parodic and entirely serious at once. If the Bible is the source of the truth, then she is indeed Eve, because she has picked Satan's flowers and fallen from an Eden of perfect belief. In the letter about the cold she transforms herself from tempted into tempter. There, Abiah is an innocent Eve, and Dickinson as the writer of fictions is implicitly identified as the tempter. In the letter to Jane Humphrey of the same week, excerpted above, in which the writer pictures herself as led astray by Satan, she also identifies herself as the tempter: "you are out of the way of temptation—and out of the way of the tempter—I did'nt mean to make you wicked—but I was—and am—and shall be—and I was with you so much that I could'nt help contaminate" (L, I, 83). Again there is a note of parody, even though the tone of the whole letter is sincerely pained: "I was—and am—and shall be" makes her wickedness as immutable as God's divinity. It disturbs her to find that the fictions she delights in are indistinguishable from the words of the "Evil one," in that she is the speaker of both, and they are equidistant from the truth. Implicitly her own fanciful words led her astray; she is self-tempted. The difference between Eve and Satan is enormous, but that she moves between the two as metaphors for herself reminds the reader that Eve became Satan's accomplice and is a tempter herself—both tempted and tempter.

Later in the same letter she speaks of her angry impatience to see Jane and again condemns herself. "Is it wicked to talk so Jane—what *can* I say that isn't? Out of a wicked heart cometh wicked words." Though hating the intervening time may be reprehensible, her friendship, the source of that animosity, is not. The wickedness may refer instead to the vivid metaphor with which she describes her impatience, just previously: "Eight weeks with their bony fingers still poking me away—how I *hate* them—and would love to do them harm! Is it wicked to talk so . . . "(L, I, 83). The danger of fictions, here or in the story about the cold, is that they tempt her to say things that she does not literally mean, but which will be read literally by others. Such talk is "wicked" only if those vividly personified weeks are really animate, but a vocabulary of hate leaves corrupting traces in the minds of writer and reader. Furthermore, the use of metaphor may itself be wicked, since orthodoxy might call fiction a falsehood.

It must have made a considerable difference to one's sense of self to have been a girl instead of a boy growing up in a context in which Biblical history was the dominant metaphorical framework in which human activity was viewed. Even if Dickinson's Puritan heritage did not plentifully reinforce the cultural prejudice that, if we are all sinners, women are a little more sinful than men, to read Genesis (and Milton) and see oneself in Eve rather than in Adam would lead to an entirely different sense of self in relation to language. Emerson's attack on orthodoxy, if that might have furnished the young Dickinson with support for her own independent views, only strengthens the identification of poetic language with a masculine tradition. By insisting on the proximity between poetic speech and the divine Word in "The Poet," Emerson makes poetry as masculine a province as does Coleridge with his inheritance of the "infinite I AM ," despite other differences in their theories of poetry. Emerson invokes the tradition that Adam was the first and best speaker when he says that the poet is "the Namer or Language-maker," who gives to every thing "its own name and not another's . . . . The poets made all the words." Dorothy Wordsworth may have been discouraged from writing poetry in part by the appropriation of poetic language by those who can consider themselves the inheritors of a masculine divinity. However unlike the God of orthodoxy Emerson's powers of divinity may be, he retains the masculinity of the verbal tradition. Eve's words are secondary and stray from the truth. Because she learns Adam's language rather than inventing it with him (Adam having named the living creatures before Eve's creation), she can learn another as well, and she learns Satan's. Satan teaches her to doubt the literal truth of the language that God and Adam share, and to interpret and demystify God's prohibition about the tree of the knowledge of good and evil. Wrong though she is to take the fruit, she proves God's words to be not literally true, because it is not, in fact, the case that "in the day that thou eatest thereof thou shalt surely die." Satan's words are no less accurate than God's: her eyes are opened, as he promises, and she learns good and evil. It is Eve's discovery that both God and Satan are fictive speakers, and that no discourse is literally true. Adam becomes the traditional symbol for literal language in which words are synonymous with meaning, but Eve is the first to question that synonymity, the first critic, the mother of irony. It is in this sense that she is similar to Satan, and in making tempter and tempted synonymous Dickinson is recognizing this aspect of her inheritance from Eve. When she talks about wickedness, then, in the context of fiction or of religion, what she fears is not the conventional notion of sin, but rather the figurativeness of language that allows even the most sincere speech to be a fiction among other fictions.

When male Romantic writers identify themselves with Satan it is in order to annex the energy of his revolt against a bland orthodoxy. In *Paradise Lost*, by the time Satan is instructing Eve in the ways of deceptive speech nothing admirable remains, but it is this aspect of Satan's history that Dickinson invokes, an entirely different paradigm from that provided by his earlier career.

An enormous change takes place in Dickinson's tone concerning tempters between the two letters of January 1850 and a letter of April of the same year. Writing again to Jane Humphrey, she extols, as she has before, the "marvellous change" that belief brings to those around her. But when she turns to her own doings, she suggests for the first time that she may be as justified as the orthodox believers. "I have dared to do strange things—bold things, and have asked no advice from any—I have heeded beautiful temp-ters, yet do not think I am wrong" (L, I, 95; 3 Apr. 1850). Whatever her belief is, she views it as a center of truth rather than as a deviation. Or rather she uses the metaphor of religious belief without any worry that she is infecting orthodoxy by pairing it with "tempters." "I hope belief is not wicked, and assurance, and perfect trust— . . . I hope human nature has truth in it—Oh I pray it may not deceive—confide—cherish, have a great faith in. . . . "

Between January and April, Dickinson wrote her first (extant) poem—a valentine addressed to a friend, dated March 4—and a prose valen-tine published in the Amherst College paper, *The Indicator*, in February. The prose valentine's exuberant effect comes from its deliberate word conscious-ness. It revels in language, using many words where one would suffice, as if the lethal fictiveness of language had become a matter of delight. "Sir, I desire an interview . . . . And not to *see* merely, but a chat, sir, or a tete-a-tete, a confab, a mingling of opposite minds is what I propose to have" (L, I, 92). Those "beautiful tempters" might be words themselves, like Whitman's "dumb, beautiful ministers," so that her use of the word "tempter" might itself be the first evidence of her own "marvellous change": one word with two happily opposite meanings. The extensiveness of her language, which both multiplies language and elevates the speaker into "Judith the heroine of the Apocrypha, and you the orator of Ephesus," is figurative speech.

That's what they call a metaphor in our country. Don't be afraid of it, sir, it won't bite. If it was my *Carlo* now! The Dog is the noblest work of Art, sir. I

may safely say the noblest—his mistress's rights he doth defend—although
it bring him to his end—although to death it doth him send!

This kind of fanciful language is exactly that which she told Abiah jokingly to
"avoid . . . as the snake;" the directive not to fear its bite might be better
directed at herself than at the "sir." The passage in effect frees her, by
parodying it, from the connection she had created between falsehood in
language and real "wickedness." The vehicle of this parody is the contrast
between harmless language and the bite of a real dog, but the last sentence in
the passage renders the dog fictive, too. Because the dog dissolves into a
nursery rhyme, there is no difference, at the level of the letter, between a
metaphoric bite and a "real" one. This glimpse of the nonreferentiality of
language has a momentary liberating effect, regardless of whether or not she
would subscribe to the theories of deconstructive criticism. The biblical
names she adopts remind the reader that her identification with Eve, earlier,
both in play and in earnest, depended on a literal reading of the Bible. If
orthodoxy depends on literal reading, then this is a declaration of freedom
from orthodoxy, and from her notion that she must define herself as an exile
from orthodoxy, either as the fallen Eve, as Satan, or as both.

The virtue of this provisional freedom from referentiality is that it
enables her to use metaphoric language without anxiety. In the letter about
the cold, fictions were dangerous only figuratively. Fictions, momentarily
personified, tell falsehoods but are not synonymous with them, and she
advises Abiah to avoid fictions "as the snake." In the April letter she uses
metaphoric language to describe her special "truth," that belief that has
resulted from heeding "beautiful tempters," showing how far she has advanced from her belief that metaphor and truth were incompatible:

> What do you weave from all these threads, for I know you haven't been idle
> the while I've been speaking to you, bring it nearer the window, and I will
> see, it's all wrong unless it has one gold thread in it, a long, big shining fibre
> which hides the others—and which will fade away into Heaven while you
> hold it, and from there come back to me
>
> (L, I, 95)

Never before has she found an explicit metaphor to be adequate for the
expression of heartfelt concerns. She emphasizes its status as metaphor by
privileging the signifier, asking her reader to believe that the golden fibre is a
tangible and visible object as well as a verbal figure. At the same time, the
image she chooses is a neat transformation of her earlier metaphor for
metaphor. The "long, big shining fibre" must be art's redeemed version of the
snake, serpentine but crafted and beautiful, issuing from and returning to the
artist rather than invading her integrity.

The snakes in the letter about the cold belong to a sequence of images of the Fall, and take their significance from this association with wickedness and with questioning literal truth. An equally traditional interpretation would be to read them as phallic images, related to but distinct from Satanic imagery. As a personal expression, the passage may or may not be about sexual fears, but what is important is that the text engages the idea of masculinity as a literary term. That Dickinson combines these two sets of significations is already an interpretive gesture. For wickedness and temptation to be characterized as masculine presents an alternative to or defense against the identification of Eve with Satan that also lurks in the passage. Instead of reading her own words as vain falsehoods, as when she says, "Out of a wicked heart cometh wicked words," identifying falsehood with masculinity would allow her to see it as alien and therefore not a reflection on herself. Her flights of fancy would be proper extravagances: moments when she borrows a language not her own. (This would hardly be a helpful paradigm for her poetic vocation, and is not long retained.)

At the same time that she identifies lies as masculine, she also sees religious orthodoxy as masculine. In the early letters about religion she limits herself to a choice between her saviour and "the world," but each alternative is equally alien to her own identity, if she characterizes them both as masculine. For the girls in her adolescent circle, "loving Christ" clearly had romantic overtones. Religion was the one permissible romance, and provided a sanctioned outlet for feelings otherwise suppressed. She loses female friends to Christ as she later loses them to husbands. Wishing she cold console Jane Humphrey for the loss of her father she says, "She has the 'Great Spirit' tho', and perhaps, she does'nt need me" (L, I, 100). A long passage about marriage in a letter to Sue Gilbert, the future wife of Dickinson's brother Austin, begins by using marriage as a metaphor for religion and turns imperceptibly to its major subject by transforming the vehicle into a new tenor. Walking with Sue's sister Mattie, we "wished for you, and Heaven. You did not come, Darling, but a bit of Heaven did, or so it *seemed* to us, as we walked side by side and wondered if that great blessedness which may be our's sometime, is granted now, to some" (L, I, 209; early June 1852). This blessedness, so far, seems to refer to a religous state of grace, but the passage continues, without a break:

> Those unions, my dear Susie, by which two lives are one, this sweet and strange adoption wherein we can but look, and are not yet admitted, how it can fill the heart, and make it gang wildly beating, how it will take *us* one day, and make us all it's own, and we shall not run away from it, but lie still and be happy!

By the end of the sentence it is clear that the subject is marriage, but it is impossible to say where the transition occurs. "It" renders all mysteries equivalent. The next paragraph is explicitly about marriage, but it uses language drawn from orthodoxy. The terms of secular romance and marriage include a sacrifice of autonomy, as does, by analogy, "loving Christ:"

> I was almost inclined to yeild to the claims of He who is greater than I. . . . I hope the golden opportunity is not far hence when my heart will willingly yield itself to Christ, . . .

> I know that I ought now to give myself away to God & spend the springtime of life in his service . . . .

(L, I, 28, 31)

This sacrifice of autonomy goes far to explain Dickinson's resistance both to marriage and to orthodox religion.

Dickinson's way of characterizing many external things as masculine—truth and falsehood, the world and its renunciation—illustrates a mind defining its own interior operations as feminine. It is also typical of a rhetorical pattern, prevalent throughout her work and not just at this early period, of rendering equivalencies from polarities. Her freedom from literal meaning originates in her sense of femininity, from her identification with Eve, and it permits her a special use of irony to draw disparate meanings from a single term. This pattern is not the same as a satanic equivalency of good and evil, even though Eve and the Tempter are closely related. If it verges on the satanic, it is only because Dickinson pursues language's own logic to that point. It is a question more of tonal than of moral values, and the manipulation of tone readily permits such divergent readings. One case in point is the way in which an apparently transparent poem invites two mutually exclusive readings. Published anonymously in 1878, Dickinson's "Success is counted sweetest" (P 67) was taken to be the work of Emerson. Slipped in to the volume of poetry Emerson published in 1876, or read in the context of the later essays, it might well be taken as a straightforward account of a pessimistic view of the doctrine of compensation. Read as early Dickinson, the poem is surely a bitter parody both of orthodox thinking and of the principle of compensation that the Emersonian reading would endorse.

> Not one of all the purple Host
> Who took the Flag today
> Can tell the definition
> So clear of Victory
>
> As he defeated – dying –
> On whose forbidden ear
> The distant strains of triumph
> Burst agonized and clear!

By compensation Emerson means a tendency in nature for all oppositions to balance out: losses are compensated for here on earth, not in heaven. In this context, the soldier is compensated for his dying by a gain in understanding. But Dickinson may be undermining the poem's ostensible moral as she utters it: "forbidden ear" suggests not just that the soldier is dying as he hears the "distant strains of triumph" but rather that he cannot hear them at all and that with his death he has purchased nothing whatsoever. The poem suggests that where Emerson would find a balance of price and purchase, Dickinson finds an equivalence of valuelessness. That the attribution of this poem could even today be mistaken is a measure of one of the challenges of reading Dickinson: it is often very difficult to know when she is being ironic and when we are to take her at her word, and often she seems to have contrived this difficulty. To speak of opposing readings of the same poem is in itself risky with Dickinson, because the poems seldom permit such comforting distinctions. But the difference between these two readings is characteristic of Dickinson's way of treating oppositeness. The poem makes its critique of an idea about oppositions, compensation, by entertaining two irreconcilable readings. It is also characteristic of a major disagreement between Dickinson and Emerson: Emerson begins with polarities and works toward reconciling them, but Dickinson works toward undermining the whole concept of oppositeness.

The language Dickinson uses to describe her idea of heaven is often the same as the language she uses to satirize the heaven of orthodoxy, so that there is only a difference of tone between heaven and one version of hell.

> "Heaven" – is what I cannot reach!
> The Apple on the Tree –
> Provided it do hopeless – hang –
> That – "Heaven" is – to Me!
> (P 239)

However, "the unknown is the largest need of the intellect." The vanishing and the elusive are genuine objects of faith and desire, as in "A Light exists in Spring" (P 812). This rare light "passes and we stay,"

> A quality of loss
> Affecting our content
> As Trade had suddenly encroached
> Upon a Sacrament.

If we suddenly recall that communion is only a transaction, belief vanishes; the vanishing light is an image of faith. But the same light is found in the nasty orthodoxy of the last stanza of poem 239: "Her teazing Purples – Afternoons – / the credulous – decoy –." The second stanza includes "The interdicted Land –" among examples of teasing heavens. This is one of several references to Jehovah's cruelty in letting Moses see but not enter Canaan. It is not Canaan itself as an image of desirability that she satirizes, but God's method of consecration, inflating the value of Canaan for others by depriving Moses, making unattainability a pure and empty status symbol.

"Success is counted sweetest" is one of many poems, early and late, that take up the theme of the relativity of knowledge, of emotion, or of achievement. These poems have largely been taken as straight forward statements of her belief, as is also true of a similar group of poems by Brontë. . . . Joy is apparently unknown without the experience of pain, and only what is inaccessible is attractive.

> Water, is taught by thirst.
> Land – by the Oceans passed.
> Transport – by throe –
> Peace by it's battles told –
> Love, by Memorial Mold –
> Birds, by the Snow.
> (P 135)

She rarely punctuates with periods, and her use of them here is the first signal of irony, as their authority and finality suggest dogmatism. The problem in the poem is that the innocent speaker seems not to know the qualitative differences among the six pairs. The first and last refer to simple and remediable absences: thirst teaches the value of water, winter teaches us to miss the birds. But to group with these innocuous forms of relativism "Transport – by throe –" is overtly bitter. Though the speaker seems to miss its power, the bland context makes the line stand out for the reader: it is not just different, but nonsensical, too.

Our appreciation of the bitterness of the line depends on our seeing its contrast to the other lines' variations on the same structure. The speaker who believes in the instructional value of relativity can do so only through deafness to the poem's tonal contrast, but we can criticize the poem's ethic of relativity only by relying on such a principle in reading the poem's language.

Two poems overtly consider the idea of oppositeness by name. "The Zeroes – taught us – Phosphorus" is, like poem 135, organized on an instructional principle, but the instruction is faulty. Not only are mild and bitter mixed indiscriminately, as if for camouflage, but some of the pairs of oppositions are simply not opposite. The speaker's critical faculties may be oppressed by orthodoxy.

> The Zeroes – taught us – Phosphorus –
> We learned to like the Fire
> By playing Glaciers – when a Boy –
> And Tinder – guessed – by power

Of Opposite – to balance Odd –
If White – a Red – must be!
Paralysis – our Primer – dumb –
Unto Vitality!
(P 689)

The exclamation marks raise a facade of false assertiveness, in the manner of the periods in poem 135. "When a Boy" denotes a time prior to cultural or linguistic differentiation, just as, in a different context ("A narrow Fellow in the Grass," P 986), the same expression denotes innocence of sexual difference. Zeroes and phosphorus, like red and white, are as opposite to him as are glacier and fire. We learn that there is no innate sense of relativity, because it must be acquired, and it can be acquired faultily. Because the poem mixes faulty and true oppositions, the final one, for which the others are a preparation, is undecidable. We may learn to value vitality by experiencing paralysis, but as in "Success is counted sweetest" that is a final frustration, not an education, and it invites an ironic reading. Or if paralysis refers to the constrictions of life on earth and vitality to a freer life after death, the logic is that of an oppressive orthodoxy that endorses suffering by reversing the meanings of life and death. Either way, the poem invites both ironic and non-ironic readings, and having established that the simple reversal of meaning is central to orthodox rhetoric, the poet allows orthodoxy's own principles to undermine themselves.

" 'Tis Opposites – entice" considers the satanic deception, corollary to this orthodox belief in deferred rewards, that whatever the believer lacks must be the good. Opposites may entice but it is because they are constructed to do so; the valuation conferred by lack is a distortion.

'Tis Opposites – entice –
Deformed Men – ponder Grace –
Bright fires – the Blanketless –
The Lost – Day's face –

The Blind – esteem it be
Enough Estate – to see –
The Captive – strangles new –
For deeming – Beggars – play –
(P 355)

The final form of these overvaluations is projection:

To lack – enamor Thee –
Tho' the Divinity –
Be only
Me –

Assuming that "Thee" has all that "Me" lacks is not far from saying that what this divine interlocutor has is what the self has too but cannot recognize. Divinity is only as powerful as the mind of its imaginer.

Most of the poems that consider the idea of opposites or of relativity admit of ironic readings, but Dickinson's use of irony is itself involved in what she criticizes. Saying one thing in order to mean its opposite is the rhetorical analogue of what she criticizes. Her ironies are so fine that it is quite hard to say if she is in earnest or ironic, and several poems do in fact celebrate what she elsewhere mocks, or, like poem 355, combine sincerity with irony. She mocks the very structure of language by writing ironically about irony. Read without irony, these poems would celebrate antithesis as the fundamental of knowledge or desire, as when transport is known by pain. Taken ironically they decry that definition of knowledge. But to take them ironically the reader must use a principle of antithesis; to decry antithesis the reader must concede antithesis. Or, in the first case, to read these as celebrations of antithesis requires that the reader become—or be, innocently—deaf to antithesis.

Poem 1036 is one of many poems about deferment whose ostensible theme is that unattainability confers value, and proximity or achievement is disappointing.

> Satisfaction – is the Agent
> Of Satiety –
> Want – a quiet Comissary
> For Infinity.

This stanza plays on the idea that one polarity demands or requires the other, not on the instructional model of poems 67, 135, and 689, but in terms of an economy of feeling. Satisfaction and satiety, used here as opposites, come from the same root, *satis* or enough. That an affective opposition ought to be or once was an identity is a self-critique of the cultural shaping of language, and threatens the poem with collapse by undermining the validity of its apparently valorized oppositions, such as want and infinity. Presenting want and infinity as a pair of opposites renders infinity a plenitude, but etymologically infinity is as negative a concept as want. The second verse complements the thought of the first by apparently opposing possession and joy:

> To possess, is past the instant
> We achieve the Joy –

All the oppositions in this poem are slightly askew. The achievement of joy may precede possession, but nothing except traditional expectation precludes joy from continuing into possession. Achieve and possess are close enough to reproximate "possess" and "the instant we achieve the Joy."

> Immortality contented
> Were Anomaly.

"Immortality contented" is presented as if it ought to be an oxymoron, since it parallels the pairing of want and infinity in the first verse, as if immortality were a process of constant desire. Anomaly usually implies deviance, more than simply difference, with negative connotations that enforce the inappropriateness of "immortality contented," but since it derives from "without law" it may have positive value here as well. To be without or outside the law, if it is the law of orthodoxy, would be freedom. The poem has used a commercial or legal metaphor throughout, in "Agent," "Comissary," and possibly "possess." If that is the kind of law that "Immortality contented" violates, then it is to the discredit of those already dubious transactions, not of the immortality. The poem would then double back and mean that satisfaction is not the agent of satiety, or that the two terms are simply returned to their original identity, cancelling the poem.

In order to show that "Immortality contented" is not an oxymoron or a self-opposition, it was necessary to show that anomaly is, in that it suggests two opposing sets of meanings. On one level the poem states that satisfaction and satiety are opposites, affectively, at the same time reminding us that they are the same, by reminding us of their common root. But these readings make sense only when opposed to first or non-ironic readings: they deny an impossibility rather than making a positive statement. Like her self-contradictory use of irony described above, this poem opposes opposition only by way of a rhetorical strategy based on oppositions.

JOANNE FEIT DIEHL

Emerson, Dickinson, and the Abyss

*He who fights with monsters should be careful lest he thereby
become a monster. And if thou gaze long into an abyss, the abyss
will also gaze into thee.*

—FRIEDRICH NIETZSCHE

Arachne, maiden of legendary au-
dacity, claimed she could weave more splendidly than the goddess Minerva
herself; the challenge ended in self-inflicted death and metamorphosis into a
spider—the cunning revenge of the Divine weaver. Dickinson betrays a
similar boldness, placing her poems against the most powerful voices of her
generation—the poets of Romanticism. Like the Romantics, she writes quest
poems, for they seek to complete the voyage, to prove the strength of the
imagination against the stubbornness of life, the repression of an antithetical
nature, and that "hidden mystery," the final territory of death. The form of
the poems reflects their subject. She writes poems of "radical inquiry," riddles
that tease the intelligence or alternatively achieve startling definitions which
testify to the authority of her own consciousness. Such authority depends on
power, and it is power that lies at the center of Dickinson's relation to
Emerson. It is from Emerson that she learns the terms of the struggle and what
she needs to conquer—to write poems that win from nature the triumph of
freedom for the imagination.

Each of us holds a particular, if hidden, resentment towards the voice
that first liberates us. How strong the antagonistic joy for Dickinson to read,
almost in "credo" form, a validation of her initial aims in Emerson's essay,
"The Poet"! The controlling image of poet as reader of the universe leads to

his observing minute particulars, studying his relation to the text, his subject-symbol, finding what will suffice as an adequate symbol for the self. The poet must be more than a scrupulous reader, for "there is no fact in nature which does not carry the whole sense of nature," and even he is part of the process itself: "We are symbols and inhabit symbols." To carry the creative emphasis further, the "poet is the Namer or Language-maker." In conclusion, all is in nature, and the force of the poet's imagination determines his success in hearing and reading the natural world. Emerson had yet to learn, in 1842, what he knew later—that such certain knowledge, a complete ability to read a text, was beyond any human poet. In "Experience," Emerson was to envision both life and the man living it as the result of illusions. The individual is limited to creating the illusion determined by his own qualities; we are left with the power to live within our self-created deceptions: "Dream delivers us to dream, and there is no end to illusion. . . . We animate what we can, and we see only what we animate. Nature and books belong to the eyes that see them." And, a little later in the essay, Emerson emphasizes the negative aspects of this personal dream: "Temperament also enters fully into the system of illusions and shuts us in a prison of glass which we cannot see."

In response to the Emerson of "The Poet," Dickinson works out her own solution as she asserts that nature is not the sacred text, ready to reveal all if we read it right. She contends not only that we can never attain to full knowledge of nature, that our view is dominated by our eye; she extends the negative cast of Emerson's opening pages of "Illusions": "There is illusion that shall deceive even the elect. There is illusion that shall deceive even the performer of the miracle. Though he make his body, he denies it." For her, nature becomes an antagonist, a deeply equivocal mystery, certainly exquisite at times, but with an exotic power that withholds its secrets as it dazzles. No matter how well one reads or imagines, nature as text withdraws and guards its final lesson; morality departs from the natural world to depend solely upon the individual. Consequently, the self perceives nature as an adversary and seeks to go beyond it into an anti- or post-naturalistic environment, pursuing questions in a self-dominated sphere that rejects the province of a communal, natural life. Finally, nature becomes not a sacred ground but a place that fails to protect, from which she must withdraw to ask other kinds of questions. Dickinson cannot accept the uneasy position Emerson maintains at the close of "Illusions": "If life seem a succession of dreams, yet poetic justice is done in dreams also." Nor can she subscribe to the conclusion to "Experience": a reiteration of justice and the rather belated assurance that "the true romance which the world exists to realize will be the transformation of genius into practical power." Abandonment of the problem fails to satisfy; nor is she temperamentally able to achieve the solace Emerson rises to attain:

"For we transcend the circumstances continually and taste the real quality of existence. . . . We see God face to face every hour, and know the savor of Nature." Such compromises appear evasions to Dickinson, and she turns from them to seek her own accommodation to the dilemma Emerson described in his "Ode to Beauty":

> I dare not die
> In Being's deeps past ear and eye;
> Lest there I find the same deceiver
> And be the sport of Fate forever.
> Dread Power, but dear! if God thou be,
> Unmake me quite, or give thyself to me!

If nature is no longer at the center and cannot hold the answers she seeks, what of vision, the significance of sight? What becomes of the crucial Emersonian "eye" if the "text" cannot be read anyway? Although vision remains a major concern, she antithetically praises what she cannot see, either because the moment is past, distant, or denied. She defines through negation the positive values Emerson had praised in "Nature," "Circles," and "The Poet." She cannot believe that "a flash of his eye burns up the veil"; and the pattern of this failure, its procedures and disappointments, assumes priority for her imagination.

> Sweet Skepticism of the Heart—
> That knows—and does not know—
> And tosses like a Fleet of Balm—
> Affronted by the snow—
> Invites and then retards the Truth
> Lest Certainty be sere
> Compared with the delicious throe
> Of transport thrilled with Fear—
> (1413)

Internal qualities developed in response to an impenetrable natural world determine her strength and inform her character; she chooses to fly "with Pinions of Disdain."

If Dickinson turns from the nature espoused by the early Emerson, denying its moral imperative, she also simultaneously relinquishes his doctrines of compensation and correspondence. No justice can be expected, no resemblance between self and the landscape maintained, once morality disappears from the universe of things. Emerson, at the age of twenty and writing for himself, stated most strongly what was to be an essential element for his own philosophical position: his ability to rise above circumstance into moments of ecstatic fulfillment. "Rend away the darkness," he writes, "and restore to man the knowledge of this principle [a moral universe], and you have lit the sun over the world and solved the riddle of life." Dickinson abjures this possibility, for when she surveys the landscape for evidence of the moral imperative she finds it lacking. Instead, Dickinson learns that nature is often capricious, disinterested, or cruel. By rejecting a moral nature, she cuts herself off from the comforts of a compensatory philosophy and a benevolent view of life which allows Emerson the privilege, when he can reach it, of escaping the ground of discouraging circumstance.

Dickinson, however, does seek correspondence between herself and nature, but her own consciousness must dictate the relationship; the landscape becomes an allegorical projection of her internal drama as her poems present a spectrum of reaction to the amorality of nature—from hope and exultation to despair. If nature cannot be relied upon as a way to approach the spiritual world and lead us from Secondary to Primary Causes, she must go by another route, approach immortality not through nature but in a direct confrontation with death. The poems' most ambitious attempt is, therefore, to provide us, the living, with the experience of hearing a voice speaking from the dead. They anticipate, observe, and follow the movements of the dying. This concentration on final moments is Dickinson's protest against the inviolate silence of death. What she wants, what "is best," the poems tell us, lies beyond her power, in realms of impossibility. It is past life that Dickinson wishes to draw her circle. If consciousness bestows power, she must carry her awareness beyond the grave, invading the forbidden territory with her voice. Emerson had asserted the potency of the energizing spirit to break through all boundaries, to rise above circumstance. Dickinson, with a daring literalism, attempts to face her central antagonist directly, to draw a circle around the fact of death. Emerson preaches the strength of the individual: "But if the soul is quick and strong it bursts over that boundary on all sides and expands another orbit on the great deep, which also runs up into a high wave, with attempt again to stop and to bind. But the heart refuses to be imprisoned; in its first and narrowest pulses it already tends outward with a vast force and to immense and innumerable expansions."

Dickinson's poems face the barrier of mortality and confront Emerson's challenge: "There is no outside, no inclosing wall, no circumference to us. . . . His only redress is forthwith to draw a circle outside of his antagonist." He perceives this power during isolated moments; the freedom of that moment from the past determines its potential for imaginative transformation: "In nature every moment is new; the past is always swallowed and forgotten; the coming only is sacred. Nothing is secure but life, transition, the energizing spirit." Her poems strive not for the moment in nature that is new but a space beyond it which provides a retrospective vision on life—the freedom of evaluation after the event. During life, however, there are moments which potentially speak of the mysteries to be disclosed in death, and it is the poet's task to witness these occasions and discover their meaning:

> The Moments of Dominion
> That happen on the Soul
> And leave it with a Discontent
> Too exquisite—to tell—
>
> (627)

The secret of the landscape will reveal itself only after life departs, when the taunts of an unknowable nature cease. Until then, "The Pleading of the Summer—" and "That other Prank—of Snow—" will not disclose their secret:

> Their Graspless manners—mock us—
> Until the Cheated eye
> Shuts arrogantly—in the Grave—
> Another way—to see—
>
> (627)

Only the thinnest of veils, life, prevents her from winning this necessary vision. Another poem, in the same packet, and most probably written in the same year, 1862, asserts Dickinson's frustration in Divine, mercantile terms which combine the bitterness of defeat with an attack on the doctrine of compensation itself:

> I asked no other thing—
> No other—was denied—
> I offered Being—for it—
> The Mighty Merchant sneered—
>
> Brazil? He twirled a Button—
> Without a glance my way—
> 'But—Madam—is there nothing else—
> That We can show—Today?'
>
> (621)

She finds other subjects, but Brazil—the ultimate exotic—remains an adequate symbol for the unifying quest of her poems. The challenge she faces is the inability to speak clearly from the other side of the grave. Deploring the inevitable silence, Dickinson will write poems that go so far as to deny death's inevitability and hover on the threshold between life and death. Prolepsis becomes a crucial strategy because it allows her to supersede the strictures of life. Moreover, passion extends to others' final moments as well; for, it is through death that the mutual condition of solipsism is simultaneously consolidated and dissolved.

Loss of belief, of a Christian or even an Emersonian faith, points toward the origins of her grim obsession:

> Those—dying then,
> Knew where they went—
> They went to God's Right Hand—
> That Hand is amputated now
> And God cannot be found—
>
> The abdication of Belief
> Makes the Behavior small—
> Better an ignis fatuus
> Than no illume at all—
>
> (1551)

Nullifying the integrity of the flame as the poem names it denies the possibility of belief. Always haunted by the forbidden, Dickinson merges memories of childhood lures, the "Flower Hesperian," with the promise of the dead. A worksheet draft written late in the poet's life specifies this preeminent concern with the moment of another's death:

> Still own thee—still thou art
> What surgeons call alive—
> Though slipping—slipping I perceive
> To thy reportless Grave—
>
> Which question shall I clutch—
> What answer wrest from thee
> Before thou dost exude away
> In the recallless sea?
>
> (1633)

The poem wants answers and is willing to clutch the question, to wrestle with the dying, for response. No other thing is denied, and the intensity of inquiry stems not from a life of despair but from an increasingly complete hegemony of consciousness that is deprived only of what it most craves to make it complete. Such extremity accounts, in large measure, for the polarities of the poems—the radically fluctuating moods that confront us as we read.

No forward or backward can be measured when the goal remains inviolate. Acknowledging that "no man saw awe," Dickinson asserts that we cannot come back bearing the vision, for "returning is a different route, The spirit could not show." Dickinson describes this geography of impossibility, a terrain one needs to cross before the journey begins: "Three Rivers and a Hill to cross / One Desert and a Sea." At the moment of completion, the fulfillment of her quest, mortality intercedes. With customary boldness, she names Death itself as the agent of usurpation; he walks off with the prize rightfully her own. In the face of this defeat, Dickinson places her poems, literally experiments that presume against the possible. She writes, "Experiment escorts us last—" and beneath "escorts" she places, then crosses out, "accosts." The polarity of feeling, the inner dialectic of what her "experiments" mean to her, cannot be more adequately conveyed than by these two words and their "correction."

Emerson challenges Dickinson to explore her power, but what saves him fails her needs. His darkest voice forms the background against which she composes poems. The opening to "Circles," an essay that deeply affected Dickinson, states the potency of expansion for the eye.

"The eye is the first circle; the horizon which it forms is the second; and throughout nature this primary figure is repeated without end. It is the highest emblem in the cipher of the world. St. Augustine described the nature of God as a circle whose centre was everywhere and its circumference nowhere. We are all our lifetime reading the copious sense of this first of forms. One moral we have already deduced in considering the circular or compensatory character of every human action. Another analogy we shall now trace, that every action admits of being outdone. Our life is an apprenticeship to the truth that around every circle another can be drawn; that there is no end in nature, but every end is a beginning; There is always another dawn risen on mid-noon, and under every deep a lower deep opens."

The possibility of a "lower deep," a more potent mystery to conquer, becomes, for Dickinson, the abyss; expansion opens into emptiness. She cannot abide the thought of fathomless depths, for they offer not opportunity but the terror of imminent destruction, an utter dissolution of the self. Emerson's faith in our capacity to expand into such depths depends upon his effect as a teacher—his ability to awaken us from our lapse, our temporary degeneracy. Only in such a state of slipping degradation are we estranged from nature and God. "As we degenerate, the contrast between us and our house is more evident. We are as much strangers in nature as we are aliens from God." He heralds the need for a liberating poet to restore us to an adequate awareness of our own possibilities. Through a series of comparisons between this sublime potential and our current condition, Emerson asserts the illimitable power lurking within: "Once man was all; now he is an appendage, a nuisance." The fault can be remedied, if only we heed his call. And throughout all the later, more sober, modulations of his thought, the belief that "intellect annuls Fate. So far as a man thinks, he is free," remains firm. In his early proclamation, "Nature," Emerson states this essential center to his future meditations: "The ruin or the blank that we see when we look at nature, is in our own eye." The material world remains subordinate to the power of the single mind, and, though he may sink into a temporary despair, or realize the necessity of accepting some principle of Fate, Emerson retains his belief in the power of the imagination to rise above despondency and conquer the conditions of life.

But there are moments in Emerson when despair takes over, and it is during these that he sounds most like Dickinson. In a journal entry marked "Skepticism," Emerson states, "There are many skepticisms. The universe is like an infinite series of planes, each of which is a false bottom, and when we think our feet are planted now at last on the adamant, the slide is drawn out from under us." Over twenty years later, he expresses the relation of the Me and the Not-Me when the false bottom slips: "There may be two or three or four steps, according to the genius of each, but for every seeing soul there are two absorbing facts,—*I and the Abyss.*" This comes closest to Dickinson's vision of the problem she confronts. Here is a struggle to know, to dive into the abyss and extract from it the knowledge she cannot win from nature or any other mediate experience. She agrees with Emerson when he remarks: "I am very content with knowing, if only I could know. That is an august entertainment, and would suffice me a great while." But the salves Emerson applies to heal the wound between "I and the abyss" remain temperamentally unavailable to Dickinson. She cannot rely on a central self, a single, inner core. When she turns to it, she finds a consciousness that hides when she approaches, an inner adversary as threatening as any she faces from outside. And so experience becomes for her, literally, a "going through peril," a walk along broken planks over the abyss of annihilation; a vertiginous threshold which offers only the terror of defeat. Though the pit remains a threat to Emerson, he marshals against it the promise of the "over-seer," one who rises above, who stands erect, and climbs "the stairway of surprise" to freedom. If "the world is nothing, the man is all," he will take advantage of his sovereignty. "Let me ascend above my fate and work down upon my world." The stance of the beholder yields him the safety he requires. To stand above and aside allows him the leisure to recollect experience. And in this act he imitates the Spirit beyond—"For it is only the finite that has wrought and suffered; the infinite lies stretched in smiling repose." The eye of the observer is the gift of the poet and offers him imaginative freedom from the circumstances of life, the pain of existence. Such a perspective serves the world, for without man it would remain only "a remoter and inferior incarnation of God, a projection of God in the unconscious." The human mind provides the consciousness that lends meaning to an otherwise un-self-conscious, hence powerless nature. Man is the vital, necessary force that unites God to his works. Moreover, if one goes deep enough into the self, he discovers this truth is applicable to all men; the Other for Emerson is the Self, whereas for Dickinson the self can and most often does become the demonic Other.

The fluid conception of Self with its boundless potency allows Emerson to push past the border of confining limitations. In "Spiritual Laws," Emerson describes his concept of a self that asserts the requisite flexibility to enact his challenge: "A man is a method, a progressive arrangement; a selecting principle, gathering his like to him wherever he goes. He takes only his own out of the multiplicity that sweeps and circles round him. He is like one of those booms which are set out from the shore on rivers to catch driftwood, or like the loadstone amongst splinters of steel." The self has a pattern, a set of tendencies, which attracts only complimentary forms to it. This fluid self becomes in Emerson's own career an evolving identity that alters its strategies but returns to address itself to fundamental questions. Dickinson's transformation of this fluid self is among her more devastating achievements: from many selves, she names two, the self and the other. This "other" is consciousness, that awful internal stranger that she must repeatedly confront. Dickinson further polarizes the internal structure, for that other self is sexualized. He embodies the masculine, prepotent force that must be at once wooed and denied.

This choosing up sides and severely narrowing options determines the intensity of Dickinson's strongest poems. Lovers and friends feed the identities of self and other, but crucial action occurs within the single, split consciousness. Such internal duality serves as a structure that governs her poems, demanding the exchange of worlds and encouraging an essentially dramatic form. This primal split in the self finds corollaries, most notably in an intense psychomachia—the struggle between the body and the soul. Self-division hardens into a basic austerity when the Emersonian multiplicity reduces to two. This process of consolidation, a toughening of position, points toward the central split between the poets themselves.

In his confrontation with Necessity, Emerson adopts specific strategies for survival. By summoning his ability to distance at least a part of the self, he is able to embrace an acquiescence that accepts the fact of a finally unknowable nature and an unalterable Fate. Saadi, the Emersonian fictive poet, maintains his cheerful equanimity because of his absence from immediate involvement; he sits a little to one side and concentrates on writing poems. The development of such an independent poet-figure is itself a part of Emerson's creation of the Observer within the self. As R. A. Yoder writes:

> The personality of the poet was a matter of long and serious concern which Emerson tried to resolve in poems, essays, and even in bits of fiction scattered through the journals. Much of the character of the emerging poet-figure is clearly autobiographical and an attempt to state his own concept of the poet's role. But gradually Emerson loosened the identification between himself and the character he created, so that in his later essays, as Whicher pointed out, there are a number of dramatic characters or alter egos who speak for different, often opposite, sets of ideas.

By contrast, although Dickinson states that the "I" of her poems is not herself but "a supposed person," this separation exists outside the province of the text; it occurs before the formation of the "I" that speaks to us so directly from the heart of her poems.

Emerson, however, rather than force solutions to what he perceives as a deepened division between the Me and the Not-Me, exploits this detach-ment which performs so incalculable a service: "What was food for remorse and regret on the plane of action, on the plane of intellection was matter for wonder. Even in his time of greatest enthusiasm some part of him had stood disengaged and aloof, and answered all interrogations, 'I, oh, I am only here to see.'" Although in times of disillusion, the privilege of spectatorship assumes a more ominous cast and threatens numbness; the relief, stasis, and aesthetic distance offered by this power earn it a permanent role within the flux of Emersonian identity.

Alternative vision—the observing eye—becomes literalized and ex-panded in Whitman's version of the self that stands apart and above. But in Dickinson's poems the self assumes neither an Emersonian nor a Whitmanian form. Her observer is potentially a spy, for his sight is directed not toward nature, the Not-Me, but focuses inward, on the self from which he grew. He most often takes the shape of an adversary, another Consciousness that inhabits her mind and whose struggle Dickinson converts to poems. This other self may be best friend or deadly enemy—a love-hate relationship that assumes priority over any external commitment.

> The Soul unto itself
> Is an imperial friend—
> Or the most agonizing Spy—
> An Enemy—could send—
>
> Secure against it's own—
> No treason it can fear—
> Itself—it's Sovreign—of itself
> The Soul should stand in Awe—
>   (683)

Despite this fundamental difference in their concepts of the Self, Emerson and Dickinson both find the origin of power within the individual. They assume a vocabulary normally ascribed to external, natural phenom-ena, and apply it to the inner life. Instances of this process of internalization recur throughout Emerson, and one does not have to look far to find him celebrating his own use of such language. Of man he declares: "But the lightning which explodes and fashions planets, maker of planets and suns, is in him." And, in what was to become a favorite trope for Dickinson, Emerson elaborates further upon the power that resides within:

"The human mind cannot be enshrined in a person who shall set a barrier on any one side to this unbounded, unboundable empire. It is one central fire, which, flaming now out of the lips of Etna, lightens the capes of Sicily, and now out of the throat of Vesuvius, illuminates the towers and vineyards of Naples. It is one light which beams out of a thousand stars. It is one soul which animates all men."

The lips of Etna and throat of Vesuvius, the oral and the volcanic, anticipate Dickinson's coupling of voice and flame. Threat of eruption, for both poets, emanates from the mouth:

> When Etna basks and purrs
> Naples is more afraid
> Than when she shows her Garnet Tooth—
> Security is loud—
>
> (1146)

Whereas Emerson and Dickinson are both drawn to the vision of an imminent power that smoulders undetected, Dickinson "personalizes" this vision. Volcanic force is no longer associated with universal man as in "The American Scholar," but, instead, with the single life. Power does not run through all of us, as Emerson maintains; furthermore, it cannot be apprehended by anyone who observes the seemingly quiet, single self. The one soul which animates all men now stands isolated and alone.

> A still—Volcano—Life—
> That flickered in the night—
> When it was dark enough to do
> Without erasing sight—
>
> A quiet—Earthquake Style—
> Too subtle to suspect
> By natures this side Naples—
> The North cannot detect
>
> The Solemn—Torrid—Symbol—
> The lips that never lie—
> Whose hissing corals part—and shut—
> And Cities—ooze away—
>
> (601)

This single life erupts irrevocably. Hidden, mysterious, still, the power floods mechanically; corals "part and shut"—destroying cities. What distinguishes this from Emerson's volcano is Dickinson's insistence on secrecy, on individuality, and on destruction. The poems will go further to identify this oral potency with both poetry and the self.

Moreover, Dickinson's practice of defining her self against Emerson's while drawing upon his language recurs in varying forms. Although she may alter the thrust of an Emersonian image or impose her own priorities on his diction, the new poem lies hidden in its parent text. Characteristically, a Dickinson poem takes an example that Emerson introduces into an essay and invests it with the strength of a subversive, anti-Emersonian vision. For instance, in his essay "Fate," Emerson develops a series of paragraphs that open with a general, declarative sentence followed by specific occasions which enumerate the forms his generalizations assume. One paragraph in this series supplants the "listing" of examples with an encapsulated narrative:

"The force with which we resist these torrents of tendency looks so ridiculously inadequate that it amounts to little more than a criticism or protest made by a minority of one, under compulsion of millions. I seemed in the height of a tempest to see men overboard struggling in the waves, and driven about here and there. They glanced intelligently at each other, but 'twas little they could do for one another; 'twas much if each could keep afloat alone. Well, they had a right to their eye-beams, and all the rest was Fate."

Emerson's example comes at the close of a series that climaxes in his assertion of our utter helplessness against the facts of nature, the fatality of our gestures against the end: "We cannot trifle with this reality, this cropping-out in our planted gardens of the core of the world. No picture of life can have any veracity that does not admit the odious facts. A man's power is hooped in by a necessity which, by many experiments, he touches on every side until he learns its arc." Emerson uses the drowning swimmers to enlist our sympathy while driving home the truth of the reality that affects us all. Dickinson's description of a related drowning is instructive.

> Two swimmers wrestled on the spar—
> Until the morning sun—
> When One—turned smiling to the land—
> Oh God! the Other One!
>
> The stray ships—passing—
> Spied a face—
> Upon the waters borne—
> With eyes in death—still begging raised—
> And hands—beseeching—thrown!
>
> (201)

One swimmer appears to *cause* the other's drowning, or, at least, offers him no help. He is clearly victorious, and at dawn returns triumphant toward shore. Dickinson shifts our attention to the "Other One," who is spied but ignored by the ships that pass as he sinks, still pleading, toward death. Emerson left his swimmers to Fate, choosing to emphasize that the glances exchanged by the drowning men could not save them, that indeed men are helpless to save even themselves in the presence of such a force; but Dickinson stresses the accountability of one swimmer for the other's death, as well as the prolonged

moment of helplessness of the drowned. Ships that pass do not even attempt
to help; they are "stray," random, without purpose, yet they do not pause;
without so much as the excuse of destination, they abandon the pleading man
to his death. The poem explodes the event, opening it to its own narrative
emphases—wrestling, human responsibility, the concentration on the eyes
in death. Paradoxically, this sharpening of focus magnifies the moment by an
act of compression. Blame is localized; the point of view partial. With these
shifts in emphasis, Dickinson renders impossible Emerson's acceptance of an
impersonal, impenetrable Fate; agencies of solution—the power of the self,
its relation to the Over-Soul, a capacity to grow erect—fail Dickinson. Her
self is split, and nature remains a mystery immune to the power of even so
masterful an intellect as her own. The mediating experience of nature
deceives more than it satisfies. She defines existence as a series of descents
into the abyss:

Emerging from an Abyss and entering it again—that is Life, is it not?

Dickinson's poems announce how it is to live on the edge of such danger. Fear
of falling assumes precedence over the possibility of flight.

A Pit—but Heaven over it—
And Heaven beside, and Heaven abroad;
And yet a Pit—
With Heaven over it.

To stir would be to slip—
To look would be to drop—
To dream—to sap the Prop
That holds my chances up.
Ah! Pit! With Heaven over it!

The depth is all my thought—
I dare not ask my feet—
'Twould start us where we sit
So straight you'd scarce suspect
It was a Pit—with fathoms under it
Its Circuit just the same
Seed—summer—tomb—
Whose Doom to whom

(1712)

The circuit of the pit (the path around it) is marked by the stages of life: the
seed = birth, summer = maturity, and the tomb of death. The cycle of life
itself walks on the edge, with no possibility of escape except a heaven that
remains tantalizingly beside, abroad, and above it. The "I" is left with awe
and the abyss, extremes that cause her to guard each step she takes as she
rounds the circle.

> I stepped from Plank to Plank
> A slow and cautious way
> The Stars about my Head I felt
> About my Feet the Sea.
>
> I knew not but the next
> Would be my final inch—
> This gave me that precarious Gait
> Some call Experience.
>
> (875)

As the danger of her position increases, as her world is reduced to heaven and the abyss, to the stars and the sea, her own figure enlarges to fill the gap. Self assumes the gigantic proportions of one who touches the extremities of the universe. The radical severity of her world demands a self that will fill "the Term between." This giantism corresponds to the aims of the expanded self that desires to measure the abyss. Thus, her poems speak with the power of an enclosed solipsism, the voice of compression. By single moments alone can Dickinson chart her course into the heart of the abyss and map her way out of it. She warns both herself and us that "slipping—is Crashe's law"; the next moment may signal another descent.

What both Emerson and Dickinson call the abyss finds at least one of its origins in Jonathan Edwards' blazing pit of Hell. The terror his description instilled in the hearts of the congregation echoes in his wayward disciples: "Unconverted men walk over the pit of hell on a rotten covering, and there are innumerable places in this covering so weak that they will not bear their weight, and these places are not seen." The void of the unknown, the mystery of the abyss, has replaced the certainty of the flames of Hell, but the central image of our own thoughtless instability as we walk on rotten planks remains. By placing the supreme power within the individual, Emerson removed much of the fear of the emptiness beneath us, but Dickinson restores to the pit its rightful terror, not by an orthodox vision of Divine retribution, but with her own forbidding gift. She would have been moved by Edwards' vision of "the dreadful pit of the glowing flames of the wrath of God," substituting only her doubt for his certainty. Identical, however, is her tenuous position, the precariousness of the self: "You hang by a slender thread, with the flames of divine wrath flashing about it. . . . " She recognizes this condition, except in her abyss the flames are self-generated, created by the power of her own imagination. Furthermore, hers is an abyss that she tells us she can enter, and so it must be an internal, deeper part of the mind to which she descends and from which she emerges through the act of writing poems.

The fact that Dickinson's abyss lies within, that it resides in her psyche, grows from Emerson's assertion that the mind contains limitless possibilities. Ironically, what Dickinson achieves by fusing the threat of the Edwardsean pit with the Emersonian faith in the self is a devastating subversion of Emersonian power. She couples the mind's power with the terrors of hell to create, in an act of daring perversion, an unfathomable creature of her own mind—a pit she must enter for her salvation but a pit that holds within it the capacity to destroy the creative self.

Dickinson, in this radical act, recalls the specter of Arachne, who claims her superiority, usurping the sovereignty of others to weave a taut web above a pit of her own making. If the points of Dickinson's web touch the bottom of the pit, they also stretch to the heaven above it. The poems alone prove the wisdom of her demonic maneuver, a power won through the subversive risk of Arachnean form.

SHIRA WOLOSKY

A Syntax of Contention

I am afraid we are not rid of God because we still have faith in grammar.
— FRIEDRICH NIETZSCHE, *The Twilight of the Idols*

T he first reviewers of Emily Dickin-
son's work pronounced it "bad poetry . . . divorced from meaning, from
music, from grammar, from rhyme: in brief, from articulate and intelligible
speech." Even Dickinson's defenders conceded these all too obvious faults.
Thomas Wentworth Higginson, having finally agreed to support the publication of *Poems*, did so with apologies. In his preface to the volume, he wrote,
"After all, when a thought takes one's breath away, a lesson in grammar
seems an impertinence." Such impertinence had, however, been his. His
thirty-year hesitation to recommend Dickinson's work was based on objections to form and grammar he here urges others to overlook. Even decades
after the emergence of Dickinson's poems, Percy Lubbock reproached her for
their "cryptic harshness, their bad rhymes and wild grammar." Harold Monro
similarly complained: "Her style is clumsy, her language is poor; her technique is appalling and there is no excuse (except that very excuse of faulty
technique) for the frequent elementary grammatical errors."

But, as critics increasingly acknowledge, Dickinson's grammar and
technique are not simply faulty, nor are they as idiosyncratic as they first
appeared. Many twentieth-century writers seem equally eccentric. "Do you
always have the same kind of feeling in relation to the sounds as the words
come out of you or do you not. All this has much to do with grammar and with
poetry and with prose," Gertrude Stein lectured in 1934. She then described

her lifelong struggle against the question mark, the exclamation point, and her preference for articles as opposed to nouns. Dickinson's sporadic rhymes, flexible metric, and irregular syntax—what John Hollander calls her "hymnody of the attic"—are features she shares with the poets who succeeded her. The similarity did not go unnoticed. As early as 1914, Harriet Monroe called Dickinson "an unconscious and uncatalogued Imagiste." Amy Lowell concurred. Although Dickinson's work was "considered only as bizarre and not at all important by her contemporaries," Lowell pronounced hers the "modern" voice crying out in the literary "desert" of mid-nineteenth-century American verse.

With time, Dickinson's poetry has come to seem less bizarre and more contemporary. Her syntax in particular has confirmed the modernity which the delay in her work's publication suggests. And yet, Dickinson's syntax and prosody continue to be seen as arbitrary or willfully cryptic—traits that are now identified with modernism as well. What David Porter, in his *Modern Idiom*, rightly calls Dickinson's "severe revision of transformational rules" is not, however, only a matter of "intensity" without "coherence of purpose." Porter sees Dickinson's as a "disintegration of meaning" deriving from an impulse to "act with arbitrary freedom." He sees her "defects of syntax" as "required by the constraints of the hymnal form," along with poor rhymes and a general failure of "lexical meanings." And he sees hers as a "divorce of language from the phenomenally experienced world [which] creates powerful effects characteristic of the extreme modern sensibility."

Dickinson's prosody, syntax, and figuration, however, remain expressive of her vision of reality and a serious attempt to engage its meanings. They are more than instances of "the significance of incoherence." Although they certainly represent a confrontation with incoherence, they represent concomitantly a resistance to it. It is this double stress that informs Dickinson's language. What must be considered is the vision that gave rise in Dickinson to such linguistic discontinuity, the disruption of the conceptual structures necessary to give order to her world, which her language records.

Dickinson's syntax constitutes an integral part of her poetic meaning. The impulse of its disorders must be sought in the image of the world she presents. And this image is indeed a disrupted one:

> Four Trees—upon a solitary Acre—
> Without Design
> Or Order, or Apparent Action—
> Maintain—
>
> The Sun—upon a Morning meets them—
> The Wind—
> No nearer Neighbor—have they—
> But God—

The Acre gives them—Place—
They—Him—Attention of Passer by—
Of Shadow, or of Squirrel, haply—
Or Boy—
What Deed is Theirs unto the General Nature—
What Plan
They severally—retard—or further—
Unknown—

[P 742]

This poem presents a world of radical disorder. A scene is given, simply and in its bare particularity. The sun rises and sets over it, an eye glances at it. But there is no hint as to its place in a wider scheme. The poem does invoke a metaperspective from which the scene could be viewed as a whole, but only to declare this perspective inaccessible. Fact and a possible pattern into which it could be meaningfully placed remain disjunct. The poem is a collection of discrete details without interconnection.

Thus, in the first stanza, there are trees, there is a field, but neither of these has any relation to the other. What traffic passes is transient: a squirrel, a boy, a shadow. This last image is for Dickinson especially ominous. A shadow is, she writes elsewhere, a presentiment that darkness is about to pass (P 764), a fleeting image of the transitory. The sun and wind also frequent the field, briefly and transiently. On the other hand, the second stanza suggests the eternal and even immanent presence of the Deity, who would stand in opposition to the brief appearance and disappearance of the other elements. But even this twists as the final stanza declares him dubious company. Instead of serving as first or final cause, tying the disparate units together, the poem closes with such a pattern absent. If God is present, he does not unite the scene. This remains a collection of isolated objects that do not cohere.

The poem's grammatical construction is as discontinuous as the scene it presents. The first, static stanza almost avoids a verb. And that verb, when it finally appears after long delay, is barely an action. Indeed, a properly transitive verb is made intransitive: "Maintain." Similarly, the final stanza circumvents a verb altogether in its main clause. The action that might have taken place is made substantive: "Deed." Only the subordinate clause has transitive verbs, and these are vague actions of even vaguer subjects: "What Plan / They severally—retard—or further—." Equally misleading is the use of an interrogative pronoun to introduce what is in fact a flat statement of lack of knowledge. "What Plan," the poet seems to ask, but she does not finally pose the question. She instead declares that the plan is unknown, an answer that is only interrogative in that it borders on accusation.

In place of any movement into which the poem's various elements can enter and mutually participate, there are series of nouns set one next to the other. These are as isolated as the solitary trees, as disconnected as general nature. In both language and nature there is lacking, and oppressive in its lack, any design that could transform this clutter into significant pattern. In these terms, the poem's syntax becomes less arbitrary. It is a function of Dickinson's sense of a world without organizing principle, a world whose parts do not cohere. Dickinson, nevertheless, hesitates to question openly an encompassing order and is reluctant to admit that she feels its lack. Her syntactic obfuscation disguises the fears of dissolution which the poem, however, traces. It expresses her doubts, even while asserting that God is indeed a "nearer Neighbor," that he oversees a design, order, or plan in general nature. The metaperspective represented by heaven and the physical world it should order remain removed from each other. No pattern emerges.

Dickinson's syntax has often attracted interpretive efforts. Brita Lindberg-Seyersted, in *The Voice of the Poet*, reviews her many oddities: incomplete sentences, ellipses of personal pronouns, relative pronouns, copulas, articles, verbs, as well as inverted or dispersed word order, ambiguous parts of speech, and strained parallel constructions. Other critics treat Dickinsonian syntax and its implications in passing, particularly with regard to her conception of time. Both George Whicher and James Reeves consider Dickinson's use of the conditional and the subjunctive as expressions of her uncertainty regarding the future: Whicher, because hers is a "state of chronic trepidation," and Reeves, because "truth to her is often provisional." But most often, Dickinson's syntax is associated with extratemporal longings. For Charles Anderson, Dickinson's subjective and uninflected verb forms express "the desire to emphasize the absolute truth of what she was saying"; for Thomas Johnson, they "universalize her thought to embrace past, present, and future."

This argument is pursued by Sharon Cameron in her book, *Lyric Time*. Cameron, like Anderson and Johnson, treats Dickinson's forms as functions of her fascination with and urge toward extratemporality. Dickinson's linguistic discontinuities are, according to Cameron, images of a wholeness which resists or negates temporal sequence. "Dickinson's utterances fragment, word cut from word, stanza from stanza, as a direct consequence of her desire for that temporal completion which will fuse all separations into the healing of a unified whole." This wholeness Cameron identifies with the concept of eternity. Citing Augustine, she asserts that "lyric poems attempt such a stasis" as he describes in the *Confessions* when he envisions a "steadfast eternity, neither future nor past, [which] decrees times future and those past." And for both Augustine and Dickinson, according to Cameron, inundation by "Torrents of Eternity" is envisioned "out of desire." Rather than constituting an actual category for Dickinson, eternity is, Cameron implies, a theoretical or aesthetic concern. It is thus Dickinson's interest in "problems of temporal boundary" that leads her to be preoccupied with death: "We might regard death as a special instance of the problem of boundary, representing the ultimate division, the extreme case, the infuriating challenge to the dream of synchrony." And synchrony leads, in Dickinson's verse, to a "disjointed syntax," a "reluctance of words to totalize themselves."

Dickinson's images of temporal stasis, however, often do not present the fact and idea of wholeness as Cameron claims. Nor is death a challenge to the dream of synchrony. On the contrary, Dickinson's notion of synchrony depended upon her beliefs about death and immortality. It is the challenge to those beliefs that her poetry registers. Far from representing the concordance and convergence of all temporal moments, Dickinson's instants are often temporal fragments, cut off from past and future and discordant with them. This Cameron admits. She identifies poems in which "the moment is severed from that which precedes and follows it." She does not, however, distinguish between static time as fragmented time and static time as an emblem of wholeness. Only the latter can be referred to Augustine, who found in the immutable world an assurance of coherence within the world of time. In Dickinson's poetry, it is exactly this image of wholeness as rooted in the immutable world that is at issue. The question is not aesthetic, although it has aesthetic implications. What Dickinson's poetry reflects is a confusion about, not an incarnation or aesthetic displacement of, eternity.

The formal aspect of temporal/eternal relations was first recognized by Augustine himself. Kenneth Burke, in *The Rhetoric of Religion*, explicates the Augustinian construction in which "time and timelessness" correspond to "the sentence as a sequence of transitory syllables and the sentence as a fixed unit of meaning." For Augustine, that unitary meaning is an image of time endlessly extended, of a present moment "ever standing (*semper stantis*) without past or future." This would seem to correlate eternity with an impulse against linguistic sequence—a correlation certainly not evident in Augustine's own work. Nor is it the case for Dickinson. Her sentence structures, when they disrupt sequence, do not necessarily signify the timelessness of eternal wholeness. The contrary is more usual. They reflect, instead, a lost sense of wholeness and consequently a sense of being lost in an extended instant which excludes, rather than includes, all past and future:

> A Pit—but Heaven over it—
> And Heaven beside, and Heaven abroad,
> And yet a Pit—
> With Heaven over it.
>
> To stir would be to slip—
> To look would be to drop—

To dream—to sap the Prop—
That holds my chances up.
Ah! Pit! With Heaven over it!

The depth is all my thought—
I dare not ask my feet—
'Twould start us where we sit
So straight you'd scarce suspect
It was a Pit—with fathoms under it—
Its Circuit just the same.
Seed—summer—tomb—
Whose Doom to whom?

[P 1712]

A topography of the pit: it is situated between an above which should define it and a below which does. The poet cites a "Heaven" over and aside and abroad, and tries to situate herself in terms of its height. But she calls her position a pit, already placing it in terms of an abyss of which she is only too aware.

The poem thus tries to ward off a terror already present. The heaven that should reassure her and make her position secure does not do so. She cannot orient herself toward it and is constantly pressed by the possibility of slipping. Any movement could be a fatal upset. Even a too careful inspection of her placement could cause the whole to collapse: "To look would be to drop— / To dream—to sap the Prop." Yet the poet clearly does look and dream. She has not kept herself from gazing into the abyss below her: "The depth is all my thought." A lost sense of the world above has already made her conscious of the fathoms below, and she is suspended between the two. She therefore remains immobile, seized by fear. Her balance depends on her feeling a heaven over her—a feeling that is already tenuous and a balance that is already tottering. And she is afraid to investigate further, lest the suspension collapse.

As is "Four Trees," this poem is strangely verbless. In the first stanza, prepositions dominate: *over, beside, abroad.* The pit is defined not by an action but as a space that seems vast and unfathomable and that cannot be negotiated. In this space, the poet's fear of movement is expressed through her use of conditional infinitive clauses: "To stir would be," "To look would be." All possible actions must be retained as only possible, for action could trigger the upset she fears. In the final stanza, inflected verbs do reappear—but either as the copula "is" or as denial of action: "I dare not ask." There are, as well, conditional verb forms. These are all forms of inaction. And the concluding lines even eclipse the copula. Such lack of syntactic modulation reduces the poem's thoughts and imagery to sudden conjunctions, appositions, and inversions.

In a poem whose subject is disorientation and a consequent immobility, an avoidance of verbs and a staccato of images is not surprising. The poem's form has its source in a sense of disorientation, as Dickinson's grasp on the orders of her universe and of her place within it becomes tenuous. Such disorientation is expressed in a technique commensurate with it. Syntax mediates the sequential relations between successive words. Verb tenses place words in time relative to each other. Agreement associates parts of speech. Prepositions, copulas, and conjunctions locate, identify, and conjoin. The disruption of syntax expresses a disruption in these relations. If a sense of sequence is threatened, the result could be grammatical.

Such result is felt here, as are the sources of disruption. The poet's dislocation is referred to a heaven which does not adequately serve her as a signpost. She cannot situate herself with respect to it and therefore feels lost. Time especially disintegrates. "Seed—summer—tomb— / Whose Doom to whom?" the poet asks. The temporal circuit of birth, maturity, and death in some sense appears "just the same" as empirical perceptions. But the value of each is determined by which term is judged a "Doom." And this for Dickinson depends on heaven. If the tomb gives way to nothingness, then this world is indeed a pit and its fathoms gape wide. But if time is heaven-directed, then she is protected from such oblivion. She can feel securely placed and able to place things in turn. Which is the case, however, is exactly the question she poses. And just posing it suffices to shatter her sense of place and time.

"A Pit" therefore presents a suspended state that is not, however, an image of eternity. It is an image of paralysis. And this paralysis is referred to a threatened sense of heaven. The poem's immobility is in fact measured against and situated in terms of heaven's immutable time, the doubt of which frames it. Such paralytic instances are common in Dickinson. In "I've dropped my Brain—My Soul is numb," her veins "Stop palsied" (P 1046). "After great pain" records a similar "Hour of Lead" (P 341), as does "Pain has an Element of Blank": "Its Infinite contain / Its Past" (P 650). These are solitary moments which cannot be mistaken for concordant wholeness.

Yet wholeness is a controlling force in Dickinson's poetic, as has often been asserted. And what is implicated is the synecdochic movement that has come to be recognized as a central Dickinsonian trope. Roland Hagenbuchle's essay on "Precision and Indeterminacy in Dickinson" identifies both synecdoche and metonymy with Dickinson's characteristic suppression of subjects, causes, and contexts: "The reader is required to supply the figurative associations himself since . . . the specific referent cannot be found in the text." Hagenbuchle sees a further movement from synecdoche ("relation of inclusion") to metonymy ("relation of cause and/or association") as a figural enactment of Dickinson's "partiality for non-representational poetry," with the metonymic connections omitted. Both Sharon Cameron and David Porter likewise pursue what Porter describes as a "metonymic distance from any possible origins in experience." Porter notes "the problem of the absent subject," and concurs that "there is no causation signified directly by her poems." To Porter, such figural patterns, like Dickinson's syntactic discontinuities, seem a "way of denying time or transcending it, of taking an utterance out of time." Cameron too cites an elimination of cause and of context in Dickinson's poetic and similarly sees it as due to an avoidance of time inherent in the structure of lyric, but present in Dickinson in an extreme form: "The synecdochic process of taking a part for the whole, common to all poetry, is exaggerated in Dickinson's characteristic use of it in which representative incompletions are placed in a larger context of verbal incompletion, . . . pushing all utterance dangerously close to a mere word tangle. . . . [Words] refuse to totalize themselves in a context, [in a] shrinking from temporal sequence that underlies such a refusal."

In Dickinson, synecdoche is a persistent figure, and its functions are a persistent concern. Effects do characteristically displace causes, which themselves remain unspecified. Antecedents are often unnamed, and both the context and the source of a poem of experience are often omitted. Above all, there is a tension between parts and wholes. But what is at stake is the very possibility of relation between part and whole, between cause and effect. The purpose is not to assert fragments or to evade time. Accomplished synecdoche would do neither. By accepting a whole which parts may represent, or into which parts may be placed, both causal continuity and temporal sequence would in fact be affirmed. And this is Dickinson's desire. The incompletion that her prosody projects is, then, not a function of temporal transcendence but of its failure. And it is not a temporal evasion, except as evasion registers the failure of transcendence—the failure of wholes to contain parts and of the eternal whole to contain temporal parts, in the synecdochic movement essential to Augustinism. It is the effort to affirm such containment, and the ironic or desperate sense of its defeat, that determines Dickinson's synecdochic figuration:

> One Blessing had I than the rest
> So larger to my Eyes
> That I stopped gauging—satisfied—
> For this enchanted size—
>
> It was the limit of my Dream—
> The focus of my Prayer—
> A perfect—paralyzing Bliss—
> Contented as Despair—
>
> I knew no more of Want—or Cold—
> Phantasms both become
> For this new Value in the Soul—
> Supremest Earthly Sum—

One blessing is asserted, one so complete that nothing else is required, so large that the very need for measure is nullified, as is the need for striving. It is both a limit and a focus at once, all-encompassing and wholly full. This totality, then, supercedes all parts. And it is accompanied by wholeness's attribute: cessation. But if at first its stopping seems to fulfill the prayer of immutability, by the second stanza, an ominous immobility is suggested instead. The paralysis of fragmented parts becomes indistinguishable from the immutable oneness of eternity.

The poem is thus itself posing the problem of containment, of its contours and its valence. The third stanza attempts to define these and to assert them positively. It dreams an achieved immunity from "Want—or Cold," temporality's condition which Dickinson would annul. That is, her blessing grants her the sense of eternity in which nothing passes away or is lacking. Eternity, however, the "new Value" claimed, is conceived not as some remote condition but as the "Supremest Earthly Sum." It is a totality in and of earth, not a separate estate. Wholeness is sought within the temporal condition.

Such an estate is indeed, as we will see, the limit of Dickinson's dream. An experience of immanent immortality would satisfy both her metaphysical longings and her metaphysical objections. The coherence of wholeness would be affirmed but not displaced into another world. The poem then pursues this dream of accomplished synecdoche, where the one earthly blessing would represent heaven, while heaven would include and place all earthly parts. But ultimately, the poem will acknowledge the phantasms it would dismiss, and dismiss its synecdochic dream as phantasm:

> The Heaven below the Heaven above—
> Obscured with ruddier Blue—
> Life's Latitudes leant over—full—
> The Judgment perished—too—
>
> Why Bliss so scantily disburse—
> Why Paradise defer—
> Why Floods be served to Us—in Bowls—
> I speculate no more—
>
> [P 756]

The poet imagines a "Heaven below" as well as one above, the line between them obscured. This life's "Latitudes" would constitute a measureless fullness, without judgment displacing it from or into another world. This one and inclusive blessing, however, founders. Bliss is scanty. Paradise is not represented or included in terrestrial parts, but deferred beyond them. And the overflowing "Floods" of the blessing remain confined, not as fullness, but inevitably and incomprehensibly as mere part.

This disruption of synecdoche's mutual predication of part and whole is a characteristic Dickinsonian strategy. Many poems reach toward such positive predication, only to admit disjunction instead. In "Before I got my eye put out," the poet poses an inner vision that would contain the whole universe, but ultimately concedes that such an attempt at containment would split her apart (P 327). Elsewhere she writes: "The Heart has narrow Banks, / It measures like the Sea" (P 928), gauging her inner magnitude against an outer one. Dickinson often engages in such measurement. And often, as here, she finds that inclusive boundlessness only appears to be such, "Till Hurricane bisect" what proves to be "insufficient Area." The hurricane is itself a figure for "An instant's Push," "A Questioning." For time itself remains the challenge whose answer is an eternity undermined, in Dickinson, by questioning.

The religious dimension of Dickinsonian synecdoche is confirmed by a poetry not her own, but with which hers has intimate ties:

My Soul forsakes her vain Delight
And bids the World farewell;
Base as the Dirt beneath my Feet
And mischievous as Hell. . . .

There's nothing round this spacious Earth
That suits my large Desire;
To boundless Joys and solid Mirth
My nobler Thoughts aspire.

Where Pleasure rolls its living Flood
From Sin and Dross refin'd,
Still Springing from the Throne of God,
And fit to cheer the mind.

Th' Almighty Ruler of the Sphere,
The glorious and the great,
Brings his own All-sufficience there,
To make our Bliss complete.

This Isaac Watts hymn bears a strange resemblance to Dickinson's idiom. Not only the images of "Bliss" and "Flood," but the notion of wholeness which they project, are Watts's subject. Watts, too, declares a "large Desire" like Dickinson's "One Blessing"; but he unequivocally identifies his with God. And God is defined in explicitly synecdochic terms. He is the all-sufficient, compared to whom the world is as nothing. For that wholeness which is God, all else is forsaken.

A further implication of synecdoche as a religious trope emerges here. Watts's image system seems not only synecdochic, but also paradoxical. To gain God, the world is forsaken. To fulfill the "large Desire," all earthly ones are displaced. "One Blessing" also proceeds paradoxically. The one blessing is not (or should not be) less, but more. Such paradoxes are, of course, the familiar Christian ones. To lose is to gain; to die to the self is to be reborn in Christ. To be blind to the world is to have spiritual sight. The inner soul is greater than the outer world. But these Christian paradoxes are essentially dialectical and implicitly synecdochic. Contradictory elements are synthesized into a final embracing unity, which is the ultimate gain of heaven and God. That synthetic whole, which is all-inclusive, reconciles contrary terms. Harold Bloom has pointed out the synecdochic impulses underlying Christian typology, in which discrete historical moments are placed into the eternal pattern of Christ's life. Synecdoche similarly governs the dialectic of Christian paradox. To lose is to gain in that the ultimate whole achieved includes and places every experience, even negative ones, which have contributed to and have become part of the final, positive totality. To die to the self is in fact to realize the full self in Christ as a member of his body. Spiritual sight supercedes and subsumes all other vision.

The synecdochic pattern of Christian paradox is visible in another Watts hymn:

> My God, my Portion, and my Love,
> My everlasting All,
> I've none but thee in Heaven above,
> Or on this Earthly Ball. . . .
>
> In vain the bright, the burning Sun
> Scatters his feeble Light;
> 'Tis thy sweet beams create my Noon;
> If Thou withdraw, 'tis night.
>
> And whilst upon my restless Bed
> Amongst the Shades I roll,
> If my Redeemer show his Head,
> 'Tis Morning with my Soul. . . .
>
> Were I possessor of the Earth,
> And call'd the Stars my own,
> Without thy Graces and thy self
> I were a Wretch undone.
>
> Let others stretch their Arms like Seas,
> And grasp in all the Shore,
> Grant me the Visits of thy Face,
> And I desire no more.

[169]

Here, divine light makes night day; and sunlight, without God, is night. To have the whole world without grace is to lose it. But grace alone fulfills all desire. The seeming whole—the sun, the world—is in each case exposed as mere part, which only has value when included in and superceded by what truly is the whole. The hymn's opening is especially suggestive. A portion of God is in fact the everlasting all; to take part in him is to attain everything.

Dickinson, in contrast, repeatedly reaches out toward an encompassing inclusiveness, only to withdraw from the attempt as she realizes the container will not in fact contain. Similarly, she often posits opposites, but rarely synthesizes them in the way of dialectic, so that they remain opposed. The one blessing emerges not as all-sufficient, but merely as one (and therefore, in a failed synecdoche, as nothing). No synthetic whole reconciles contrary terms. Wholeness, both as synecdochic and as dialectical resolution, fails to emerge, leaving only ironic incompletion.

Yet Dickinson continues to yearn toward wholeness, whose value is never renounced. Its continuing pressure on her is suggested by the hymnal form itself, which so pervades her work. That Dickinson's versification is firmly based in Isaac Watts's *Psalms, Hymns, and Spiritual Songs* has been well demonstrated by Thomas Johnson. Dickinson's metric, accordingly, falls into the common meter of alternating eight- and six-syllable lines; the long meter of eight syllables to the line; the short meter of two lines of six syllables, followed by one of eight and one of six; and variations upon them traditional to hymnody. Metric itself can be considered a "part of grammar," as Harvey Gross writes in *Sound and Form in Modern Poetry*. As such, it too "articulates relationships among objects, qualities, and actions," especially with regard to temporal orders. Metric functions as "images of time . . . grasped and understood by human awareness. . . . It is rhythm that gives time a meaningful definition, a form." "One Blessing" is itself a poem in common meter. The introduction of the hymnal mode, associated as this must be with affirmations of faith, in a poem of disruption is noteworthy. It opens the general question of the tensions implicit in her use of hymnody to express not faith but uncertainty, with the confusion and hostility this gave rise to in Dickinson's mind.

This tension is particularly evident in a poem whose subject, diction, and metric is decisively hymnal, but whose purport is a denial of doubt which argues its presence:

> My Faith is larger than the Hills—
> So when the Hills decay—
> My Faith must take the Purple Wheel
> To show the Sun the way—
>
> 'Tis first He steps upon the Vane—
> And then—upon the Hill—
> And then abroad the World He go
> To do His Golden Will—
>
> And if His Yellow feet should miss—
> The Bird would not arise—
> The Flowers would slumber on their Stems—
> No Bells have Paradise—

How dare I, therefore, stint a faith
On which so vast depends—
Lest Firmament should fail for me—
The Rivet in the Bands—

[P 766]

A consistent common meter prevails in this poem, whose opening figure is especially hymnlike. It declares a faith greater than the greatest natural phenomena and implies an ascent from things of nature to things of spirit. Hills and sun stand as emblems of eternity. And if hills do alter, the sun's circuit assuredly never fails. This first stanza does introduce dissonant notes. "When the Hills decay" assumes deterioration to be nature's most salient trait—and only Dickinson's expert eye could see in the millennial process of geological change an instance of the transitory. Even the sun, adopted as a more secure figure of eternity, is somewhat acknowledged to be, in this, figural. Faith must still "take the Purple Wheel" and "show the sun" its way toward symbolizing permanence. Nevertheless, the first stanza argues for some movement from the perception of nature's objects to intimations of immortality.

The poem thus accepts its own figure of eternity and in the second stanza joins omnipresence to sempiternity. The sun's circuit encompasses vane and hill and the world at large. It is only in the third stanza that the dissonant note emerges into prominence. The sun figure comes to signal, through negativity, not an immutable order but a pressing sense of its possible failure. The sun's stride might break; its circuit comes to suggest an image of eternity confounded. With its overthrow falls every other process: in nature, as seen metonymically in the failure of birds to return and flowers to bloom, and in supernature, with the silencing of heaven's bells. This last image is in fact redundant. It is the failure of heaven that the sun's broken movement signals and that has priority. As the final stanza demonstrates, what is at issue is the faith in heaven's immutability. It is this that determines the poet's perception of all orders in nature, the sun among them.

This final stanza in some sense reasserts the hymnal stance of the poem's opening. But it does so in contrary fashion. Faith is not so much affirmed as declared necessary. The poet cannot dare to "stint" her belief in the everlasting, lest the admission of heaven's failure unleash all the forces of dissolution she thus far only suspects to be ascendant in her world. "Firmament" is, for her, the "Rivet in the Bands." A belief in eternity is what holds all things together. Its breaking apart would dissolve all else. The hymnal metric is, therefore, not merely ironic. The poem's statement verges on unfaith and a palpable sensing of its consequences. But it draws back from apostasy. The regular common meter continues to assert the organization and regularity which the poet never quite relinquishes.

Dickinson's forms are therefore more closely involved with conflict than they are linguistic representations of wholeness, although they attempt to retain their grasp on wholeness—one origin, in fact, of their conflict. They raise, above all, the question of temporal orders. That Dickinson's relation to time was highly problematic has often been discussed. Clark Griffith, for example, in *The Long Shadow*, argues that Dickinson found her world over-whelmingly threatening, cruel, and chaotic:

> In her poetry, nature is capable of conferring moments of great ecstasy. But the moments prove fleeting and transitory. They tantalize the observer, lull her feelings into false security. Suddenly, they pass, to be followed by periods when nature glares back with a chilling hostility.

This spectacle of impermanence terrified Dickinson. Nature seemed to her, as Allen Tate points out, a disintegrating force characterized by corruption and decay. Time passes, things change, and above all, they die. Dickinson had a profound sense of time's transiency and found it exceedingly alarming. "I feel that life is short and time fleeting, and that I ought now to make my peace with my maker," she wrote in one of her earliest letters. Soon after, she again wrote, "We take no note of time, but from its loss" (L 13). As in "My Faith is larger than the Hills," nature could not provide her with an assurance of stability. It, instead, suggested to her the possibilities of constancy's default. To her, time represented in its motion the very epitome, not only of loss, but of deception. Its beauties and its joys were nothing more than mere vanishing semblances. To her, then, "Day" was composed of:

> A morning and a noon
> A Revelry unspeakable
> And then a gay unknown
> Whose Pomps allure and spurn
> And dower and deprive
> And penury for Glory
> Remedilessly leave.
>
> [P 1675]

Morning and noon here do not merely pass away. They betray and delude, so that even their positive beauties are subverted and finally negated. The gay revelry, even when announced, is already revoked as "unspeakable" and "unknown." What initially seems to be terms of Emersonian ecstasy—wel-coming "as it were in flashes of light . . . sudden discoveries of profound beauty and repose" even if they are fleeting—are here deflationary. The ascent is in fact descent. The pomps spurn even as they allure; the sequence of "dower and deprive" which the sun's diurnal arc traces for the poet is not even linear, but a simultaneous undermining. In the end, glory has not only been displaced by but is shown to have never been anything but a penury without remedy.

Against this spectacle of change and loss, Dickinson opposed eternity. Her whole ability to comprehend time was eternity-dependent and was so in several senses. To Dickinson, eternity was a unitary, immutable other world, standing beyond time as both its end and its totality. As such, it determined her primary conceptual categories: causality, axiology, teleology. Eternity as the end of time provided the telos toward which every moment was directed, in terms of which the position and importance of every moment relative to other moments could be established, and within which, as within an inclusive sum, every event would take its place. Eternity thus guaranteed the sequence, value, and purpose of the temporal process—and of the linguistic process as well. For through these causal, axiological, and teleological categories Dickinson not only structured but also ultimately articulated her world. Dickinson's verse dramatizes her dependence on eternity with regard to each of these conceptual categories and reflects, in its formal fissures, the consequences of doubting them for both perceptual and linguistic orders. Eternity thus emerges as a center of contention. Without it, the dissolution so often attributed to her work would indeed ensue. She therefore struggled incessantly to retain not only a notion of but a faith in eternity. It is the tension between the threat of disorder, which the doubt of eternity represented, and the inability to dispel such doubt altogether, which her language registers.

First, Dickinson's sense of causal coherence was derived from her belief in an immutable world. She saw the end of time as providing a vantage point from which to look back on life's discrete events and in terms of which those events could be placed in sequence. They would become linked in perceivable succession, and the pattern through which each moment leads into the next would become evident. "Retrospection," she writes, "is Prospect's half" (P 995). Retrospect in fact makes prospect possible. The ability to negotiate time progressively depends upon a belief that on review all the different events will be situated:

> The Admirations—and Contempts—of time—
> Show justest—through an Open Tomb—
> The Dying—as it were a Height
> Reorganizes Estimate
> And what We saw not
> We distinguish clear—
> And mostly—see not
> What We saw before—
>
> 'Tis Compound Vision—
> Light—enabling Light—
> The Finite—furnished
> With the Infinite—
> Convex—and Concave Witness—

Back—toward Time—
And forward—
Toward the God of Him—
[P 906]

As in so many poems, Dickinson projects forward to an ultimate
stance (often, as here, that of death) in order to project back to her present
moment—now seen, however, from a posterior viewpoint. Dickinson, that
is, would read time backwards. She attempts to establish her moments as at
once viewed and reviewed. She thus "Reorganizes Estimate" from the backward stance of the tomb. From the end, we see "what We saw not" and do not
see "What We saw before." Then, time and eternity, the finite and infinite,
together form a "Compound Vision." Time, seen retrospectively, emerges as
a continuum forward toward the God who directs it. With such a retrogressive
progression the relative place of each moment emerges into cohesive shape.

The relative value of each moment emerges as well. "Admirations"
become distinguished from "Contempts." Each event is not only organized
and integrated but also weighed and judged. The tomb is more than the last
point in a continuum from which to look back. It constitutes and encompasses all time at once. Not just end, but end as synecdochic wholeness
provides the retrospective stance that makes forward motion possible and
that determines its axiology. And only such final totality allows time's
"Contempts" to be borne. The temporal differentiation that Dickinson found
so unacceptable and that seemed a continual incremental loss would be
justified only if it were a function of temporal wholeness. "Chaos" is described
in one poem as a voyage in which there is not "even a Report of Land— / To
justify—Despair" (P 510). Without terminus, the journey seems senseless;
and terminus must, as well, be validating. Final stance finally serves as the
only redemption from traumas which Dickinson felt to be absolute, even as
they were daily:

The Days that we can spare
Are those a function die
Or Friend or Nature—stranded then
In our Economy

Our Estimates a Scheme—
Our Ultimates a Sham—
We let go all of Time without
Arithmetic of him—

[P 1184]

Loss of function, friend, or nature, all inevitable, will deprive the poet
of sequence, unmask her judgments as mere schemes, and declare her "Ultimates" to be sham endings and sham values that neither explain nor justify—
unless she have an "Arithmetic" of time. Time's arithmetic, an impressive
figure for prosody, here entails the totality that governs linguistic and empiri-

cal pattern. On it, Dickinson's ability to compute, comprehend, and evaluate duration depends. Without it, duration scatters, leaving the poet stranded.

Both the coherence and values eternity bestows are in turn aspects of a teleological framework which establishes the purpose of events. Frank Kermode, in *The Sense of an Ending,* posits teleological formulation as a human imperative. "There is still a need to speak humanly of a life's importance in relation to it," writes Kermode, "a need in the moment of existence to belong, to be related to a beginning and to an end." And, in the traditional Christian structure, the end was identified with a world of Being, of Divinity, of timeless unity, against which the world of time was measured: "We have a creation of which the law relating to forms is a law of change and succession, and a Creator whose realm and forms are changeless and non-successive." Their interrelation becomes centered on the end point at which they merge or on the particular moments in time that may serve as teleological emblems.

It is in moving toward a telos that experience achieves, for Dickinson, both logical succession and value. Her "inclination toward aftermath" is therefore not "simply an unexplained but persistent leaning." It is integral to her conceptual grasp of reality's structure as it is integral to her poetic structure—which is why Dickinson's poems must so often be read backwards from their end. And it is as telos that Dickinson's eternity ultimately functions:

> Each Life Converges to some Centre—
> Expressed—or still—
> Exists in every Human Nature
> A Goal—
>
> Embodied scarcely to itself—it may be—
> Too fair
> For Credibility's presumption
> To mar—
>
> Adored with caution—as a Brittle Heaven—
> To reach
> Were hopeless, as the Rainbow's Raiment
> To touch—
>
> Yet persevered toward—sure—for the Distance—
> How high—
> Unto the Saints' slow diligence—
> The Sky—
>
> Ungained—it may be—by a Life's low Venture—
> But then—
> Eternity enable the endeavoring
> Again.
>
> [P 680]

The progressive qualification of this poem only dramatizes the poet's need for its assertions. The poem opens with a positive declaration—"Exists in every Human Nature / A Goal"—but each subsequent stanza qualifies this statement. The goal is "Embodied scarcely to itself." "Credibility's presumption" could "mar" it, for it is not easily believed. It must be "Adored with caution." "To reach" it "Were hopeless." But in spite of qualification, the goal is "persevered toward." The fourth stanza seems to move beyond hesitation into reaffirmation. The sky is then attained, through whatever distance, by the "Saints' slow diligence," and the final stanza specifies the hope that makes the effort possible. Even if the goal remains beyond life's reach, eternity will "enable the endeavoring / Again."

This conclusion would be more convincing if the poet had not, in the poem's course, presented both goal and eternity as unattainable, as hopeless to reach as would be a rainbow. The relation between goal and process remains complicated: complications in which the poem's prosody shares. This enacts the tension between goal and process. Each stanza delays its syntactic completion until its end and only then is its sense apparent: "Exists . . . A Goal . . . Credibility's presumption to mar." In each case, subject and complement are inverted, so that the intention is hidden until the end. Even then the statement is not always clear. And the strange spondees at each stanza's end, comprising the poem's only metrical regularity, serve to emphasize these conclusions of thought, while against the stanzas' rhythmic alterations, they do not quite establish any conclusive regularity.

This prosody underscores the goal as that which governs process. It also underscores how tenuous relations between goal and process can be. Syntactically, inverted complements lead to confusion as to the subject left behind; conceptually, the significance of what has gone before depends entirely upon an end that remains beyond it and that remains unknown. Life's close may in fact be closure, a cessation of time rather than its completion. This makes the end suspect. "Advance is Life's condition," the poet writes, and the "Grave but a Relay." But it may be that the grave is in fact a "terminus," and then it is "hated" (P 1652). And were the grave indeed terminus, all process would disintegrate for Dickinson. In "Each Life," the uncertain proceeding and confusion as to ends show the space that could open between them, even as the poem gropes toward assertion of process governed by end.

But poems that retain a sense of ending, while foreseeing in their structure the possibility of its collapse, give way to poems in which such a collapse does occur. The poet is then faced with a chaos that inundates and a complete loss of sequence. She experiences what it is like to venture "Down Time's quaint stream / Without an oar," what it is like to sail with "Our Port a secret / Our Perchance a Gale" (P 1656). All is arbitrary, and no known end guides. Temporal definition is then lost. The poet, finding that her "Sum" has fallen into "schism," finds that she has "wrecked the Pendulum" (P 1569).

Spatial definition is likewise effaced. Experience becomes a "Boundlessness" whose "Location is Illocality" (P 963). Infinity is no longer a redeeming but a disorienting realm:

> From Blank to Blank—
> A Threadless Way
> I pushed Mechanic feet—
> To stop—or perish—or advance—
> Alike indifferent—
>
> If end I gained
> It ends beyond
> Indefinite disclosed—
> I shut my eyes—and groped as well
> 'Twas lighter—to be Blind—
>
> [P 761]

The end cited here is conditional and transforms "beyond" from a designation of place—the other world—into "beyond" as a dependent and indefinite adjective: beyond what the poet can gauge. But without the reference point provided by an end, movement becomes impossible. Movement necessarily entails measure, a distance negotiated from one point to another. Here, however, instead of points, there are blanks. Thus motion can only be "Threadless," without delineation. Neither stopping nor advancing nor even perishing can be distinguished, because all relations that could define them have been lost. The poem concludes with a subtle Dickinsonian inversion of the familiar religious paradox by which external darkness may be spiritually bright. Writes Isaac Watts:

> My God, my Life, my Love,
> To thee, to thee I call.
> I cannot live if thou remove,
> For thou art all in all.
>
> Thy shining Grace can cheer
> This Dungeon where I dwell;
> 'Tis Paradise when thou art here,
> If thou depart, 'tis Hell.
>
> [170]

Here darkness is subsumed into the experience of God's totality, the spiritual illumination which cancels all blindness. But in Dickinson the religious dialectic breaks apart. Blindness is not paradoxically vision. When space has no definition, to see or not become functional equivalents—except that blindness raises no doomed expectations. Blindness is therefore chosen, but as a darkness which remains itself: an incomplete dialectic unsynthesized into any all-inclusive divine light.

The loss of wholeness threatened here finally comes to be defined by Dickinson as a place of despair:

> No Man can compass a Despair—
> As round a Goalless Road
> No faster than a Mile at once
> The Traveller proceed—
>
> Unconscious of the Width—
> Unconscious that the Sun
> Be setting on His progress—
> So accurate the One
>
> At estimating Pain—
> Whose own—has just begun—
> His ignorance—the Angel—
> That pilot Him along—
>
> [P 477]

Despair is a "Goalless Road" along which the traveler proceeds but has no sense of progression. He travels unaware of distance as marked by the sun in a space without demarcation. Only the pain that comes with loss of direction serves to measure his movement and comprises the space of his journey. In this space, advance is impossible. The way is circular, and even if he hurried he could never complete it. A goalless road cannot be compassed, for it has no end.

In fear of finding herself in the untraversable space of such despair, Dickinson stops short of a declared unbelief in ends or in the structure that provided her with a teleology. Outright rejection of her faith would thrust such dislocation upon her. She therefore tries to retain her hold upon belief. Yet firm belief continues to elude her. The "Angel" of her journey thus remains, if not apostasy, then "Ignorance." But even uncertainty acts as a "pilot" toward the realm of dissolved limits which the poet tries to resist.

This mediate position gives rise in Dickinson to conflicting and often contradictory statements, which have caused her to be categorized in turn as a mystic and as an apostate. She is, on the one hand, included among ecstatic if unorthodox poets "filled with love for the beauty they perceive in the world of time," and who are "neither fearful nor morbid in facing death." Or, in a more orthodox manner, she is said to have discovered herself "elected to receive the grace of God." On the other hand, the religious doubts she so often expresses have led her to be seen as having renounced her faith and, most often, replaced it with a belief in her own powers, especially those employed in her art. She is then said to have embraced poetry, in the Arnoldian mode, in religion's stead. Heaven becomes for her a "poetic faith"; "Imagination's fictions rescue the world."

Even Albert Gelpi, who recognizes Dickinson's ambivalence, sees it as finally resolved in a transferral from a reliance on heaven to a reliance on the self. He notes that Dickinson referred to herself as both a "pagan" and a "Puritan spirit" and discusses at length in *The Mind of the Poet* her inability to accept wholeheartedly the theological inheritance of New England while remaining under its influence. But, according to Gelpi, "lack of commitment to external absolutes drove the search within, pivoted the mind to turn and turn upon itself." As a result, "her basic motive—the highest motive that the will could command—was comprehension: to know and feel as intensely as possible."

Dickinson, however, never lost her commitment to external absolutes, nor were intense knowledge and feeling her motives. She could not accept a personal and subjective meaning as substitute for an external one operating through objective creation. If the world lacked order, then so did her personal existence. A dispassionate exploration for the sake of abstract knowledge hardly corresponds to the urgency of her poetry. Gelpi is correct in refuting the claims of biographers that "passing years and the death of friends forced a serene acceptance of immortality." But his assertion that "much of the time she would have been satisfied with the stoicism . . . which neither feared extinction nor prized redemption" assumes a resolution to a conflict never resolved. Emily Dickinson feared extincton. She prized redemption. She desperately wished for some assurance that the passing of time was an orderly process and that apparent dissolution was in truth a patterned unfolding. About this she was neither serene nor stoic.

Dickinson's therefore remained a "religion / That doubts as fervently as it believes" (P 1144). She was poised between a faith she could not embrace and an apostasy too terrible to be finally asserted. In a very early letter, she had already described this condition. Identifying herself with the Satan of Job, she felt left to "Pause, and ponder, and ponder, and pause, and do work without knowing why—not surely for this brief world, and more sure it is not for heaven." Unable to accept heaven, she was left only with this brief world, which, however, without heaven, seemed a dreadful place indeed. Thus, in the same letter, she returned to belief:

> What shall we do when trial grows more, and more, when the dim lone light expires, and it's dark, so very dark, and we wander, and know not where, and cannot get out of the forest—whose hand to help us, and to lead, and forever guide us, they talk of a "Jesus of Nazareth," will you tell me if it be he?
>
> [L 36]

Dickinson's doubts tempted her to forsake God. But her needs impelled her toward faith in him. Neither stance could triumph, but they could not be reconciled.

"Christian eternity," writes Octavio Paz, "was the solution to all contradictions and anguish, the end of history and of time." Modern conceptions of time have accepted the rectilinear and irreversible temporal scheme of the Christian model. But it has eliminated both creator and end. Paz cites Jean Paul's *Dream: Speech of Christ, from the Universe, That There is No God* in this shift of temporal archetype. In contrast with the Enlightenment attack on Christianity, which still "postulated the existence of a universal order" and believed that "an intelligent necessity, divine or natural, moved the world," Jean Paul sees contingency and unreason as a result of the death of God. He does not accept a mechanistic universe. His world is convulsive: "The universe is chaos because it has no creator." Paz compares this vision with the dark night of the mystics, in which we feel "adrift, abandoned in a hostile or indifferent world." But, he adds, it is a night without end. The rejection of an eternal world in which all things achieve their absolute state, for good or evil, and of the God who orders the created world in terms of these absolutes threatens to transform cosmos into chaos. And the modern age has rejected the eternal world. Paz defines modernity as an age of criticism, especially in its tendency to criticize the Christian temporal archetype: "Christianity postulated an abolition of the future by conceiving of eternity as the place of perfection. Modernity begins as a criticism of Christian eternity."

In Emily Dickinson, the beginning of this criticism is apparent. And she is aware of its consequences. Her whole sense of coherence, of meaning, and of purpose in the world depended upon the Christian schema in which all things move toward a meaningful end. Earth and heaven should form a pattern that encompasses all experience. This pattern meant, for Dickinson, the difference between chaos and order. But the parts of the pattern would not fit together. Eternity remained a mystery her faith could not penetrate. Consequently, she saw before her an abyss of utter confusion:

> More than the Grave is closed to me—
> The Grave and that Eternity—
> To which the Grave adheres—
> I cling to nowhere till I fall—
> The Crash of nothing, yet of all—
> How similar appears—
>
> [P 1503]

Dickinson here does not reject Christian eternity. Her critique does not draw conclusions. Nor does she declare the death of God. But she is uncertain about his presence. The grave, with all its secrets, is closed to her. Her faith cannot quite negotiate the distance between life and death. And she has glimpsed the crash that would follow a complete loss of faith. In this, she glimpses the vision of Nietzsche's madman who, in *The Gay Science*, raves about the death of God:

Whither are we moving now? Away from all suns? Are we not plunging continually? Backward, sideward, forward, in all directions? Is there any up or down left? Are we not straying as through an infinite nothing? Do we not feel the breath of empty space?

Emily Dickinson, even from uncertainty rather than apostasy, feels this breath of empty space. She feels its disorientation and knows that if it becomes her vision, she will be lost in a world without backward or forward or any direction. She will cling to nowhere and fall through nothing.

The disorientation Dickinson here senses becomes, after Nietzsche, a familiar vision. Dickinson shares with her successors a critical attitude toward inherited metaphysical frameworks, an attitude her forms register. Nietzsche himself had considered the relation between our language and our conceptual categories. "The basic presuppositions of the metaphysics of language" he considers especially to involve causality, with its "concept of transcendent being everywhere projected by thought." And Nietzsche suggests that these are supported above all by our linguistic habits: "After all, every word we say and every sentence speak in its favor." In Dickinson's work, sentences no longer speak in its favor with the same force. Dickinson does not deny the metaphysical world or the structures built upon it. But she admits the possibility of such denial. And for her, this threatens to transform the cosmos into a space empty of significance, as the motions of the heavens lead her to an overwhelming question:

> The Moon upon her fluent Route
> Defiant of a Road—
> The Star's Etruscan Argument
> Substantiate a God—
>
> If Aims impel these Astral Ones
> The ones allowed to know
> Know that which makes them as forgot
> As Dawn forgets them—now—
>   [P 1528]

This poem begins with empirical observation. The lunar path appears "Defiant of a Road," arbitrary, following no appointed route. As to the stars, if their movements "Substantiate" a divine order—and the verb tense remains conditional with an ellipse of the modal "might"—the "Argument" remains "Etruscan." Etruscan, says the dictionary, is the extinct language of Etruria, not known to be related to any other language. Thus, the star's message, if it attests the existence of God, cannot be understood; and the order this would imply remains invisible to the poet. The facts, as they are perceived by the unprejudiced eye, do not necessarily support a belief in divine supervision of the universe.

The second stanza moves into a conditional assessment of the perceived facts. The sidereal movements may have a purpose. They may not be simply random. But if not, the knowledge is restricted and is not accessible to us. As to who may be in possession of it, the poem is ambiguous. The inverted sentence order and unspecified pronoun of the opening lines only confuse. "The ones allowed to know" may be the "Astral Ones," the stars themselves, whom dawn "forgets" as day eclipses the night sky. But elsewhere Dickinson had written of the dead soul: "Even Nature herself / Has forgot it is there" (P 1344). The ones who are "as forgot" may be the dead, whom "Dawn," the living day, forgets in their eternal night. The dead have been initiated into the mystery of eternity. This is the mystery on which the aim of the stars ultimately depends, and the dead may know the answer to the question posed by the universe. But whether the stars or the dead are possessors of this knowledge, it remains their exclusive property. Those who live on earth must continue to question. Nevertheless, except for the initiating "If" of the stanza, this would be a statement of faith. At least heavenly beings know. But the stanza is set in the conditional and remains a hypothetical statement of a possible answer to which, in any event, the living have no access.

Dickinson is questioning here all those assumptions about time, order, and aim without which her universe becomes inconceivable. The mere suspension of faith in teleology and theology, which is implicit in the empirical first stanza and the conditional second stanza, represents a threat of disintegration. This threat is reflected in the poem's language. George Steiner, in his writings, is repeatedly concerned with the way in which "syntax mirrors or controls the reality concept" of a given culture:

> So much of that characteristic Western sense of time as vectored flow, of sequential causality, of the irreducible status of the individual, is inseparable from the bone structure, from the lucid . . . patterns of Indo-European syntax. We can locate in these patterns the substrata of past-present-future, of subject-verb-object, of pronominal disjunction between ego and collectivity that shape so many elements in Western metaphysics, religion, and politics.

A cohesive sentence structure posits and reflects a belief in time as a sequential, causal continuum, and in space as an integrated, interrelating system. In this poem, sentence structure is savaged, with its ellipses of the copula and modal auxiliaries of verbs, inversions of sentence order, and persistent ambiguities. If the sense of time as "vectored flow" and "sequential causality" is, as Steiner suggests, inseparable from the "lucid patterns of Indo-European syntax," this tortuous syntax suggests a challenge to such coherence, as does the poem's argument.

"The Moon upon her fluent Route" looks forward to the era initiated by Nietzsche. It peers into the vision of aimlessness and disorder which Nietzsche made his theme. Its language is consequent to that vision in its fragmentation, its disruption of sequence, and, not least, its linguistic imagery. Dickinson proposes, as does the Nineteenth Psalm, a linguistic trope for heavenly motion. The lunar orbit is a "fluent Route," the astral pattern is an "Etruscan Argument." But, unlike the psalmist, Dickinson implies that they are so in a code difficult to decipher. This shift to a universe conceived as linguistic, like the poem's language, can be seen as part of the reassessment of metaphysical assumptions the poem implies. Its epistemological problems ultimately raise questions concerning the processes of signification within linguistic systems, with an increased attention on language as a realm in its own right. In this, Dickinson heralds the universe of modern poetry, which is increasingly linguistic even as its forms are increasingly difficult.

For Dickinson, traditional explanations no longer quite explain, and the world, therefore, threatens to become inexplicable. The model of eternal wholeness, of concordant time, becomes for her problematic as a paradigm for the temporal unfolding that is essentially different from it but that is, for her, dependent upon it. And if order depends upon eternity as end, the doubt of it could lead to order's collapse. In Dickinson's forms, the effects of such a possible collapse are felt; in her poetry and her poetic, its causes can be traced, as can her attempts either to reaffirm her inherited teleology or to conceive an alternative one.

Dickinson's language thus reflects both her need to affirm structures for her world and her recognition that traditional structures had grown insecure, which she shares with later writers. Her own attempts to erect new structures from or instead of those available to her remained, to a great degree, a struggle between acceptance and rejection of the beliefs she had inherited. The difficulty of her verse reflects this struggle and is no less accidental than the difficulty of the verse written after her. Because of her tantalizing reclusion, critics tend to overlook objective contexts for Dickinson's work. At most, some relate her religious uncertainty to a general transition in American Calvinism, and these still focus on her personal religious sensibility. Emily Dickinson was certainly the most private of poets. But if her beliefs were shaken, this is because her world shook them. For her period, not unlike our own, was characterized by change, instability, and above all, war.

Chronology

1830   Born December 10, in Amherst, Massachusetts, to Emily Narcross Dickinson and Edward Dickinson. The poet was the second of three children, being a year younger than her brother, William Austin, and two years older than her sister, Lavinia.

1840   Enters Amherst Academy, together with Lavinia.

1847   Enters Mount Holyoke.

1850   Reads Emerson's *Poems* (of 1847).

1855   November, start of long illness of mother.

1856   Marriage of William Austin Dickinson to Susan Gilbert.

1861   Newspaper printing of "I taste a liquor never brewed."

1862   Newspaper printing of "Safe in their Alabaster Chambers." Start of correspondence with Thomas Wentworth Higginson.

1864   Newspaper printings of "Some keep the Sabbath going to church" and "Blazing in gold, and quenching in purple."

1866   Newspaper printing of "A narrow fellow in the grass."

1870   First meeting with Higginson, when he visits Amherst.

1873   Second visit of Higginson to Amherst.

1874   Death of father.

1875   Mother stricken with paralysis.

1878   Printing of "Success is counted sweetest," attributed by some to Emerson.

1882   Death of mother.

1884   Death of Judge Lord, who was perhaps the most important of her attachments.

1886   Death on May 15, two days after losing consciousness.

1890   First publication of *Poems*.

Contributors

HAROLD BLOOM, Sterling Professor of the Humanities at Yale University, is the author of *The Anxiety of Influence, Poetry and Repression* and many other volumes of literary criticism. His forthcoming study, *Freud: Transference and Authority*, attempts a full-scale reading of all of Freud's major writings. He is the general editor of *The Chelsea House Library of Literary Criticism*.

CHARLES R. ANDERSON retired in 1969 as Caroline Donovan Professor of English at Johns Hopkins University. Besides his work on Dickinson, he is known for his writings on Melville, Thoreau and Henry James.

ALBERT GELPI is Professor of English at Stanford University. His best known book is *The Tenth Muse*, a study of American poetry.

DAVID PORTER is Professor of English at the University of Massachusetts, Amherst. His books include *The Art of Emily Dickinson's Early Poetry, Emerson and Literary Change* and *The Modern Idiom*.

ROBERT WEISBUCH is Professor of English at the University of Michigan, Ann Arbor, and has written extensively on American and modern literature.

SHARON CAMERON is Professor of English at Johns Hopkins University, and is a widely recognized authority upon nineteenth century American literature.

MARGARET HOMANS teaches English at Yale. Her *Women Writers and Poetic Identity* will be followed by a book on women writers in the Victorian period.

JOANNE FEIT DIEHL teaches English and American Literature at the University of California, Davis, and is the author of *Dickinson and the Romantic Imagination*.

SHIRA WOLOSKY teaches English at Yale. Her book on Dickinson, *A Voice of War*, will be followed by a study of Paul Celan and Jewish tradition.

Bibliography

Anderson, Charles R. *Emily Dickinson's Poetry: Stairway of Surprise*. New York: Holt, Rinehart and Winston, 1960.

Blake, Caesar R. and Wells, Carlton, F., eds. *The Recognition of Emily Dickinson*. Ann Arbor: The University of Michigan Press, 1964.

Cambon, Glauco. "Emily Dickinson's Circumference." *Sewanee Review* 84:342–50

Cameron, Sharon. *Lyric Time: Dickinson and the Limits of Genre*. Baltimore: The Johns Hopkins University Press, 1979.

Capps, Jack L. *Emily Dickinson's Reading: 1836–1886*. Cambridge, Mass.: Harvard University Press, 1966.

Chase, Richard. *Emily Dickinson*. New York: William Sloane Associates, 1951.

Cody, John. *After Great Pain: The Inner Life of Emily Dickinson*. Cambridge, Mass.: Harvard University Press, 1971.

Cunningham, J. V. "Sorting Out: The Case of Dickinson." *The Southern Review* 5, no. 2:436–56.

D'Avanzo, Mario. "Dickinson's 'The Reticent Volcano' and Emerson." *American Transcendental Quarterly* no. 14:11–13.

Davis, Thomas M., ed. *Fourteen by Emily Dickinson*. Glenview, Ill.: Scott, Foresman and Co., 1964.

Diehl, Joanne Feit. *Dickinson and the Romantic Imagination*. Princeton: Princeton University Press, 1981.

Donoghue, Denis. *Emily Dickinson*. Minneapolis: The University of Minnesota Press, 1966.

Eitner, Walter H. "Emily Dickinson's Awareness of Whitman: A Reappraisal." *Walt Whitman Review* 22:111–15.

Ford, Thomas W. *Heaven Beguiles the Tired: Death in the Poetry of Emily Dickinson*. University, Ala.: University of Alabama Press, 1966.

Franklin, R. W., ed. *The Manuscript Books of Emily Dickinson*. 2 vols. Cambridge, Mass.: Harvard University Press, Belknap Press, 1981.

Frye, Northrop. *Fables of Identity: Studies in Poetic Mythology*. New York: Harcourt, Brace and World, Inc., 1963.

Gelpi, Albert J. *Emily Dickinson: The Mind of the Poet*. Cambridge, Mass.: Harvard University Press, 1966.

Gilbert, Sandra M. and Gubar, Susan. *The Madwoman in the Attic: The Woman Writer and the Nineteenth-Century Literary Imagination*. New Haven: Yale University Press, 1979.

Griffith, Clark. *The Long Shadow: Emily Dickinson's Tragic Poetry*. Princeton: Princeton University Press, 1964.

Hagenbüchle, Roland. "Precision and Indeterminacy in the Poetry of Emily Dickinson." *Emerson Society Quarterly: A Journal of the American Renaissance* 74: 33–56.

Homans, Margaret. *Women Writers and Poetic Identity*. Princeton: Princeton University Press, 1980.

Johnson, Thomas H. *Emily Dickinson: An Interpretive Biography*. Cambridge, Mass.: Harvard University Press, 1964.

————, ed. *Selected Letters*. Cambridge, Mass.: Harvard University Press, Belknap Press, 1971.

————, ed. *The Complete Poems of Emily Dickinson*. Boston: Little Brown and Co., 1960.

————, ed. *The Poems of Emily Dickinson*. 3 vols. Cambridge, Mass.: Harvard University Press, Belknap Press, 1958.

Johnson, Thomas H. and Ward, Theodora, eds. *The Letters of Emily Dickinson*. 3 vols. Cambridge, Mass.: Harvard University Press, Belknap Press, 1958.

Keller, Karl. *The Only Kangaroo Among the Beauty: Emily Dickinson and America*. Baltimore: The Johns Hopkins University Press, 1979.

Kher, Inder Nath. *The Landscape of Absence: Emily Dickinson's Poetry*. New Haven: Yale University Press, 1974.

Laverty, Carroll. "Structural Patterns in Emily Dickinson's Poetry." *Emerson Society Quarterly: A Journal of the American Renaissance* 44: 12–17.

Leyda, Jay. *The Years and Hours of Emily Dickinson*. New Haven: Yale University Press, 1960.

Lindberg-Seyersted, Brita. *The Voice of the Poet: Aspects of Style in the Poetry of Emily Dickinson*. Cambridge, Mass.: Harvard University Press, 1968.

Lubbers, Klaus. *Emily Dickinson: The Critical Revolution*. Ann Arbor: University of Michigan Press, 1968.

Lucas, Dolores Dyer. *Emily Dickinson and Riddle*. DeKalb, Ill.: Northern Illinois University Press, 1969.

MacLeish, Archibald; Bogan, Louise; and Wilbur, Richard. *Emily Dickinson: Three Views*. Amherst: Amherst College Press, 1960.

Miller, Ruth. *The Poetry of Emily Dickinson*. Middletown, Conn.: Wesleyan University Press, 1968.

Porter, David. *The Art of Emily Dickinson's Early Poetry*. Cambridge, Mass.: Harvard University Press, 1966.

Rosenbaum, S. P. *A Concordance to the Poems of Emily Dickinson*. Ithaca: Cornell University Press, 1966.

Sewall, Richard. *The Life of Emily Dickinson*. 2 vols. New York: Farrar, Straus and Giroux, 1974.

————, ed. *Emily Dickinson*. Englewood Cliffs, N. J.: Prentice-Hall, Inc., 1963.

Sherrer, Grace B. "A Study of Unusual Verb Constructions in the Poems of Emily Dickinson." *American Literature* 7: 37–46.

Sherwood, William. *Circumference and Circumstance: Stages in the Mind and Art of Emily Dickinson*. New York: Columbia University Press, 1968.

Ward, Theodora. *The Capsule of the Mind: Chapters in the Mind of Emily Dickinson.* Cambridge, Mass.: Harvard University Press, Belknap Press, 1961.

Weisbuch, Robert. *Emily Dickinson's Poetry.* Chicago: The University of Chicago Press, 1975.

Whicher, George. *This Was a Poet.* New York: Charles Scribner's Sons, 1938.

Wolosky, Shira. *Emily Dickinson: A Voice at War.* New Haven: Yale University Press, 1984.

Yetman, Michael. "Emily Dickinson and the English Tradition." *Texas Studies in Literature and Language* 15, no. 1: 129–47.

Acknowledgments

"Despair" by Charles R. Anderson from *Emily Dickinson's Poetry: Stairway of Surprise* by Charles R. Anderson, copyright © 1960 by Charles R. Anderson. Reprinted by permission.

"Seeing New Englandly: From Edwards to Emerson to Dickinson" by Albert Gelpi from *Emily Dickinson: The Mind of the Poet* by Albert Gelpi, copyright © 1965 by the President and Fellows of Harvard College. Reprinted by permission of Harvard University Press.

"The Early Achievement" by David Porter from *The Art of Emily Dickinson's Early Poetry* by David Porter, copyright © 1966 by the President and Fellows of Harvard College. Reprinted by permission of Harvard University Press.

"The Necessary Veil: A Quest Fiction" by Robert Weisbuch from *Emily Dickinson's Poetry* by Robert Weisbuch, copyright © 1975 by University of Chicago. Reprinted by permission of the University of Chicago Press.

" 'A Loaded Gun': The Dialectic of Rage" by Sharon Cameron from *Lyric Time* by Sharon Cameron, copyright © 1979 by The Johns Hopkins University Press, Baltimore/London. Reprinted by permission of the Johns Hopkins University Press.

"Emily Dickinson and Poetic Identity" by Margaret Homans from *Women Writers and Poetic Identity* by Margaret Homans, copyright © 1980 by Princeton University Press. Reprinted by permission of Princeton University Press.

"Emerson, Dickinson, and the Abyss" by Joanne Feit Diehl from *Dickinson and the Romantic Imagination* by Joanne Feit Diehl, copyright © 1981 by Princeton University Press. Reprinted by permission of Princeton University Press.

"A Syntax of Contention" by Shira Wolosky from *Emily Dickinson: A Voice of War* by Shira Wolosky, copyright © 1984 by Yale University Press. Reprinted by permission.

Index